A
CHRISTIAN'S
GUIDE
TO CRITICAL
THINKING

A CHRISTIAN'S GUIDE TO CRITICAL THINKING

Henry A. Virkler, Ph.D.

Wipf & Stock
PUBLISHERS
Eugene, Oregon

Wipf and Stock Publishers
199 W 8th Ave, Suite 3
Eugene, OR 97401

A Christian's Guide to Critical Thinking
By Virkler, Henry A.
Copyright©1993 by Virkler, Henry A.
ISBN: 1-59752-661-4
Publication date: 6/9/2005
Previously published by Thomas Nelson Publishers, 1993

To Joshua,
who has always been
a critical thinker.

Contents

Acknowledgments

I would like to thank Victor Oliver, Lila Empson, and Marie Sennett for believing this book could be useful to the Christian community and for their practical help in making it become a reality.

I also would like to thank Dr. Timothy A. Deibler, colleague and friend at Liberty University, for his many helpful suggestions.

Part One

INTRODUCTORY QUESTIONS AND CONCEPTS

CHAPTER 1

How Do We Come to Know Truth?

Christians rarely think about the process by which we decide that certain conclusions are true and others are false. Because we are not consciously aware of those processes, we sometimes accept conclusions that lack adequate support. The goal of this book is to help you as a Christian to develop a fuller understanding of how to decide to accept or reject truth claims.

The academic term associated with what we will be doing is *epistemology*. Epistemology is the study of how we conclude that certain things are true. We could divide epistemological models into descriptive models and normative models. A *descriptive model* describes how an individual comes to accept certain things as true and other things as untrue. It probably varies somewhat for each individual. A *normative model* is one that prescribes certain processes that one should go through in reaching the decision whether a certain proposition, statement, or claim is true or not.

The normal way we decide whether or not to accept something as true happens subconsciously. It might include the following steps (this is a descriptive epistemological model):

1. We begin the process of incorporating new truth when we read or hear new information from an authority source (parent, teacher, book, television or radio program, etc.).

2. We compare that information with our past experience. If the new information is compatible with our past experience, we generally accept it.

3. If the new information is incompatible but seems insignificant to us, we usually reject it. If we cannot easily reject it we may distract ourselves from the dissonance it creates by focusing on other things.

4. If the new information is incompatible and significant, the dissonance between the incompatible pieces of information initiates a complex process. This process may either go on internally or in an interaction with others, depending on how much we trust our own powers of reasoning versus how much we depend on others to help us reconcile cognitive problems.

5. If we are primarily people-centered, we are likely to discuss this apparent incompatibility with people whose judgment we respect and trust. We may continue the process of seeking out people until we have found a resolution that makes sense to us, have decided that one of the conflicting pieces of information is invalid and can be rejected, or concluded that no one has developed a resolution at this time.

6. If we are primarily intrapsychically-oriented we will prefer to do our own research, examining data until we have found a resolution that makes sense to us, have decided that one of the conflicting pieces of information is invalid and can be rejected, or concluded that we can find no way of satisfactorily resolving the discrepancy now.

Obviously, the people-centered versus intrapsychically-oriented problem-solvers are not as different as this comparison represents them. Members of both groups may discuss the apparent contradiction with others, and members of both groups may do personal research: the difference is in the proportion of time spent in these two activities. The first few steps of a normative epistemological model are similar to the descriptive model and might go as follows:

1. We begin the process of incorporating new truth when we read or hear new information from an authority source (parent, teacher, book, television or radio program, etc.).

2. We compare that information with our past experience. If the new information is compatible with our past experience, we generally accept it. (This is not necessarily a valid step to take, for both our past experience and the new information may be compatible but invalid. Since we cannot re-examine every conclusion we have made whenever new data comes in, this is probably necessary for psychological survival.)

3. If the new information is incompatible with our previous experience but seems insignificant to us, we may distract ourselves from the dissonance it causes by focusing on other things. (Again this is not necessarily a valid step to take from the standpoint of truth, but we realistically can deal only with a finite amount of dissonance at one time. Therefore, it is reasonable to focus on that information and those tasks that are most important.)

4. If the new information is incompatible and the dissonance is significant, a problem-solving process should be initiated. Figure 1-1 illustrates the key activities in this process.

The normative model in Figure 1-1 suggests that there are two sources of valid data from which we normally should draw our conclusions—Scripture and sense data. We can use the rules found in *hermeneutics*, principles for interpreting

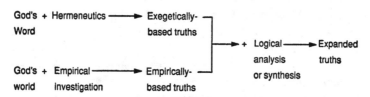

FIGURE 1-1. Problem-solving process.

the Bible, to draw accurate conclusions from scriptural data. Similarly, we can use *empirical research techniques and statistical analysis* to draw conclusions from the sense data around us. Through *logical analysis and synthesis* (the right half of the diagram above) we can expand the conclusions that we have gained from our exegetical or empirical investigations. For example, Scripture and experimental psychology each gives us insight into human motivation. By integrating the findings from both fields, we gain a more comprehensive understanding of motivation than we would from either field alone.

5. Using these three processes, we attempt to find a resolution to the apparent incompatibility. We may ask those whom we respect for their input regarding a resolution, but we accept their input only if it correctly uses these three processes. A resolution, even if put forward by a respected mentor, should not be accepted unless it is derivable from these epistemological processes.

There is an obvious difference between problem solving done unthinkingly through habit compared with that done by someone who has studied the process of learning. It lies with the intentionality with which the latter person uses the methods of hermeneutics, research design and statistics, and logical analysis or synthesis in arriving at one's conclusions.

WHY IS IT IMPORTANT TO UNDERSTAND THESE THREE PROCESSES?

Results of the Failure to Understand Hermeneutics

Failure to understand hermeneutical principles can cause us to interpret Scripture improperly, which in turn can lead to spiritual problems in our own life and in the lives of those who follow our example.

For example, within the charismatic movement several years ago a speaker told his audiences that if they only had adequate faith, they could manifest any of the charismatic gifts whenever there was a need for them in their life situation.[1]

One Christian whom I know believed this man and ventured out in faith to heal the sick and do other deeds of kindness. He soon found that he was unable to manifest these gifts, even in those situations where there seemed to be a clear need for them. As he continued to pray and seek these gifts, he became depressed. He eventually became angry with God, and almost abandoned his faith.

The problem lay, not in this person or his faith, but in the hermeneutics of his teacher. The question of whether or not charismatic gifts are for today is a matter of some debate, which we'll not attempt to resolve here. However, regardless of the stance we take on that issue, there is clear scriptural teaching about charismatic gifts that could have spared this believer many months of unnecessary spiritual conflict and suffering.

First Corinthians 12 teaches that when the Holy Spirit gives gifts, no one is given them all. The Holy Spirit gives the gifts individually as He chooses, not as we think we need them (v. 11). We are each given one or more but not all of them, so that we recognize that we need everyone in the body of

Christ (vv. 7–10, 14–26). In the last few verses of the chapter the apostle Paul asks several questions, using the Greek word *mē*. When a Greek speaker included this word in a question it meant that he or she expected the answer "no." So these verses are best translated "All are not workers of miracles, are they? All do not have gifts of healings, do they? All do not speak with tongues, do they? All do not interpret, do they?" (vv. 29b–30 NASB). If this Christian leader had more carefully applied hermeneutical principles, or if this believer had the hermeneutical training to reexamine his teaching, he could have avoided much unnecessary anguish.

Results of the Failure to Understand Research Design and Statistics

Failure to understand research design and statistical analysis can keep us from being able to separate valid from invalid research. It also may cause us to become skeptical of all research especially when we hear researchers arriving at very different conclusions. We may fail to recognize that some researchers design their studies better than others and that a difference in design quality may be causing the seemingly-incompatible results. Failure to understand research design may cause us to conduct research that is invalid and believe we have proven something that we have not.

For example, a pastor who was studying for his doctor of ministry degree designed and led a nine-week course in his church to help several depressed parishioners. After the program was over all group members agreed that they felt less depressed. The pastor concluded that he had developed a program that reduced depression.

This pastor's experiment lacked adequate empirical controls in several areas, of which I will only discuss two here. (Chapters 4 and 5 will give more detail about the requirements for valid empirical research.) The pastor's study lacked a control group, so it is impossible to know whether the reported decrease in depression was due to the course he had designed or to other factors. The group meeting caused the participants to have increased attention from the pastor and increased interaction with each other: both factors could have decreased group members' depression. Many depressions become less intense over a period of two months. Therefore it is impossible to know whether the decrease in group members' depression was due to the pastor's group or to other factors.

Furthermore, the pastor's design did not control for "demand characteristics." *Demand characteristics* are either subtle or explicit clues that the experimenter or the experimental situation itself gives. These clues enable research subjects to know how they should behave in order to be "good" subjects. The parishioners knew that the pastor wanted to design a project that would decrease depression. They also believed that if the project were successful it would help their pastor receive his doctorate. In this kind of situation, their report of less depression after the project may be due entirely to their desire to be "good" parishioners and help their pastor receive his degree. The changes may be unrelated to the ingredients in his program.

Results of Other Research and Sampling Errors

There are other results of not understanding research and statistical procedures. Since few people understand the issues of sampling and generalization, these matters are frequently not discussed in newspaper or magazine articles. For example, we have all heard of Kinsey's sexual research in the 1950s and probably assumed that any research quoted as widely as his must be valid. Yet Kinsey's research with five thousand males included large percentages who were in prisons, mental hospitals, or who were homosexual.[2] Thus it is invalid to generalize from Kinsey's sample to the general population although writers have done this in the intervening years, causing some normal males to feel that they were abnormal.

Another result of lack of knowledge about research design is that, when writers or speakers mention widely discrepant research results, people become suspicious of the validity of all research. One research study released in early 1990 said that there is a positive correlation between drinking more than two cups of coffee per day and heart problems; a few months later another study claimed to find no such linkage. This might lead us to wonder whether we can trust anything researchers say.

As another example, in 1987 Shere Hite reported that her survey of several thousand women indicated that 75 percent of women married five years or longer had had or were having an affair.[3] However, Andrew Greeley reported in 1990 that 90 percent of those women he had surveyed said they had been faithful during their present marriage.[4] How are we to know which is more accurate? Are 75 percent of women unfaithful, or 10 percent?

An awareness of the factors necessary for valid research design can help us understand why there may be such drastic differences among research results. It also can help us evaluate which results are probably more accurate. When you complete this book you should be able to make some decisions about the likely validity of Hite versus Greeley and the contradictory coffee-drinking research.

Results of the Failure to Understand Logic and Logical Errors

Failure to understand logic and logical fallacies may cause us to be unable to refute someone who draws a persuasive but invalid conclusion from a situation or set of data. The following paragraph gives an example of how this can happen.

Barney Smith assumes that there is more crime in his new neighborhood than in his old. What is his reason? The newspaper in his new neighborhood usually has more columns describing local crime than did the newspaper in his old neighborhood.

Barney is reaching an incorrect conclusion because of an unspoken, probably unconscious, assumption. He is assuming that the newspaper space devoted to crime reporting is an equivalent measure of the crime rate across the two communities. This is not true. There are two reporters in his new community who are very aggressive in covering all the crime in the area. Thus the newspaper in the second community carries more crime stories; Barney assumes it has a higher crime rate than his previous community. Unspoken, incorrect assumptions can lead to invalid conclusions unless one can recognize them and replace them with more accurate assumptions.

"Wasn't the visiting minister's sermon on marriage excellent?" Jim asked his friend Ted. "Oh, I didn't think much of it," Ted replied. "I've heard that his first wife divorced him."

What is the logical error Ted is making? Ted is making an *ad hominem* fallacy. An *ad hominem fallacy* is an argument that criticizes another argument (or sermon) based on the character or life situation of the speaker. The points about marriage made by the guest minister are either valid or invalid and nothing about his character or life situation changes that. His character and life situation may affect whether he should function as a minister, but they do not affect the validity of his message. Ted may miss important insights that he could gain from this minister and others were it not for his *ad hominem* approach to them.

INTENDED AUDIENCE FOR THIS BOOK

Several groups of Christians may benefit from reading this book. First, Christian liberal arts colleges aim to help students learn information in their area of specialization and also understand the process of thinking and reasoning. This book is intended to help them with that second process.

Second, this book may be useful to those pastors who are designing doctor of ministry projects. A few years ago I spent some time researching the ministry projects done by pastors in doctor of ministry programs. Though doctoral level supervisors had approved these projects, many of the projects (as the one discussed in this chapter) lacked even the most basic empirical requirements. Thus these pastors and their supervisors believed they were proving things they were not. The thousands of hours spent doing these projects were scientifically worthless because of inadequate design. By reading the second and third parts of this book and by consulting with someone skilled in research design and statistical analysis, these projects could become an extremely valuable resource contributing to our knowledge of Christian mental health. In addition to pastors in doctor of ministry programs, the information in these sections also may be useful to college students who want an introduction to research design.

Third, this book may be useful to any Christian who is concerned with how to think more carefully about the processes by which he or she comes to accept truth. Sometimes we Christians are more gullible than non-Christians because we are honest in what we say and expect others to be likewise, an assumption that is not always justified. There is a biblical mandate for us, particularly those of us called to Christian leadership (e.g., pastors, elders, deacons, Sunday school teachers) to be well-versed in discerning truth and being able to refute error (Eph. 4:11–15; Titus 1:7–9).

Fourth, this book may be a useful guide as an adult Sunday school elective. Although the focus of some chapters is not on biblical material, the purpose of the book (that we all become more discerning Christian thinkers) is compatible with the purpose of most adult Sunday schools.

GOALS OF THIS BOOK

Let me begin by stating what are *not* the goals of this book. This book is not intended to encourage people to become hypercritical vigilantes, always scanning their environment for minor deviations from truth. Several years ago I attended a conference of evangelical theologians. At a meal I sat close to a young man with a newly-acquired Th.D. As the meal progressed, this person's entire conversation centered on finding what he considered errors in the thinking or theology of those around him. With a smile of smug satisfaction, he would conclude his conversation with one person and turn to someone else. Although his neighbors at the table had many positive things they might have discussed with him, he focused exclusively on finding something wrong with their thinking. I certainly would not encourage anyone to emulate his behavior.

This book is not intended to encourage anyone to become a chronic skeptic. There are those who delight in the philosophy of chronic skepticism. They enjoy finding arguments that appear to prove that we can never be certain about any truth. They invent brilliant, cynical syllogisms that are difficult to refute.[5]

Chronic skepticism about ever knowing the truth about anything is an example of taking a correct idea so far that it becomes false. It is true that we occasionally make mistakes in our sense perceptions. However, through consensual validation (verification by others) or through validation by instruments that examine the same data we are sensing, we may, with a high degree of certainty, affirm that we are perceiving reality correctly. Our entire legal system is based on the premise that people can perceive and remember reality accurately. If a chronic perceptual skeptic truly believes what he says, he probably should give up driving or riding in automobiles, for between the errors in his perceptions and the perceptual errors of other drivers he is taking an extremely great risk to travel in this manner. The reality that only a small percentage of drivers have accidents on any given day attests to the fact that our senses are usually accurate.

The skeptic also may argue that language is an inadequate vehicle for conveying truth. This criticism fails to distinguish between comprehensiveness and truth. It is true that language does not convey all of an experience or a concept. There are always components of an experience that we miss, or that occur within our unconscious or subconscious minds, or that lie beyond the range of our vocabulary to describe. On the other hand, we do not necessarily need more. If we were to describe everything that we experienced in full detail, our lives would become markedly inefficient. We consider a verbal description adequate if what it says is an accurate reflection of reality and if it describes the major components of that experience. God does not claim that Scripture explains and describes everything there is to know about Him and our heavenly home. However, He does claim that it makes verbal statements about Him and about heaven that are accurate enough for Him to call them true (e.g., John 1:14–17; 8:14; 19:35; Rev. 22:6). If God is willing to call noncomprehensive statements written in human language true, then probably we are not on unsafe ground to do likewise.

Negatively, then, the goals of this book are not to encourage hypercriticism nor chronic skepticism. Positively, the goals of this book are to enable you to identify fallacies in biblical interpretation, research design, statistical analysis, logical deduction and induction, and be able to replace those fallacies with appropriate thinking and analysis. And, with those skills, to be able to affirm truth, not dogmatically, but with the quiet assurance that you are accurately interpreting God's Word and God's world.

Part Two

INTERPRETING GOD'S WORD

CHAPTER 2

Hermeneutical Principles I

Whenever we listen to someone speak or when we read what someone has written, we automatically (but unconsciously) apply interpretive principles to try to understand what he or she means. When that person is speaking in a different language and out of a different culture we become more consciously aware of the interpretive efforts we must make to understand them. If we are reading a difficult book, we may go back and reread a section two or three times to understand the meaning clearly. Hermeneutics is the identification of the principles used to properly interpret someone else's communication. As used within a seminary setting, hermeneutics is the study of the principles necessary to interpret God's Word correctly.

Hermeneutics is not something that we use only in the rarefied atmosphere of academia. It is a codification of the processes we use constantly at some level to understand others. Hermeneutics is particularly important as we study Scripture because there are significant historical, cultural, linguistic, and philosophical differences between ourselves and the people to whom God originally gave the Bible.

A basic and important issue in the study of hermeneutics is the question—"Is it possible to specify what constitutes the meaning of a text?" Does a text have more than one possible interpretation or meaning? To help you think through this issue for yourself, read the following exercise and write out your answers.[1]

EX 1: The Naphtunkians' Problem

Situation: You once wrote a letter to a close friend. On route to its destination the postal service lost your message (this was not the U.S. Postal Service, of course). Your message remained lost for the next two thousand years, amid nuclear wars and other minor historical transitions. One day it is discovered and examined. Three literary experts from the contemporary Naphtunkian society translate your letter, each working separately. They arrive at three different meanings. "What this means to me," says Tunky 1, "is..." "I disagree," says Tunky 2. "What this means to me is..." "You're both wrong," claims Tunky 3. "My interpretation is the correct one."

Resolution: As a dispassionate observer viewing the controversy from your celestial (we hope) perspective, what advice would you like to give the Tunkies to resolve their differences? We will assume that you were a reasonably articulate communicator and that you were both sane and sober at the time you wrote the letter.

1. Is it possible that your letter has more than one valid meaning? If your answer is "Yes," go to (2). If "No," go to (3).

2. If your letter can have a variety of meanings, is there any limit to the number of valid meanings it can have? If there is a limit, what criteria would you propose to differentiate between valid and invalid meanings?

3. If your letter has only one valid meaning, what criteria would you use to discern whether Tunky 1, 2, or 3 has the best interpretation? If you, for example, decide that Tunky 2's interpretation is better, how would you justify this to Tunkies 1 and 3?

If you have not spent at least fifteen minutes trying to help the Tunkies resolve their problem, go back and see what you can do to help them. The problem they are wrestling with is foundational to everything else in chapters 2 and 3. After you have done that, turn to the Answers to Exercises section in the back of this book and compare your thoughts with mine.

AN OVERVIEW

If the Tunkies want to understand your meaning accurately, they probably will have to do several things. First, they must understand the historical and cultural context in which you were writing. For example, if you mentioned Watergate, they could misunderstand this as something related to hydroelectric dams unless they had familiarized themselves with the significant events in twentieth-century American politics.

They also would need to understand the words you used and the grammatical constructions of twentieth-century English to understand your intended meaning accurately. Third, you might have made reference in your letter to things you had discussed in previous letters. If so, the Tunkies would gain a clearer picture of your intended meaning in this letter if they had access to those previous ones.

Fourth, if you used any literary forms or genres, such as allegories, parables, poems, or figures of speech, it would be important for the Tunkies to know what these literary forms were and how to interpret them properly. Last, if there had been significant cultural changes between the time you wrote the letter and its discovery, while the letter's meaning would not change, there might be a change in how that meaning would be applied considering those cultural changes.

These same five steps can be applied when interpreting God's Word. These steps, with technical names and brief explanations, follow:

1. *Historical-cultural and contextual analysis:* Study any elements of the history, culture, and context that may shed light on God's intended meaning.

2. *Lexical-syntactical analysis:* Study the words (lexicology) and the way the author related these words to each other (syntax) to help you better understand the author's intended meaning.

3. *Theological analysis:* How does what God has revealed before and after this passage help us understand what He meant here?

4. *Literary (or genre) analysis:* What are the genres being used in this passage and what are the rules for interpreting them properly?

5. *Application across times and cultures:* In what ways, if any, should a biblical command be modified when translating it into a culture where behavioral norms may differ substantially?

In the remainder of this chapter we shall take up the first two of the five steps and treat them in more depth.

HISTORICAL-CULTURAL AND CONTEXTUAL ANALYSIS

There are three major substeps in doing a historical-cultural and contextual analysis. These are (1) Discover the general historical and cultural milieu of the writer and his audience, (2) Identify the purpose(s) the author had in writing this book, and (3) Understand how the passage you are studying fits into its immediate context. We will examine each of these substeps, and their substeps, in turn.

Discover the General Historical-Cultural Milieu

There are three basic questions we can ask to help us understand the general historical and cultural situation of a book or passage.

1. What is the general historical situation facing the human author and his audience? For example, as we learn about the intense cruelty and depravity of the Ninevites, we can understand more easily why Jonah didn't want to go as a prophet to them and why he went into a rather juvenile sulk when they repented and God spared them.

2. What knowledge of customs will clarify the meaning of given actions or given commands? In Mark 7, Jesus upbraided the Pharisees for their practice of Corban. Whatever does Corban mean?

Corban was a culturally and religiously accepted practice under which a man could declare that all his money would go to the temple treasury when he died. Therefore, since all his money belonged to God, he claimed he was no longer responsible for caring for his aging parents. Jesus criticized people who abused the practice of Corban, charging that they were using a Pharisaic tradition to render God's command (to honor one's father and mother) of no account. Clearly, unless we understand the custom of Corban, we will be unable to understand Jesus' meaning in this passage.

3. What was the level of spiritual commitment of the audience? The audiences to which God spoke through Scripture were sometimes righteous but discouraged, sometimes self-righteous but spiritually dead, sometimes spiritually unfaithful, sometimes anxious or misguided because of incorrect doctrine they had been taught. By knowing the audience we can better grasp the intended message.

Identify the Specific Purpose(s) of a Book

Within this step it is helpful to learn (when possible) the identity of the writer, to whom he was writing (e.g., believers, unbelievers, apostates, professing believers who were

exhortation: emphatic urging of particular action

in danger of becoming apostate), and the writer's relationship to those to whom he was writing.

It is also important to identify the author's intention in writing this book. This is very similar to how you might figure out the purpose a friend had for writing to you. You can generally tell this in one of three ways: (1) sometimes your friend will tell you directly, (2) sometimes you can discern this by the exhortations your friend gives you, and (3) sometimes you can figure this out by what he or she chooses to focus on and omit.[2]

For example, Luke tells us in Luke 1:1–4 and Acts 1:1 that his purpose in writing was to present an orderly account of the beginning of the Christian era. John tells us in John 20:31 that his purpose was to present an account of Christ's ministry so that men might believe. The book of 1 Peter is an exhortation to stand fast amid persecution (5:12).

We can sometimes tell a biblical writer's purpose through the exhortations he gives us. Throughout the book of Hebrews the author intersperses exhortations and warnings to Jewish believers not to return to Judaism, but to stay true to their newfound profession of faith.

Third, the purpose of a book sometimes is obvious from the issues the author omits or focuses on. The writer of 1 and 2 Chronicles, for example, does not give a complete history of all national events during Solomon's reign and the divided kingdom. He selects events that illustrated that Israel can endure only as she remains faithful to God's commandments and His covenant.

Develop an Understanding of the Immediate Context

If a Tunky was to take a sentence out of your letter and interpret it without any concern for the sentences around it, you probably would be inclined to cry "Foul!" You might be even more inclined to do so if that Tunky "interpreted" the meaning of your sentence without taking the time to study your culture or your language. To interpret in such a way is *eisegesis,* where Tunky is reading his meaning into your text, rather than reading your meaning out of the text *(exegesis).*

Another word for what Tunky would be doing is "proof-texting." Prooftexting generally is regarded as an invalid method of Bible study because it fails to do this very important step of understanding a passage within its immediate context. There are several questions that can help us develop an understanding of the immediate context.

1. What are the major blocks of material within this book and how do they fit together as a whole?

2. How does the passage under consideration contribute to the flow of the author's argument? There is usually a logical or theological connection between any two adjacent passages (God did not free-associate!). To interpret a verse or passage as God intended it to be understood, we must take the time to see how it fits into what He said just before and after this verse. (How many sermons have you heard where the pastor reads a single verse and immediately launches into his message? If he were to read the verse in context the passage sometimes would not sustain the message he planned to preach.)

3. Decide whether the author's perspective is *noumenological* or *phenomenological.* (If you are familiar with Kant's definitions of the *noumenal* and *phenomenal* realms, please put those definitions aside and use the definitions I am giving to understand the following paragraphs.) These words are a mouthful, but they contain an important distinction. To view something noumenologically means to see it as God would see it (to see it in its entirety). To view something phenomenologically means to view it as a human being would see it (to have a more limited perspective). For example, God can

see the entire universe at once (a noumenological perspective). If we look into a telescope we see only a small portion of the universe (a phenomenological perspective).

Robert Newman and Herman J. Eckelmann discuss one important example of this distinction in perspectives. Newman and Eckelmann both have graduate training in astronomy and theology. They have written a book titled *Genesis One and the Origin of the Earth.* Here they describe the latest astronomical theories regarding the origin of the universe and of our solar system. They propose that, if our solar system developed as theorized, and if God had described the formation of the earth as it might seem to a person who had been there to observe it, we would possess a description exactly like that found in Genesis 1. In other words, Genesis 1 probably is a phenomenological description of the origin of our planet.

The description of the Flood found in Genesis 6 through 9 could be either a phenomenological or a noumenological description, with important implications. For example, if we understand the phrases "all flesh died" and "all the high hills were covered" noumenologically (as God would see the earth), this would suggest that God was describing a universal flood. If we interpreted those phrases phenomenologically, they would mean "all the animals that I could see died" and "all the high hills that I could see were covered." If this is a phenomenological description it could support either a local flood or a universal flood.

Notice that this option does not hinge on whether one accepts the Bible as the inspired Word of God, inerrant in what it affirms. Rather, it hinges on whether God was intending to describe the Flood from a noumenological or a phenomenological perspective. If He is intending this to be understood phenomenologically, we misinterpret the passage if we interpret it noumenologically, and vice versa. (Incidentally, there is much work to be done on discerning when God is speaking

noumenologically and when phenomenologically throughout
Scripture.)

4. Is this passage *descriptive* or *prescriptive* truth? Descriptive passages describe what happened and what was
said at a given time. When they contain statements made by
God the Father or the Lord Jesus, these statements are
obviously true. When they contain statements by men, the
statements are sometimes true, sometimes not. When they
contain statements by Satan, these usually contain a small
amount of truth mixed with a large amount of error.

When descriptive passages recount actions without comment, nothing should be inferred from this recounting beyond
the fact that the events occurred. Because Genesis 1' recounts incestuous behavior between Lot and his two daughters without comment is not an endorsement of incest. Even
though Acts 4 describes believers entering into a voluntary
kind of socialism, it does not mean that we should do also or
that we should not. Because Acts 1:15–22 records Peter
preaching a sermon in which he used two passages from the
Psalms totally out of context, this should not be taken as an
encouragement for us to do likewise. Descriptive passages
only describe what happened or what was said—no more, no
less.

Prescriptive passages, by contrast, prescribe what we should
or should not do. Sometimes they prescribe or prohibit behavior for one individual, sometimes for a group. To find out
whether a prescription applies to us, we need to review the
context to identify whom the biblical author is addressing,
and then decide whether we belong to that group. There may
be times when a prescription is definitely given to New Testament believers and yet may not apply to us. For example,
in 1 Corinthians 11 Paul prohibited the Corinthian church
from having a love feast (a fellowship supper) before taking
communion. We can assume that Paul probably intended this

as a prohibition for the Corinthian church only; the various epistles to other churches contain no similar prohibitions. The abuse of the fellowship supper prior to the Lord's Supper was apparently a specific problem at one church, therefore the prohibition applies to them alone.

5. What is the teaching focus of this passage and what represents only an incidental detail? Some major heresies throughout church history did not maintain this important distinction. For example, a major teaching of the allegory of Christ as the Vine (John 15) is that we derive the power to live spiritual lives from Christ, not from ourselves. Using an incidental detail as a teaching focus, one group of early theologians (later branded heretics) declared that since Christ is the Vine, and because vines are part of the created order, it follows that Christ is part of the created order. The Pelagians of the early fifth century did a similar thing with the story of the prodigal son. They argued that since the prodigal son repented and returned to his father without the aid of a mediator, it follows that we do not need a mediator.

An important way to protect yourself from this error is to read a passage in context, identify the point or points the biblical author was trying to make, and then not take other details of the text and make teaching points out of them. Remember that if you try to make points that the biblical author was not intending, you are doing eisegesis rather than exegesis.

6. Identify whom the biblical author is addressing in this passage. An anecdote that you may have heard makes this point well. A young man was searching frantically for God's will and decided to follow the leading of whatever Scripture he opened. The first passage that fell open was concerning Judas in Matthew 27:5 who "went away and hanged himself." The second passage was Luke 10:37 which said, "Go and do

likewise." The third was John 13:27 which read, "What you are about to do, do quickly."

LEXICAL-SYNTACTICAL ANALYSIS

To review briefly, understanding the history, culture, and immediate context of a scriptural passage is the first major step in ascertaining God's intended meaning. Lexical-syntactical analysis is the second major step. *Lexical-syntactical analysis* is the study of the meaning of individual words (lexicology) and the way the author combined those words (syntax) to discern more accurately his intended meaning.

Alexander Carson emphasized the importance of lexical-syntactical analysis in the interpretive process when he said:

> No man has a right to say, as some are in the habit of saying, "The Spirit tells me that such or such is the meaning of a passage." How is he assured that it is the Holy Spirit, and not a spirit of delusion, except from the evidence that the interpretation is the legitimate meaning of the words?[3]

Lexical-syntactical analysis is a more complicated process than historical-cultural analysis because it involves working with foreign languages. This task is obviously easier if you know Hebrew and Greek. However, with the Bible study tools that we now have available, it is possible for those who have no understanding of Hebrew or Greek to do meaningful word studies. This final section of chapter 2 will describe the steps involved in lexical-syntactical analysis.

STEPS IN LEXICAL-SYNTACTICAL ANALYSIS

The General Literary Form

Identify the general literary form. The literary form of a writing shows the way an author meant his words to be interpreted. A writer composing poetry uses words in a different way than he does when writing prose. For example, when King David said "I filled my bed with my tears," he didn't intend those words to be taken literally. Recognizing poetry as such becomes particularly significant when we realize that one-third of the Old Testament is poetry. To interpret these passages as if they were prose can cause us to misunderstand the author's meaning.

For purposes of our analysis at this point, it is sufficient to speak of three general literary forms—prose, poetry, and apocalyptic literature. Apocalyptic writing occurs primarily in Daniel and Revelation: apocalyptic writers frequently used words symbolically. Writers of prose and poetry generally used words in literal and figurative ways. In prose the literal usage predominated; in poetry figurative language was used most often. Newer translations frequently place poetry in stanzas so that it can be more easily identified and interpreted as such.

The Author's Theme

Trace the development of the author's theme and show how the passage under consideration fits into the context. You have already begun this step under contextual analysis. I include it here because an understanding of the context often shows us the definitions this author was intending in this passage. Also, studies of words and grammar can become so absorbing (or mind-boggling) that we can get lost. The best way to stay oriented when doing word and grammatical studies is to have a clear sense of the author's argument before and after the passage under examination.

Natural Divisions of the Text

Identify the natural divisions of the text. The main conceptual units (sentences and paragraphs) and transitional statements reveal the author's thought process and therefore make his meaning clearer.

The chapter and verse divisions that are so prominent in our Bibles today were not part of the original Scriptures. A helpful priest added these several centuries after the Bible was written to aid in locating passages. Although verse divisions serve this purpose well, the standard verse-by-verse division of the text has the disadvantage of dividing the author's thoughts unnaturally.

Imagine for a moment having someone write you a letter in normal longhand. Before sending it, however, he or she rewrites the letter in columns. In addition he or she inserts numbers, sometimes between sentences, but sometimes in the middle of them. After each number he or she starts a new paragraph heading.

How much more difficult do you think it would be for you to follow the development of your friend's thoughts in the second letter than in the first? Probably most of us would agree that the unnatural structure of the second would seriously distract us from understanding our friend's thoughts.

In modern English, writers usually organize ideas within sentences and paragraphs. The first sentence in a paragraph serves either as a transition from one idea to the next or as a thought that the author will develop in the following sentences. We usually understand written ideas in this way. Several newer translations have de-emphasized the verse numberings (by making them smaller), and have placed the ideas in sentence and paragraph format. This change makes it easier to follow the flow of the author's thoughts.

Connecting Words

Identify the connecting words within the paragraphs and sentences. Connecting words include conjunctions, prepositions, and relative pronouns. They often show the relationship between two sections of material or two of the author's thoughts. Some examples of important connecting words include "for," "because," and "therefore."

Word Meanings

Decide what the individual words mean. Any word that survives long in a language begins to take on a variety of meanings. We call these various meanings *denotations.* Whenever you look in a dictionary and see several definitions of a word, each preceded by a number, you are viewing the denotations of that word.

For example, if you look up the word *green* in a dictionary, you might see a paragraph similar to the following: 1. Having the spectrum color between blue and yellow. 2. A plant in leaf. 3. Not fully mature, unripe. 4. Unskilled in experience or judgment. 5. Pale, sickly, wan.

Besides having denotations, words have *connotations.* A connotation is an implied meaning or an emotional significance that is usually unstated. A word having multiple denotations also may have multiple connotations. When the word *green* refers to a color, it probably has a neutral connotation for most people unless, perhaps, they are Irish. Denotations 4 and 5 in the entry above have negative connotations.

Finding the Denotations of Ancient Words

There are three primary ways to find the denotations of an ancient word. The first is to study how people used this word elsewhere in the secular and religious literature of the time. A second way is to study synonyms, looking for points of comparison and contrast. When doing this it is important to recognize that communication is fluid, and that words do not have rigid, nonoverlapping meanings. For example, two of the Greek words for love (*agapao* and *phileo*) generally do have distinctive meanings (as in John 21:15–17); however, biblical writers sometimes used them as synonyms (Matt. 23:6; 10:37; Luke 11:43; 20:46).

A third method for determining word meanings is to study *etymology*. A word's etymology is its historical development, its roots, and its historically and culturally conditioned usage over time. We use etymological studies somewhat less today than in the past for two reasons. First, it is often unclear what were the historical roots of a word. Second, word meanings often change significantly within one or two hundred years, so that there is no clear connection between the present use of a word and the meaning of its ancestral roots. Therefore the most helpful way to identify the various denotations of a word is to find out the meanings it had at the time the biblical passage was written.

Tools for Discovering Denotations

Concordances. An exhaustive concordance lists all the occurrences of a given word in Scripture (a concordance that is not exhaustive lists some, but not all, passages in which it occurs). For example, the English word *peace* occurs some 400 times in our English Bibles. Our word *peace* is a translation of several different Hebrew and Greek words. If you have *Strong's Concordance* or another one patterned after Strong, beside each reference containing the word *peace* you will find a number. This number refers you to either a Hebrew or Greek section in the back of the concordance. These sections contain short (two- or three-line) definitions of Hebrew and Greek words. Thus, with only a concordance and the ability to follow the numbering system you can do modest word studies.

Theological Wordbooks. You can do much more extensive word studies (again without having to know Hebrew or Greek) by investing in two more sets of tools. For Hebrew words,

the *Theological Wordbook of the Old Testament,* edited by
R. Laird Harris, Gleason Archer, and Bruce Waltke is excellent. Once you have found the appropriate number in Strong
(or in another concordance patterned after Strong), you simply take that number to the index of the *Theological Wordbook,* and it will tell you where you will find a discussion of
that word. The *Wordbook* devotes one-half page to most
words, so that you acquire a good idea of the major denotations of any word you study.

For Greek words there is a similar process that can be
used. *The New International Dictionary of New Testament
Theology,* edited by Colin Brown is an excellent study tool.
Begin by looking up the Greek word you wish to study in the
back of Strong or a comparable concordance. There you will
find the Greek word sounded out in English letters that help
you know what the Greek word would sound like (this is
called *transliteration*). At the end of volume 3 of this set you
will find these transliterated Greek words (in English alphabetical order using English letters) and a list of pages in which
the *Dictionary* discusses that particular word. These descriptions are longer than the ones for the Old Testament and
editors have arranged the *Dictionary* so that words with similar meanings are discussed in the same section. In this way
the nuances of various words become more clear.

Other Tools. There are other books that can help you do
short word studies without requiring an understanding of Hebrew or Greek. These include Bullinger's *Critical Lexicon
and Concordance* and Vine's *Expository Dictionary of Biblical
Words.* Interesting discussions of synonyms can be found
in R. B. Girdlestone's *Synonyms of the Old Testament* and
R. C. Trench's *Synonyms of the New Testament.* These tools
are somewhat dated. A new study tool that gives short to
moderate length definitions is *The Expository Dictionary of
Bible Words* by Lawrence O. Richards.

Discovering the Author's Intended Denotation

Although a word may have several possible denotations, a writer or speaker usually intends to use a single denotation at a specific place in his conversation or writing. If a friend takes a ride on the American Scream Machine and I say to him as he staggers off that he looks a little green, I do not mean that he looks leafy, or unripe, or that we could place him on the color spectrum between blue and yellow. My intention is to suggest that he doesn't look very healthy and to ask whether he'd like to sit for a few moments.

Therefore, once we have identified the possible denotations of a word, we must find some way of narrowing them down to the one the author intended here. The most helpful guide to use is the context. Usually reading several verses before and after the passage you're studying will identify the author's intended denotation.

Second, look at definitions or explanatory phrases the author himself gives. For example, 2 Timothy 3:16–17 states that God gave Scripture so that "the man of God may be perfect" (KJV). What does Paul mean by *perfect* here? Does he mean sinless? Incapable of error? Incapable of error or sin in some specific area? The best answer is supplied by Paul's own explanatory phrase immediately following—"that the man of God may be perfect, throughly furnished unto all good works." In this context Paul meant for this word, interpreted by the King James Bible translators as *perfect,* to convey the idea of being thoroughly equipped for godly living.

Third, the subject and predicate of a sentence may each explain the other. For example, the Greek word transliterated *moranthei,* found in Matthew 5:13, can mean either "to become foolish" or "to become insipid." How do we find Christ's intended denotation here? In this instance the subject of the sentence is salt, and so the second denotation ("if the salt has lost its savor") is the correct one.

Fourth, look at parallelism if it occurs within the passage. As mentioned earlier, one-third of the Old Testament (and some of the New Testament) is poetry. One characteristic of Hebrew poetry is parallelism, a feature that may shed light on the meaning of words that are in question.

Hebrew parallelism can be categorized into three basic types: synonymous, antithetic, and synthetic. In *synonymous parallelism* the second line of the stanza repeats the content of the first, but in different words. Psalm 103:10 is an example:

> He does not treat us as our sins deserve
> or repay us according to our iniquities.

In *antithetic parallelism* the idea of the second line sharply contrasts with that of the first line. Psalm 37:21 provides an example:

> The wicked borrow and do not repay,
> but the righteous give generously.

In *synthetic parallelism* the second line carries further or completes the idea of the first line. Psalm 14:2 is an example:

> The LORD looks down from heaven on the sons of men
> to see if there are any who understand, any who seek
> God.

Thus, if a passage is poetry, recognition of the type of parallelism employed may give clues to the meaning of the word in question.

Fifth, decide whether the author is using a figure of speech. Sometimes authors use words or phrases in ways that deviate from simple, normal speech in order to produce a vivid impression. When these phrases are figures of speech, the author does not intend for them to be interpreted literally. If a figure persists and becomes widely accepted within a culture, it becomes an idiom (something peculiar to that culture or language). Some English examples of figures of speech or idioms are these:

- His eyes were bigger than his stomach.
- This fog is as thick as pea soup.
- I'm broke.
- The White House said . . .
- We'll hit Athens about 2 P.M.
- She made the cake from scratch.
- The thermometer is going up.
- The furnace has gone out.
- Take a bus (a bit of an armload).
- I'd better get off the phone so I don't tie up the line.

Notice there are two figures of speech in the final sentence.

As we can see from the above list, we use figures of speech and idioms frequently. Figures of speech convey a definite meaning just as surely as does normal prose. To say that something is a figure of speech does not imply that the meaning of the phrase is ambiguous.

An interpretation of a figure of speech using the normal denotations of a word will usually result in a radical misunderstanding of the author's intended meaning. For example, if I were to interpret literally the phrase "It's raining cats and dogs," I would seriously misinterpret the meaning of this phrase.

Figures of speech are common in the biblical text. One procedure that can be used to identify them is to consult Bullinger's *Figures of Speech Used in the Bible.* Index 3 of Bullinger's book will show whether there are any figures of speech in a passage and will provide appropriate explanations. Bullinger's book must be used with discretion. It represents his personal judgments and knowledge of Hebrew and Greek figures of speech. It does, however, provide a large amount of important and useful information.

Sixth, study parallel passages. To understand the meaning of an obscure word or phrase, look for additional data in clearer parallel passages. It is important, though, to distinguish between verbal parallels and real parallels. *Verbal parallels* are those that use similar words but are discussing different ideas (the similarity is more verbal than real). The discussions of God's Word as a sword, found in Hebrews 4 and Ephesians 6, is an example of a verbal, but not a real, parallel. Hebrews 4 speaks of the Bible's function as a divider that differentiates between those who are truly obedient to its message and those who profess obedience but inwardly remain disobedient. In Ephesians 6, Paul also speaks of the Bible-as-a-sword, but in this instance refers to it as a defensive weapon to be used against the temptations of Satan (v. 11). Christ used the Word in this way when Satan tempted Him in the desert.

In contrast to verbal parallels, *real parallels* are those that speak of the same idea or same event. The author may use different words, but is discussing the same idea. The marginal references found in many Bibles are intended to yield real parallels, although occasionally such references seem to be more verbal than real. The best way to decide whether two passages are verbal or real parallels is to examine carefully the context of each.

In summary, six ways of ascertaining the specific intended denotation of a word in a given passage are these: (1) study the context; (2) look at definitions or explanatory phrases the author gives; (3) use the subject and verb to explain each other; (4) look at parallelism if it occurs in the passage; (5) decide whether the author was using a figure of speech; and (6) study parallel passages.

Syntax

Study the syntax (or grammar) of the passage. This is probably the most difficult step to do without a knowledge of Hebrew and Greek. *Syntax* deals with the way an author expresses himself or herself through grammatical forms. Each language has its own structure. One of the problems that makes learning another language so difficult is that the learner must master not only the word definitions and pronunciations of the new language, but also new ways of arranging and showing the relationship of one word to another.

English is an analytic language: word order is a guide to meaning. For example, nouns normally precede verbs, which normally precede direct objects or predicate adjectives. We say "the tree is green" rather than another combination of those words. Hebrew is also an analytic language, but less so than English. Greek, in contrast, is a synthetic language: we understand meaning only partially by word order and much more by word-ending or case-ending.[4]

If you wish to try to do grammatical studies, there are several tools that can be helpful in discovering what information syntax can contribute to your understanding of the author's intended meaning.

Interlinear Bibles. These Bibles contain the Hebrew or Greek text with the English translation printed between the lines (therefore the name *interlinear*). By juxtaposing the two sets of words, you can identify the Greek or Hebrew word you wish to study further. (Those who are proficient in Hebrew and Greek can, of course, go directly to the Hebrew or Greek texts rather than to interlinears.)

Analytical Lexicons. Often the word you encounter in the text is some variation of the root form of the word rather than the root word itself. For example, in English you might encounter various forms of the verb *to speak:*

spoke
spake
had spoken
will speak
will have spoken

Nouns also may take on different forms and play different roles within sentences.

An analytical lexicon does two primary things: (1) it identifies the root word of which the word in the text is a variation, and (2) it identifies which part of speech the variation is. For example, if the word you wished to study were the Greek word *thumon,* by looking in an analytical Greek lexicon you would find that this is the accusative singular of the word *thumos,* which means "anger" or "wrath."

Hebrew and Greek Grammars. If you are unfamiliar with the meaning of the term "accusative singular" to describe the form of a word, a third set of syntactical aids will be valuable. Hebrew and Greek grammars explain the various forms that words can take in their respective languages, and the meaning of the words when they appear in one of these forms. Respected Hebrew grammars include Gesenius's *Hebrew Grammar* and J. Weingreen's *Practical Grammar for Classical Hebrew.* Greek grammars include A. T. Robertson's *Grammar of the Greek New Testament in the Light of Historical Research* and Blass and Debrunner's *Greek Grammar of the New Testament and Other Early Christian Literature.* Grammars that may be easier for laypersons to use include *Hebrew Syntax: An Outline* by Ronald J. Williams, and *Hidden Meaning in the New Testament* by Ronald Ward.

Share Your Results Simply and Clearly

When doing lexical-syntactical analysis we need to guard against allowing pride to affect the results of our work. There is a sense of satisfaction that results whenever we use the tools of lexical-syntactical analysis to dig out the meaning of an obscure passage or to show how two seemingly contradictory passages can be reconciled. The temptation may be to impress others with our intelligence and ability to study the Hebrew and Greek. A better way to impress people is by using our study to help them clearly understand God's intended meaning in the passage under study.

RESOURCES FOR DOING HISTORICAL-CULTURAL AND CONTEXTUAL ANALYSIS AND LEXICAL-SYNTACTICAL ANALYSIS

Rather than having to discover all the above information yourself, Bible scholars have already done much of this work for you in books called *expository commentaries*. These books usually address many questions that we've asked under historical-cultural and contextual analysis. The author also will do a lexical-syntactical analysis of the words he or she believes are most significant.

Because these books contain much technical and academic information, they usually do not make for spellbinding reading. You may not find that they challenge you spiritually. However, this is not the purpose of an expository commentary. The purpose of a commentary is to help you understand what the biblical message meant to its original recipients. It is up to you, as a Sunday school teacher or Bible study leader or writer, to develop the application that meaning has for us today, and to motivate whomever you are working with to implement that application in their own lives.

Below are some excellent sources of reliable commentary on the Bible. Their authors write so that non-Hebrew and Greek scholars can benefit from them:

NIV Study Bible: Obviously not an expository commentary, but an excellent study Bible that does many things expository commentaries do, only less extensively (Zondervan).

Expositor's Bible Commentary Series: edited by Frank Gaebelein (Zondervan). These are, in my opinion, the finest commentaries available today.

Tyndale Old Testament Commentary Series: edited by D. J. Wiseman (InterVarsity Press).

Tyndale New Testament Commentary Series: edited by R. V. G. Tasker (Eerdmans).

A FINAL QUESTION

You might be asking yourself, "Why go through all the work of learning to do historical-cultural, contextual and lexical-syntactical analysis if I can already find this work done for me in an expository commentary?" There are several reasons it is valuable for you to know this process yourself. Here are three:

1. Some of your most important conversations with non-believers and with believers who are struggling (perhaps because of a misinterpretation of a text) will be spontaneous. You will not have the opportunity to go back and read several commentaries. The helpfulness you can provide in many of these situations depends on the extent to which you have mastered these hermeneutical principles and can use them without reference to other sources.

2. Sometimes expositors do not answer the questions you have. If you can read only what expositors have written, you will not have the ability to research the questions or controversies that are important to you. Sometimes expositors avoid complex and controversial issues because of the difficulty of finding a solution that incorporates the legitimate points that various parties have raised. If you do not know how to do your own analysis, you will reach a dead end (notice the

figure of speech) if your expositor fails to discuss it. You also may be frustrated if you are certain that his or her analysis is invalid, but cannot show why.

3. Sometimes expositors will disagree. When this occurs how are we to decide which exposition to endorse? We need skills of interpretation to make our own judgments.

After becoming familiar with the hermeneutical principles covered thus far, you probably can determine when an expositor is failing to consider one or more important interpretive principles or when another interpretation is a more adequate one hermeneutically. This approach is preferable to the one in which you choose an expositor because he agrees with what you already believe.

SUMMARY OF CHAPTER 2

Historical-Cultural and Contextual Analysis

1. Discover the general historical and cultural milieu of the writer and his audience.
   a. What is the general historical situation facing the human author and his audience?
   b. What knowledge of customs will clarify the meaning of given actions or given commands?
   c. What was the level of spiritual commitment of the audience?
2. Identify the purpose(s) the author had in writing the book by:
   a. noting explicit statements or repeated phrases.
   b. observing exhortations he gives.
   c. observing issues the author omits or focuses on.
3. Understand how the passage fits into its immediate context.
   a. Identify the major blocks of material in the book and show how they fit into a coherent whole.

   b. Show how the passage fits into the flow of the author's argument.

   c. Decide if the author's perspective is noumenological or phenomenological.

   d. Distinguish between descriptive and prescriptive truth.

   e. Distinguish between incidental details and the teaching focus of the passage.

   f. Identify who the biblical author is addressing in this passage.

Lexical-Syntactical Analysis

1. Identify the general literary form or genre.
2. Trace the development of the author's theme and show how the passage under consideration fits into the context.
3. Identify the natural divisions (sentences and paragraphs) of the text.
4. Identify the connecting words within the paragraphs and sentences and show how they aid in understanding the author's progression of thought.
5. Decide what the individual words mean.
   a. Identify the multiple meanings (denotations) a word possessed in its time and culture.
   b. Determine the single meaning intended by the author in a given context.
6. Analyze the syntax and show how it contributes to an understanding of the passage.
7. Put the results of your analysis into nontechnical, easily-understood words that clearly convey the author's intended meaning.

EXERCISES

[Please do not cheat yourself by ignoring these exercises. We rarely learn to do anything by just reading about it, whether it be softball or

geometry or debating. Fully half of what you will learn from this book will come from thinking through these exercises, then comparing your results with the suggested answers at the back of this book.]

EX 1: Included within chapter 2.

EX 2: A Christian author was discussing the way to discover God's will for one's life and made the point that inner peace was an important indicator. He based his argument on one verse—Colossians 3:15, "Let the peace of Christ rule in your hearts." Would you agree with his use of this verse to make this point? Why or why not?

EX 3: A well-known Christian counselor was writing about the problem some people have of continually saying "yes" when they want to say "no." Many of these people eventually explode in anger because of all their pent-up frustration. This counselor suggested:

> Always being Mr. Nice-Guy, and then turning your real feelings into stomach acid is self-defeating. You may get what you want—for the moment—by lathering [submitting to the expectations of] others, but you don't like yourself for it.
> Consider putting out what you're feeling in simple honesty. As Jesus put it, "Let your yes be a clear yes, and your no, no." Anything else spells trouble.

Do you believe Jesus was talking about assertiveness in the passage paraphrased by this author (Matt. 5:33–37)? Why or why not?

EX 4: A Christian lost his job during a period of economic recession. He and his wife interpreted Romans 8:28 ("All things work together for good" NRSV) to mean that he lost his job in order that God might give him a better-paying one. Consequently he turned down several lower-paying or equal-paying job opportunities and remained on unemployment for two years before returning to work. Do you agree with his way of interpreting this verse? Why or why not?

EX 5: Hebrews 10:26–27 states: "If we deliberately keep on sinning after we have received the knowledge of the truth, no sacrifice for sins is left, but only a fearful expectation of judgment and of raging fire that will consume the enemies of God." A person comes to you extremely depressed. A week ago she willfully and deliberately stole some merchandise from a local store, and now, on the basis of the above verses, believes there is no possibility of repentance and forgiveness (this was not the first occurrence). How would you counsel her?

EX 6: You have just finished telling someone that you do not agree with the oracular use of Scripture (consulting the Bible by opening it and applying the first words one reads as God's instructions to him or her). You disagree with the oracular use of Scripture because it generally interprets words without regard to their context. This person argues that God has often used just this method to bring him or her comfort and guidance. How would you reply?

EX 7: Most people assume that the girl spoken of in Matthew 9:18–26 was dead, but there are some reasons to believe that she was comatose rather than dead.

(a) What lexical-syntactical factors would you consider as you attempt to deal with this question?

(b) What factors suggest she was dead? Evaluate the strength of these factors.

(c) What factors suggest she was comatose rather than dead? Evaluate the strength of these factors.

(d) Do you think she was comatose or dead?

EX 8: A great deal of discussion by Christians on the topic of anger has been based on Ephesians 4:26 ("Be angry, and yet do not sin" NASB). Analyze this verse and decide whether you think Paul was affirming human righteous anger here.

EX 9: There has been much discussion concerning the nature of "worldly" (neurotic?) versus godly guilt (2 Cor. 7:10) among Christian psychologists. Applying your knowledge of hermeneutics to this particular text, differentiate between the two as best you can.

EX 10: Some Christian groups and colleges maintain a very strong stand on the issue that Creation took six literal twenty-four-hour periods. They often believe that to do otherwise suggests a less-than-faithful adherence to the biblical record. Do a word study of the Hebrew word for day (*yom*) as used in the early chapters of Genesis. What does your word study indicate regarding the question of whether Creation occurred in six days or six periods of unspecified duration?

CHAPTER 3

Hermeneutical Principles II

Hermeneutics is a study of the principles involved in correctly understanding God's intended meaning in Scripture. In the last chapter we studied two important steps in that process. In the first step we must study the history, culture and context as a way of more accurately discerning God's intended meaning. In the second step we must develop an understanding of the words and grammar God chose to use as He spoke through a human author.

In this chapter we will look at three more important steps in the process. First we will examine the process of theological analysis—studying how what God has written before and after a particular passage helps us understand the passage under study. Second, we will look at literary analysis—how the different genres and literary devices of the biblical period, such as similes, metaphors, parables, and allegories—affect the way we should understand an author's words. Third, we will look at how to translate biblical stories and commands into our own time and culture in a way that neither subtracts from nor adds to an author's intended meaning.

THEOLOGICAL ANALYSIS

The first question asked in theological analysis is "How does this passage fit into the total pattern of God's revelation?" It immediately becomes evident that another question must first be answered, namely, "What is the pattern of God's revelation?"[1]

There are several theories about the best way to understand the nature of God's relationship to humanity throughout salvation history. Some students of Scripture believe God has changed His ways of relating significantly. Other students believe that His manner of relating has remained essentially the same. The first group puts a primary emphasis on discontinuity, with a secondary emphasis on continuity. The second group puts a primary emphasis on continuity, with a lesser emphasis on discontinuity.

Dispensationalists are one theological group who, particularly in the past, have placed more emphasis on discontinuity. Many dispensational theologians of the last ten to fifteen years have moved to a position which places less emphasis on discontinuity and more emphasis on continuity within the dispensations. Two theological groups that place more emphasis on continuity are Lutheran and reformed theologians. The spectrum of positions is represented in Figure 3-1.

Why Is the Continuity-Discontinuity Issue Important?

Those who believe that the nature of God's relationship to humanity has been continuous generally view all Scripture as relevant for the believer today. They see a basic unity between themselves and believers in both the Old and New Testament. Those who believe the nature of God's relationship to humanity has been more discontinuous generally view the Old Testament, and sometimes even the New Testament

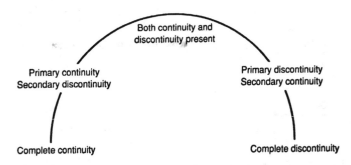

FIGURE 3-1. Theories regarding the nature of God's
relationship to mankind.

before the Crucifixion, as less applicable to believers today.
For example, Lewis Sperry Chafer in *Dispensationalism* stated
that the only Scriptures addressed specifically to Christian
believers are the gospel of John (particularly the Upper Room
Discourse), the book of Acts, and the Epistles.[2]

Ultradispensationalists (who are a small group within Evan-
gelicalism) take an even more discontinuous position. They
believe Acts and the Epistles describe three different church
dispensations (other dispensationalists usually believe there
is only one). The first dispensation existed when the church
was primarily Jewish. The second occurred when the church
was a mixture of Jews and Gentiles. The third church dispensation occurred at the end of Acts, when the church had
become primarily Gentile. Ultradispensationalism teaches that
the portions of Scripture that are primarily applicable to believers today include only those parts of Acts and those Epistles written to those in the third church dispensation.

Thus the position we take on the continuity-discontinuity
issue is of major importance as we attempt to answer the
question, "How does what I am studying in this passage
relate to what God has said before and after it?" The position

we take on this issue is also going to be of major importance
as we try to decide the relevance and applicability of commands and teachings given to believers widely separated from
us in time. We will examine four of these theories in more
detail.

Dispensationalism

Dispensationalism is one of those theories that people seem
either to "swear by" or "swear at"; few take a neutral position. Writers have called dispensationalism "the key to rightly
dividing the Scriptures"[3] and alternatively "the most dangerous heresy currently to be found within Christian circles."[4]

Scofield defined a dispensation as "a period during which
man is tested in respect of obedience to some specific revelation of the will of God."[5] Most contemporary dispensational
writers stress the idea of various stewardship arrangements
rather than time periods. The pattern of God's relationship to
humanity occurs in three regularly repeated steps: (1) God
gives humanity a specific set of responsibilities, (2) humans
fail to live up to those responsibilities, and (3) God responds
in mercy by giving a different set of responsibilities, that is, a
new dispensation. (Dispensations are sometimes called "economies." When theologians use the word "economy" in this
way it refers to God's management of human affairs in a
specific way. Therefore one may speak of dispensations or of
divine economies.)

Dispensationalists recognize between four and nine dispensations. The most common numbers are seven and eight. The
following description of seven dispensations, summarized from
Charles C. Ryrie, is typical of many dispensational writers:[6]

Dispensation of Innocence or Freedom. This dispensation
existed when Adam and Eve were in a state of innocence. It
ended when they sinned. The Bible describes this in Genesis
1:28—3:6.

Dispensation of Conscience. During this period "obedience to the dictates of conscience was man's chief stewardship responsibility." It ended as man became increasingly wicked and God brought judgment through the Flood. The Bible describes this dispensation in Genesis 4:1—8:14.

Dispensation of Civil Government. During this dispensation God gave humans the right to capital punishment, implying with it the right to develop human government. Instead of scattering and filling the earth, people expressed their rebellion by building the Tower of Babel. God's judgment came through the confusion of languages. The Bible describes this period in Genesis 8:15—11:9.

Dispensation of Promise. This dispensation covered the time from the patriarchs until the emergence of Moses. It received this name because of God's promise to Abraham of a land and of subsequent blessings. The Bible describes this period in Genesis 11:10—Exodus 18:27.

Dispensation of Mosaic Law. This period lasted from the time of Moses until the death of Christ. During this time God gave commandments covering all phases of life. Israel's repeated failure to abide by these commandments led to division of the nation and eventually to bondage. The Bible describes this dispensation in Exodus 18:28—Acts 1:26.

Dispensation of Grace. During this period (including the present) humanity's responsibility is to accept Christ's atonement for their sins. This age will end with humanity's rejection of God's gift, leading to the Tribulation. The Bible describes the dispensation of grace in Acts 2:1—Revelation 19:21.

Dispensation of the Millennium. During the millennial kingdom, man's responsibility will be obedience to the personal rule of Christ. (Dispensationalists generally believe the Millennium to be a literal 1000 years when Christ will be physically present on earth to rule all humanity.) After this period there will be a brief final rebellion. God subdues this rebellion

and then initiates the Final Judgment. The best-known biblical passage describing the Millennium is Revelation 20.

There are some differences between dispensational laypersons (particularly those raised on the "old" Scofield Reference Bible) and contemporary dispensational theologians. A
common belief among older dispensational laypersons is that
the dispensations of law and grace represent two different
means of salvation. People base this view, in part, on some
notes in the original Scofield Reference Bible.[7]

Most dispensational theologians, however, probably would
agree with Ryrie's statement that

> The *basis* of salvation in every age is the death of Christ;
> the *requirement* for salvation in every age is faith; the
> *object* of faith in every age is God; the *content* of faith
> changes in the various dispensations [italics his].[8]

Everyone saved in any dispensation has been saved through
the death of Christ, although Old Testament believers, by
offering sacrifices that pointed forward to Christ, probably
understood this role of the Messiah dimly, if at all. Therefore,
the content of faith changes, or becomes progressively clearer,
throughout the dispensations.

The second major change during the dispensations is the
rules for obedient living. Those rules given under the dispensation of Mosaic Law have changed considerably under the
dispensation of grace. This raises a question: "Do the rules
given to people under one dispensation apply to believers in a
subsequent dispensation?"

Some dispensationalists believe that commandments given
in one dispensation apply to believers in consecutive ones in
some way. However, dispensationalists have not clearly articulated the specifics of this. At the other end of the spectrum
would be those dispensationalists who believe that nothing in

one dispensation applies to those in later dispensations.[9] Working out a rationale for whether and how this is to be done represents an important, unfinished task for dispensationalists.

Clearly, if dispensationalism is a valid way of understanding the history of God's relationship to humanity, it is an extremely important hermeneutical tool. Scofield would be right in saying that we cannot rightly divide the Word of God unless we know the dispensation in which God gave a specific command, the dispensation we are in, and the relationship between the two. On the other hand, if dispensationalism is a theory forced onto Scripture rather than one that is derived from it, there is a very real danger that by relegating much of Scripture to previous dispensations, we may be minimizing the relevance of Scriptures that we should be applying to our lives.

The following six books contain much useful information on dispensational theory. The first three authors agree with dispensational theory; the last three present critiques of it.

Lewis Sperry Chafer, *Dispensationalism*
C. C. Ryrie, *Dispensationalism Today*
C. I. Scofield, *Rightly Dividing the Word of Truth*
Louis Berkhof, *Systematic Theology*, pp. 290–301
William E. Cox, *An Examination of Dispensationalism*
George Eldon Ladd, *Crucial Questions About the Kingdom of God*

Three more recent books on this issue are:

John Feinberg, (ed.), *Continuity and Discontinuity: Perspectives on the Relationships Between the Old and New Testaments*
Daniel P. Fuller, *Gospel and Law: Contrast or Continuum, the Hermeneutics of Dispensationalism and Covenant Theology*
Vern S. Poythress, *Understanding Dispensationalists*

Lutheran Theology

Luther believed that to achieve a proper understanding of Scripture we must carefully distinguish between two parallel and ever-present truths in Scripture: Law and Gospel. Law refers to God in His hatred of sin, His judgment, and His wrath. Gospel refers to God in His grace, His love, and His salvation.

Both aspects of God's nature exist side by side in Scripture. The Law reflects the holiness of God's character: if He were to dispense with it, He would become an amoral rather than a holy God. Grace is God's response to the fact that man can never meet the standard of holiness the Law demands.

One way of distinguishing Law and Gospel is to ask, "Is this speaking judgment on me?" If so, it is Law. In contrast, if a passage brings comfort, it is Gospel. Using these criteria, decide whether the following passages would be considered Law or Gospel:

1. "The LORD then said to Noah, 'Go into the ark, you and your whole family, because I have found you righteous in this generation'" (Genesis 7:1).
2. "Jesus replied: 'Love the Lord your God with all your heart and with all your soul and with all your mind'" (Matthew 22:37).
3. "Whoever believes in the Son has eternal life, but whoever rejects the Son will not see life, for God's wrath remains on him" (John 3:36).

(Answers: 1. Gospel, 2. Law, and 3. Gospel; Law)

For Lutheran theologians, Law and Gospel reveal two integral aspects of God's personality—His holiness and His grace. Thus they view Law and Gospel as inseparable parts of salvation history, from the story of Adam and Eve's sin to the close of the Millennium.

Law and Gospel have continuing purposes in the lives of both unbelievers and believers. For the unbeliever the Law condemns, accuses, and shows him his need for the Lord. For the believer the Law continues to show our need for grace, and gives guidelines for daily living. The Gospel shows the unbeliever a way of escape from condemnation; for the believer it serves as a motivation to keep God's moral law.

The careful differentiation between, but maintenance of, both Law and Gospel has been an important hermeneutical tool and hallmark of Lutheran preaching. The Lutheran position places strong emphasis on continuity. God continues to respond to man with both Law and Grace as He has from the very beginning of human history. Law and Grace are not two different epochs of God's dealing with man, but are integral parts of His every relationship. For further reading on the Lutheran position, I recommend the following two books:

P. Althaus, *The Theology of Martin Luther*

C. F. W. Walther, *The Proper Distinction Between Law and Gospel*

Covenantal Theology

Another framework that focuses on continuity rather than discontinuity in salvation history is covenantal theology. Covenantal theologians view all biblical history as covered by two covenants, a covenant of works until the Fall, and a covenant of grace from the Fall to the present. (Some reformed theologians speak of a third covenant—the covenant of redemption—that was made in eternity past. This was an agreement between the Father and the Son, in which the Father pronounced the Son to be Head and Redeemer of the elect, and the Son voluntarily agreed to die for those whom the Father had given him.)

The *covenant of works* is that agreement between God and Adam that promised Adam life for perfect obedience and death as the penalty for disobedience. The *covenant of grace* is the agreement between God and a sinner in which God promises salvation through faith, and the sinner promises a life of faith and obedience.[10] All Old Testament, New Testament and contemporary believers are part of the covenant of grace.

Some students of Scripture believe that covenantal theologians minimize the difference between the Old and New Testaments. Covenantal theologians respond to this criticism by making several points. First, God saved Old Testament believers by grace just as He did New Testament believers; therefore they can both be accurately considered under the covenant of grace. Second, the many comparisons between the Old and New Testaments in the book of Hebrews never describe them as antithetic. The change is from a good covenant relationship to an even better one. The idolatrous Israelites had rejected the good covenant that God had offered in the Old Testament (a covenant of grace). God replaced it with another covenant of grace even more gracious than the original one. One can further describe the relationship as one that looked forward to its fulfillment, and one that had experienced the fulfillment itself. The blood of bulls and goats could never take away sin finally and absolutely, but simply acted as a down payment until Christ came as the perfect atonement (Heb. 10:1–10). Therefore, covenantal theologians conclude, the Old and New Testament covenants are synthetic rather than antithetic. Both are covenants of grace, one built on the gracious promises of its predecessor.

A second criticism brought against covenantal theology is that the Old Testament speaks of several covenants—a pre-Flood Noahic covenant (Gen. 6:18); a post-Flood Noahic covenant (Gen. 9:8–17); an Abrahamic covenant (Gen. 15:8, 18;

17:6–8); a Mosaic covenant (Ex. 6:6–8); a Davidic covenant (Ps. 89:3, 4, 26–27); and a new covenant (Jer. 31:31–34). Considering this, is it proper to speak of one covenant of grace rather than several covenants? If there are several covenants, is not covenantal theory almost the same as dispensational theory?

Although covenantal theologians recognize each of these individual covenants, there are several differences between covenantal and dispensational conceptions of salvation history. In response to the first issue above, the covenantal conception of salvation history emphasizes continuity: a general covenant of grace overshadowed each specific covenant. God has called human beings by grace, justified them by grace, and adopted them into His family by grace ever since the Fall. Thus covenantal theologians believe it is accurate to group these individual covenants under the more general heading of the covenant of grace.

Dispensational theologians place more emphasis on discontinuity. While most of them would agree that salvation has always been by grace, they also believe that there are significant changes regarding God's commands for obedient living that occur across the dispensations. Although some recent dispensational theologians are now stressing the continuity between the dispensations, previous dispensational theologians emphasized the differences. Humanity's responsibilities within each dispensation are a different type of test from the previous one. Thus when humans weren't obedient to God when given the responsibility of following conscience (second dispensation), God gave them the responsibility of obedience through government.

Covenantal theologians place more emphasis on the additive rather than the disjunctive nature of the covenants. For example, the post-Flood Noahic covenant was consistent with the pre-Flood covenant; it simply filled in more details of the grace relationship. Similarly, the Mosaic covenant did not abolish the Abrahamic one; rather, the Mosaic covenant added to the Abrahamic (Gal. 3:17–22). Thus, starting from the same biblical data and very similar views of inspiration and revelation, dispensational and covenantal theologians have arrived at moderately different views of salvation history. These views are reflected in different theological analyses of all passages other than the Epistles.

The following four books present further information on covenantal theory: the first three authors are covenantal theologians. The fourth author critiques covenantal theology.

Louis Berkhof, *Systematic Theology*, pp. 262–301

J. Oliver Buswell, Jr. *Systematic Theology*, vol. 1: pp. 307–320

E. W. Hengstenberg, "The New Covenant," in *Classical Evangelical Essays in Old Testament Theology*, ed., W. C. Kaiser, Jr.

C. C. Ryrie, *Dispensationalism Today*, pp. 177–191

The Epigenetic Model

The epigenetic theory views divine revelation as analogous to the growth of a tree from a seed, to a seedling, to a young tree, and then to a fully grown tree. We can contrast this model with one that likens divine revelation to the building of a cathedral piece by piece. A cathedral when half built is an imperfect cathedral. A tree when half grown can be a perfect tree. The epigenetic theory views God's self-disclosures as never being imperfect or errant, though later disclosures may add further information.

The idea of progressive revelation, which is almost unanimously held by evangelical scholars, is highly consistent with the epigenetic theory. *Progressive revelation* is the concept that God's revelation gradually increased in definiteness, clarity, and fullness over time, even as a tree increases its girth and root and branch structures over time. The trunk and branches of a tree grow in several directions simultaneously. So also humanity's knowledge of God, Christ, salvation, and the nature of human beings grew simultaneously as God's revelation progressed.

In some important ways, the epigenetic model may be viewed as a middle road between dispensationalism and covenantal theology. Covenantal theologians often criticize dispensationalists of minimizing the essential unity of Scripture. Dispensationalists contend that covenantal theologians fail to maintain important distinctions that should be maintained (e.g., the difference between Israel and the church). A model that is responsive to both criticisms would emphasize the unity of salvation history but allow for valid differentiation as well. The epigenetic model, with its unified trunk but variegated branch structure, provides one such model.

Kaiser, who has encouraged the acceptance of the epigenetic model, suggests that the idea of God's promise might serve as the central organizing concept within this model. He describes the promise as God's pledge to do or be something for the Old Testament Israelites, then for future Israelites, and eventually for all nations. This promise gradually becomes more defined and differentiated. Branches of the promise include: (1) material blessings for all humans and animals; (2) a special seed to humankind; (3) a land for a chosen nation; (4) spiritual blessings for all nations; (5) a national deliverance from bondage; (6) an enduring dynasty and kingdom that will one day embrace a universal dominion; (7) a forgiveness of sin; and others.[11] The promise thus extends from the past to the present and into the future.

The promise doctrine is not the only possible central organizing principle that could be suggested for the epigenetic models. Lutherans probably would want to suggest that Christ be the central concept. J. Barton Payne might have suggested

"God's testament" as a candidate. Others might suggest God's grace, in all its manifestations, as a possibility.

Doing Theological Analysis

The discussion up to this point has been preliminary to the steps of doing theological analysis. Remember that theological analysis involves understanding how what God said before and after the passage you are studying enhances your ability to understand His intended meaning in the passage. Here are my recommended steps for doing theological analysis.

1. *Select the view of salvation history that you believe best fits the biblical data.* You may have grown up in a church that does not emphasize any of the views mentioned in this chapter. It could be argued that we all interpret Scripture based on some view of salvation history, whether we're conscious of this or not. Therefore it's probably best to use your conscious mind to evaluate these four possibilities and any others of which you may be aware. Then make a decision about which one best fits the scriptural data.

2. *Identify the implications of this view for the passage you are studying.* For example, if you choose a view of salvation history that is primarily discontinuous, this will have certain implications for how you would explain and apply a passage in the Old Testament. Those implications will be different if you choose a view of salvation history that is primarily continuous.

3. *Assess the extent of theological knowledge available to the original recipients of the letter.* What previous knowledge had they been given? (Some authors of hermeneutics textbooks refer to this previous knowledge as the "analogy of Scripture" or the "analogy of antecedent Scripture.") Good biblical theology texts may prove helpful in this regard. (Biblical theology and systematic theology books are organized somewhat differently. Biblical theology texts discuss passages based only on the theological understanding the recipients

had available to them at the time. ~~Systematic theology~~ texts discuss issues based on everything known about that topic from all of Scripture.)

4. *Decide what meaning the passage possessed for its original recipients in light of the knowledge available to them.*

5. *Identify the additional knowledge about this topic that is available to us now because of later revelation.* (Authors of hermeneutics textbooks sometimes refer to this as the "analogy of faith.") Systematic theology texts and Bible dictionaries will often prove helpful in acquiring this type of information. If you prefer to do your own research directly rather than depending on someone else, *Nave's Topical Bible* lists relevant Scriptures on 20,000 topics.

LITERARY ANALYSIS

Good communicators use a variety of literary devices for illustration, clarification, emphasis, and maintenance of audience interest. Some common literary devices and genre found in Scripture include similes, metaphors, parables, proverbs, and allegories.

E. D. Hirsch likens various types of literary methods to games: to understand them properly it is necessary to know what game you are playing. It is also necessary to know the rules of that game. Conflicts in interpretation arise because (1) readers disagree about what game is being played, or (2) they disagree about the proper rules for playing that game.[12] Fortunately for us, careful literary analysis has yielded a substantial body of knowledge concerning the characteristics of these literary forms and the principles necessary to interpret them properly.

Two of the simplest literary devices are similes and metaphors. A *simile* is simply an expressed comparison: it typically uses the words *like* or *as* (for example, "The kingdom of heaven is like. . . ."). The emphasis is on some point of similarity between two ideas, groups, actions, etc. The author keeps the subject and the thing being compared separate (for example, not "The kingdom of heaven is. . . ." but rather "The kingdom of heaven is like. . . .").[13]

A *metaphor* is an unexpressed comparison: it does not use the words *like* or *as*. The author intertwines the subject and the thing which he is comparing to it. Jesus was using a metaphor when He said, "I am the bread of life," and "You are the light of the world." Although Jesus identifies the subject and its comparison as one, He does not intend His words to be taken literally. Christ is not a loaf of bread any more than we are Sylvania light bulbs. Because of their compact nature, an author uses similes and metaphors to stress a single point. For example, Christ is the source of sustenance for our spiritual lives; Christians are to be examples of godly living in a sin-darkened world.

A *parable* can be understood as an extended simile. The author indicates that he is making a comparison, he explains the subject and the thing compared more fully than in a simile, and he keeps them separate. Similarly an *allegory* can be understood as an extended metaphor: the author does not use the words *like* or *as*, and he intermingles the subject and the thing being compared.

A *proverb* is a short, pithy statement that contains an important spiritual insight. Because of their highly condensed forms, proverbs usually have a single point of comparison or principle of truth to convey. Pressing a proverb in all its incidental points usually results in going beyond the author's intention. For example, when King Lemuel says of the virtuous woman that "she is like the merchants' ships" (Prov. 31:14 KJV), he did not intend this to be a statement about her girth. She is like the ships of the merchants because she goes various places gathering food for the needs of her household.

Thus proverbs, like similes and metaphors, usually convey a single intended point of comparison. They also are not intended to say all there is to say about a given topic or situation. Each kernel of truth contained in a proverb should be applied only within the context of all the other truths God has given us in His Word.

Understanding the Literary Sophistication of the Biblical Writers

We need to be aware that the biblical writers and their audiences were not sophisticated literary scholars. They were not aware of the distinctions we have just drawn, and did not always observe those distinctions. The most common Hebrew and Greek words referring to these genres were used quite fluidly. D. A. Carson says that the Hebrew word *masal* can refer to "proverbs, maxims, similes, allegories, fables, comparisons, riddles, taunts, and stories embodying some truth."[14] Similarly, the word translated parable (*parabole*), can refer to a proverb, a profound or obscure saying, a non-verbal symbol or image, an illustrative comparison without a story, and (the situation that we usually associate with the word parable), an illustrative comparison that includes a story.[15]

Therefore we need to be careful not to expect in Scripture the same kind of precision in formulating parables and allegories that we might expect from a twentieth-century English professor. We can describe certain characteristics that frequently appear in such stories, but then realize that any "rule" that we make about the structure or interpretation of these genres is likely to be broken by the biblical speakers or authors more than once.

Parables

As mentioned above, parables are like extended similes in structure. They usually include the words "like" or "as." The speaker usually keeps the subject and the thing to which it is being compared separate (e.g., "the kingdom of heaven is like a man who sowed good seed in his field.") Usually the speaker tells the story first, and tells the interpretation, if there is one, at the end (see Isaiah 5:1–7). Usually there is a single point of comparison (a focal idea); but sometimes some details also will have significance as they relate to that focal idea.

For example, the focal point of the parable of the soils is that the preaching of the Word will meet with varying receptions in the lives of those who hear it. Jesus then goes on in His parable to elaborate on four types of reception. There are those who have hardened their hearts against the message, and there will be no chance for it to take root. There are those who receive the message with enthusiasm, but have not taken it into their lives at a deep level. When pressure comes, they quickly fall away. There are others who gladly take the Gospel into their hearts, but then allow the love of money and cares of this world to choke out their spiritual vitality. The fourth category are those who gladly receive the message and go on to produce much spiritual fruit.

Notice how the details that are significant are all related to one focal idea. This is different from the structure of an allegory, where there may be several significant details, but they may fall in a line as the allegory develops rather than around one focus.

Allegories

Allegories are like extended metaphors in structure. They do not include the words "like" or "as." The author usually intertwines the subject and the thing with which it is being compared, rather than presenting the story first, and following it with an interpretation. Psalm 80:8–16 (comparing Israel to a vine) contains an example of an allegory. It is useful to compare Psalm 80:8–16 with Isaiah 5:1–7. Both passages treat the same subject matter, but Psalm 80 does it through an allegory and Isaiah 5 does it using a parable.

A parable usually has a single focal idea; details of the parable (such as the four kinds of soil) have meaning as they relate to that focal idea. In an allegory there may be several important ideas, and they do not necessarily converge. They may simply appear in linear fashion as the allegory unfolds.

For example, let's examine the allegory of Christ the Good Shepherd found in John 10:1–18. The context for this story was Jesus' healing of the blind man, who had responded to Him in faith as the true Shepherd (see John 9). The Pharisees questioned the man, who persisted in his belief in Jesus. The Pharisees (wonderful "shepherds" that they were) then excommunicated him.

Jesus was very angry with these false shepherds (read verses 39–41). In His indignation He told this story (John 10:1–5), but because of its highly condensed nature, His audience didn't understand His meaning. In response Jesus retold the story, giving more details (vv. 7–18). Here are some of His major teaching points:

1. Jesus is the means of entry for salvation. Those who come to God through Him will be saved (vv. 7 and 9).

2. Those who came before Him were thieves and robbers. Thieves (*kleptes*) are those who steal through subtlety and trickery. Robbers (*lestes*) are those who steal through violence and plundering. (An exact identification of the thieves and robbers is impossible. Thieves—those who steal through subtlety and trickery—may be a reference to the Pharisees. Robbers—those who steal through violence and plundering —may be a reference to some of the cruel governors Rome placed over the nation of Israel. The two groups together refer to those who by pretense or violence attempt to gain

control of the sheep. There is a sharp contrast between Jesus and the false shepherds. The false shepherds tend the sheep, not for the good of the sheep, but to gain something for themselves from the sheep. Jesus comes to the sheep so that they might have abundant life (vv. 8 and 10).

3. There is a contrast between Jesus the Good Shepherd and the hirelings. He is willing to lay down His life for the sheep: they run away because they care more for themselves than for the sheep (vv. 11–13).

4. The word *ginosko* means "to know"—"to have a relationship of trust and intimacy with someone." Jesus has an intimate personal relationship with both the sheep and the Father, and the sheep have a personal relationship with Him. By omission, it is implied that the false shepherds have neither (vv. 14–15).

5. Verse 16 is Jesus' prophecy that there are other sheep who are not of this fold, whom He would call into the fold. This is probably a prediction that He would call Gentiles into the family of believers (v. 16).

6. Jesus says that He will lay down His life voluntarily. The Pharisees will not take it from Him, but He will give His life for the sheep of His own volition (vv. 17–18).

There are three reasons why this story is considered an allegory rather than a parable. First, the six points listed above are more linear than structured around a single focus. (Some might argue that the focus was the Good Shepherd. However, look also at the second and third reasons.) Second, the meaning of the story is implicit within the story, rather than added as a separate section at the end. Third, the story sounds like an expanded metaphor: it does not use the words "like" or "as."

An Important Caveat

Because the biblical writers and speakers did not have formal rules for distinguishing parables and allegories, their use of these genres may not follow all the distinctions that we have made in the last few pages, nor should we expect them to do so. It is better to look at each of these illustrative stories in their historical context. Then ask yourself, "What were the author's intended points as he told this story?" This is not as subjective a process as it might sound. Usually, by examining the structure of the story in context, it quickly becomes evident what point(s) the speaker was intending to make.[16]

Probably there is no genre in Scripture that is more prone to eisegesis than parables. Many pastors are fond of taking a well-known parable, looking at the incidental details, and coming up with creative sermons based on those details. The points that they develop are often biblical points, and the sermons may be edifying to many in the audience. Hermeneutically, though, the biblical speaker or writer never intended to be teaching the points the pastor or teacher derived from that passage. Walter C. Kaiser says of such preaching: "Great sermon, wrong text." We call the situation in which a speaker derives many more points from a parable than the biblical author intended "allegorizing a parable."

I will not discuss the biblical genres of types, prophecy and apocalyptic here because that would take us too far afield of the purposes of this book. If you are interested in these genre, you may consult my larger book on hermeneutics—*Hermeneutics: Principles and Processes of Biblical Interpretation,* or one of the following books:

Gleason Archer, Paul Feinberg, Douglas Moo, and Richard Reiter, *The Rapture: Pre-, Mid-, or Post-Tribulation?*
Robert Clouse, ed., *The Meaning of the Millennium*
Patrick Fairburn, *The Typology of Scripture*
R. Ludwigson, *A Survey of Biblical Prophecy*
Leon Morris, *Apocalyptic*

J. Barton Payne, *Encyclopedia of Biblical Prophecy*
J. Dwight Pentecost, *Things to Come*
Merrill Tenney, *Interpreting Revelation*
John Walvoord, *The Millennial Kingdom*

Summary of Steps for Interpreting These Genres or Literary Devices

1. Do a historical-cultural and contextual analysis.
2. Do a lexical-syntactical analysis.
3. Do a theological analysis.
4. Identify the literary genre and apply an appropriate analysis.
   a. Look for explicit references that show the author's intent regarding the method he was using.
   b. If the text does not explicitly identify the literary form of the passage, study the characteristics of the passage to ascertain its form.
   c. Apply the principles of genre analysis carefully but not rigidly.
      (1) Similes, metaphors and proverbs: look for the single point of comparison.
      (2) Parables: identify the focal teaching and the details of significance surrounding it.
      (3) Allegories: look for the multiple points of comparison intended by the author.
5. State your understanding of the meaning of the passage.
6. Check to see whether your stated meaning "fits" into the immediate context and total context of the book. If it doesn't, recycle the process.
7. Compare your work with that of others.

APPLYING THE BIBLICAL MESSAGE ACROSS CULTURES

This topic is not a part of hermeneutics per se. Hermeneutics studies the author's intended meaning. In this section we will address the question, Once we understand the author's intended meaning, how do we apply that meaning in another time and culture? In this section I will propose two methods. One can be used when dealing with narrative portions of Scripture, i.e., the stories. The second can be used when examining prescriptive passages, i.e., those that teach theology or prescribe behavior that Christians either should or should not do.

Principlizing: An Alternative to Allegorizing Biblical Narratives

When we are in a position where we have to teach or preach from a narrative portion of Scripture, a simple retelling of the story is generally an ineffective and insufficient expository method. By itself such a method leads to a "B.C. message," a message that had meaning for its original recipients but which fails to seem relevant to believers today. What we need is an expository method that makes the narrative portions of Scripture relevant for contemporary believers. It should do this without making the text say something the original author did not intend it to say. Principlizing is one method of doing this.

Principlizing is an attempt to discover in a narrative the spiritual, moral, or theological principles that have relevance for the contemporary believer. Principlizing rests on the assumption that the Holy Spirit chose those historical incidents that are recorded in Scripture for a purpose—to give information, to make a point, to illustrate an important truth, etc. Principlizing is a method of trying to understand a story so that we can recognize the original reason the Holy Spirit included it in Scripture, the principles He wanted to teach.

Allegorizing gives meaning to a story by assigning symbolic significance to its details that the original author never intended. (For example, one allegorist expounded the story of Herod killing all the boy babies in Bethlehem who were two years old and under in the following way. He said that the story meant that Binitarians and Unitarians will surely perish, but Trinitarians will be saved.) In contrast, principlizing seeks to derive its teachings from a careful understanding of the story itself.

Methodologically, the approach is the same as in the exegesis of any biblical passage. We should carefully observe the historical circumstances and cultural customs that help us understand the significance of actions and commands. We should identify the purpose of the book within which the narrative occurs, and also the immediate context surrounding the narrative. We should survey the state of theological knowledge and commitment.

When we have done all these things, we can understand the meaning of the story, in its original setting. Finally, based on that understanding, we attempt to articulate the principle(s) illustrated by the story, principles that continue to possess relevance for the contemporary believer. An example of principlizing follows.

An Analysis of the Temptation Process

A framework for understanding the process of temptation can be drawn from the story that recounts the first such enticement, as found in Genesis 3:1–6. The text reads as follows:

> Now the serpent was more crafty than any of the wild animals the Lord God had made. He said to the woman,

"Did God really say, 'You must not eat from any tree in the garden'?"

The woman said to the serpent, "We may eat fruit from the trees in the garden, but God did say, 'You must not eat fruit from the tree that is in the middle of the garden, and you must not touch it, or you will die.'"

"You will not surely die," the serpent said to the woman. "For God knows that when you eat of it your eyes will be opened, and you will be like God, knowing good and evil."

When the woman saw that the fruit of the tree was good for food and pleasing to the eye, and also desirable for gaining wisdom, she took some and ate it. She also gave some to her husband, who was with her, and he ate it.

Significance of the Actions

Maximizing the Restriction

Satan's temptation of Eve can be understood in six steps, steps that we can see in Satan's temptations of believers today. Verse one records the first step. We may paraphrase the Hebrew in the following way: "Now the serpent was more crafty than any wild creature that the Lord God had made. He said to the woman: 'Is it really a fact that God has prohibited you from eating from all the trees of the garden?'"

What is the dynamic here? Why did Satan ask this question? He obviously knew what God had said to Adam and Eve, or he couldn't have asked what he did. Also, he deliberately distorted what God had said, "Is it really a fact that God has prohibited you from eating of *all* the trees of the garden?" Satan's ploy is obvious: he was getting Eve to take her eyes off all the things God had given her to enjoy, and to focus on the one thing that God had forbidden. There were probably a thousand pleasurable things Eve could have done in the garden, but now she has focused all her attention on the one thing she is not supposed to do. We might call this first step maximizing the restriction.

Minimizing the Consequences

Eve was now psychologically prepared for Satan's next step. In response to Eve's statement that God said that eating of the fruit of the tree would result in death, Satan boldly declared: "You will not surely die." The results of such-and-such an action won't really be as bad as God has said. This might be called minimizing the consequences of sin. Satan minimized the consequences of sin in two ways: first, by telling Eve that the consequences of sin would not be as bad as God has said they would be, and second, by eventually focusing her attention so completely on the tree that she forgot the consequences entirely (v. 6).

Mislabeling the Action

The third step Satan took might be called mislabeling the action. In verse 5 he says: "For God knows that when you eat of it your eyes will be opened, and you will be like God, knowing good and evil." Here Satan planted the suspicion in Eve's mind that it was not because the fruit of the tree would injure her that God had forbidden her to eat it. It was because He did not wish her to be like Himself. Satan deftly removed his temptation from the category of sin by relabeling it. In this instance, he relabeled partaking of the fruit as a way of expanding her consciousness. She would become a more complete person if she tried it once. Before this time Eve had thought of the forbidden action as disobedience: now she sees it as a necessity if she is to become a complete and mature person.

Mixing Good and Evil

Satan then quickly added another aspect to his temptation, an aspect that might be called mixing good and evil. Verse 6 reads: "The woman saw that the fruit of the tree was good for food." C. S. Lewis has commented that evil is often a perversion of something good that God has created. In this instance Satan added potency to his temptation by mixing good with evil: Eve saw that the tree was good for food.

Mixing Sin with Beauty

We find the fifth aspect of Eve's temptation in the middle part of verse 6: "She saw that the fruit of the tree was . . . pleasing to the eye." This might be called mixing sin with beauty. Temptation often comes wrapped in something beautiful, something that appeals to our senses and desires. It is often necessary to think twice before we recognize that a beautiful object or goal is really sin in disguise. In this incident Eve didn't discriminate between the beautiful package and the sinful contents that the package contained.

Misplacing One's Trust

Finally Eve took a sixth step: the narrative tells us that "she saw that the fruit of the tree was . . . desirable for gaining wisdom." In essence she swallowed the devil's lie. This step might be called misplacing one's trust. Although this may seem like an insignificant point in the temptation process, it is perhaps the most crucial. In effect, by accepting Satan's statement, Eve was calling God a liar, though she might not have recognized those implications in her action. She accepted Satan as the truth-teller and God as the prevaricator: by partaking of the fruit she was implicitly stating her belief that Satan cared more for her welfare than God did. Yielding to the temptation implied that she accepted Satan's analysis of the situation instead of God's.

Application

Many of the same dynamics of Eve's temptation are present in Satan's temptations of believer's today. With only brief introspection we can often identify in our own temptations his tactics of maximizing the restriction, minimizing the consequences, mislabeling the action, mixing good and evil, and mixing sin with beauty. A minister or teacher or discussion leader can use whatever methods are appropriate to his role to help those who are listening to apply these new awarenesses to their lives.

Guidelines for Principlizing

1. Principlizing focuses on those principles implicit in a story that are applicable across time and cultures. The details may change, but the principles remain the same. For example, Satan may continue to tempt us by maximizing a restriction, but is not likely to do so by using a fruit tree.

2. When deriving the meaning of a story as a basis for principlizing, the meaning must always be developed from a careful historical-cultural and lexical-syntactical analysis. The meaning we derive must be the author's intended one.

3. From a theological standpoint, the meaning and principles derived from a story must be consistent with all other teachings of Scripture. An inductive principle drawn from a narrative that contradicts the teaching of another scriptural passage is invalid.

4. Principles derived by this method may be either universally applicable or not. For example, it is valid to say that Satan sometimes uses the above methods to tempt believers today. It would be invalid to say that he always uses these methods, or that he uses only these methods.

5. Texts have only one meaning, but may have many applications. Principlizing is a method of application. The meaning is the author's intended one, but the applications of that mean-

ing may refer to situations that the author, in a different culture, never envisioned. For example, I have written a book on affairs in which I apply this six-step process to the situation of extramarital temptation in twentieth-century America. This is an application that Moses probably never envisioned.

Moses intended to give us a narrative account of the first temptation—not a psychological analysis of the temptation process. In order for our application of the text (through principlizing) to be valid, it must be firmly grounded in, and thoroughly consistent with, the author's intention. Thus if the author's intention in a narrative passage was to describe an event of temptation, it is valid to analyze that passage to understand the sequence and process of that particular temptation and then see how it might apply to our lives. It would be invalid to generalize from that same text principles about the way temptation always occurs, since the author did not intend the text to be the basis of normative doctrine.

Translating Biblical Commands from One Time and Culture to Another

To what extent are biblical commands to be understood as culturally-influenced and thus not binding on believers today? If some commands are to be binding and others are not, how can we develop a method for knowing which ones are in which category?

At one end of the spectrum are those interpreters who believe that often both the scriptural principle and the behavioral command that expresses that principle should be modified in light of historical changes. At the other end of the spectrum are those who believe that scriptural principles and their accompanying behavioral commands always should be applied literally within the church today. Many believers adopt a position somewhere between these two views.

Most evangelical churches have, by their actions, implicitly agreed that some biblical commands are not to be adopted wholesale into our time and culture. For example, Paul commands believers to greet one another with the holy kiss five times (Rom. 16:16; 1 Cor. 16:20; 2 Cor. 13:12; 1 Thess. 5:26; 1 Peter 5:14) yet very few churches observe this command today. Also, few Protestant churches observe the command for women to wear veils when praying (1 Cor. 11:5). Few churches practice footwashing as spoken of in John 13:14, because the changing cultures and times have lessened the need and significance of the practice.

More controversially, some evangelical churches now have women who preach, although Paul stated in 1 Timothy 2:12 that he permitted no woman to teach or have authority over men. Many evangelicals, men and women alike, are wondering whether the traditional husband-wife roles delineated in Ephesians 5 and other passages are to be continued in our culture and time. The question of whether practicing homosexuals should be accepted by churches or ordained to the ministry is causing tremendous uproar in certain denominations. Churches are struggling with several other issues as well.

Most evangelical Christians have accepted the view that some scriptural commands are culturally limited while others are not. It then becomes necessary to develop some criteria for distinguishing between those commands that continue to apply and those that do not. If our procedure is not to be simply arbitrary—one where we dismiss those commands and principles with which we disagree and retain those with which we agree—we must develop criteria, (a) the logic of which can be shown, (b) that can be consistently applied to a variety of issues and questions, and (c) the nature of which we draw from Scripture or, at least, show to be consistent with Scripture.

Establishing a Theoretical Framework for Analyzing Behavior and Behavioral Commands

First postulate: A single behavior usually has ambiguous significance for the observer. For example, I may look out my study window and see a man walking up the street. I do not know whether he is (a) getting some exercise by taking a walk, (b) on his way to catch a bus, or (c) leaving home after an argument with his wife.

Second postulate: Behavior takes on more meaning for the observer as he ascertains more about its context. As I observe the man more closely, I hypothesize that he is a student on his way to a class because of his age, dress, briefcase, and books. However, I also observe a woman, apparently his wife (because of similar clothing styles) following about fifteen feet behind him, walking with her head down. I immediately wonder whether they have been fighting, and she is following him in an attempt to pacify him. I dismiss this hypothesis when I recognize that the clothing styles show that this couple is from a culture where it is normal and expected that the wife walk a certain distance behind her husband whenever they are together in public.

Third postulate: Behavior that has a certain meaning in one culture may have a totally different significance in another. In American society, for a woman to follow her husband at a distance of fifteen feet, with her head down, would usually suggest a problem in their relationship. In another culture, this behavior may be normal and expected. (For many other examples of behavior that has different meanings in different cultures, see Edwin Yamauchi, "Christianity and Cultural Differences," *Christianity Today,* June 23, 1972, pp. 5–8.)

Let us examine the implications of these three postulates.

First, the meaning of a single behavior cannot be understood apart from its context. By analogy, the meaning of (and principle behind) a behavioral command in Scripture cannot be understood apart from the context of that command.

Second, the meaning behind a given behavior can be more accurately understood the more one knows about the context of that behavior. Similarly, the more we know of the context of a behavioral command, other things being equal, the more accurately we can understand the meaning of (and the principle expressed by) that command.

Third, since a given behavior in one culture may have a different meaning in another culture, it may be necessary to change the behavioral expression of a scriptural command to translate the principle behind that command from one culture and time into another.

Two aspects of biblical commands need to be differentiated: the behavior specified, and the principle expressed through the specified behavior. For example, the holy kiss greeting (behavior) expressed brotherly and sisterly love (principle).

In making transcultural applications of biblical commands, three alternatives can be considered:

1. Retain both the principle and its behavioral expression.
2. Retain the principle but suggest a change in the behavioral expression of that principle in our culture.
3. Change both the principle and its behavioral expression, assuming that both were culture-bound and are therefore no longer applicable.

For example, let us look at the custom of the veiling of women as an expression of voluntary submission to their husbands (1 Cor. 11:2–16). Commentators have taken three approaches.

1. Retain both the principle of submission and its expression through the use of veils.
2. Retain the principle of submission but replace veiling with another behavior that more meaningfully expresses submission in our culture.

3. Replace both the principle of submission and all expressions of submission with a more egalitarian philosophy, believing that the idea of hierarchy within the family is a culture-bound one.

Thus the analysis of biblical commands into principles, and behaviors that express those principles, possesses little worth unless there are some means for differentiating between those principles and behaviors that are culture-bound and those that are transcultural.

Guidelines for Discerning Whether Principles Are Transcultural or Culture-bound

First, find the reason given for the principle. For example, we are to love one another because God first loved us (1 John 4:19). We are not to love the world and its values, because love of the world and love of God are mutually exclusive (1 John 2:15).

Second, if the reason for a principle is culture-bound, then the principle may be also. If the reason has its basis in God's unchanging nature (His grace, His love, His moral nature, or His created order), then the principle itself probably should not be changed.

Guidelines for Discerning Whether Commands (Applications of Principles) Are Transcultural or Culture-Bound

First, when a transcultural principle is expressed through a behavior that was part of the common cultural habits of the time, the behavior may be modified, even though the principle remains unchanged. For example, Jesus modeled the principle that we should have an attitude of humility and willingness to serve one another (Mark 10:42–44) by washing the disciples' feet (John 13:12–16), a familiar custom of the day. We retain the principle, although it is possible that there are other ways to express that principle more meaningfully in our culture.

As another example, James argued that believers should not show partiality in the church meeting by having the rich sit in chairs and the poor sit on the floor (James 2:1–9). We retain the principle of nonpartiality, but the application of the principle takes on different dimensions in our time and culture.

Second, when a practice that was an accepted part of a pagan culture was forbidden in Scripture, this is probably to be forbidden in contemporary culture as well, particularly if Scripture grounds this command in God's moral nature. Examples of practices that pagan cultures accepted but which God forbade in Scripture include fornication, adultery, spiritism, divorce, and homosexual behavior.

Third, it is important to define the intended recipients of a command, and to apply the command with care to other groups. If God gave a command to one church only, this may show that God meant it to be a local rather than a universal command (for example, Paul's prohibition of a fellowship supper before communion).

Some Suggested Steps in Translating Biblical Commands from One Culture and Time to Another

1. Discern as accurately as possible the principle behind the given behavioral command. For example, Christians are to judge individual sin within their local community of believers because, if unchecked, evil will have an effect upon the entire community (1 Cor. 5:1–13, especially v. 6).

2. Discern whether the principle is timeless or time-bound (transcultural or culture-bound). I have offered some suggestions for doing this in the preceding section. Since Scripture roots most biblical principles in God's unchanging nature, it

seems to follow that a principle should be considered transcultural unless there is evidence to the contrary.

3. If a principle is transcultural, study the nature of its behavioral expression within our culture. Will the behavioral expression given then be appropriate now, or will it be an anachronistic oddity?

There is a very real danger of conforming the biblical message to our cultural mold. There are times when the expression of a God-given principle will cause us to behave in ways different from non-Christians (Rom. 12:2), but not needlessly so, not for the sake of difference itself. The criterion for whether a behavioral command should be applied in our culture should not be whether it conforms to modern cultural practices, but whether it adequately and accurately expresses the principle God intended.

4. If the behavioral expression of a principle should be changed, suggest a cultural equivalent that would adequately express the God-given principle behind the original command. For example, J. B. Phillips suggests that "Greet one another with a hearty handshake" may be a good cultural equivalent to "Greet one another with the holy kiss." For further discussion of this oriental custom, see Fred Wright, *Manners and Customs in Bible Lands* (Chicago: Moody Press, 1953), pp. 74–75.

If there is no cultural equivalent, it might be worthwhile to consider creating a new cultural behavior that would meaningfully express the principles involved. (In a similar but not strictly analogous manner, some contemporary wedding ceremonies express the same principles as more traditional ones, but in creative and meaningful new ways.)

5. If after careful study the nature of the biblical principle and its attendant command remain in question, apply the biblical precept of humility. Occasionally, even after careful study of a given principle and its behavioral expression, we

still may remain uncertain about whether it should be considered transcultural or culture-bound. If we must decide to treat the command one way or the other but have no conclusive means to make the decision, the biblical principle of humility can be helpful. After all, would it be better to treat a principle as transcultural and be guilty of being overscrupulous in our desire to obey God? Or would it be better to treat a transcultural principle as culture-bound and be guilty of breaking a transcendent requirement of God?

If we isolate this humility principle from the other guidelines mentioned above, it could easily be misconstrued as ground for unnecessary conservatism. The principle should be applied only after we have carefully tried to decide whether a principle is transcultural or culture-bound, and, despite our best efforts, the issue still remains uncertain. This is a guideline of last resort and would be harmful if used as a first resort.[17]

SUMMARY OF CHAPTER 3

Theological Analysis

1. Select the view of salvation history that you believe best fits the biblical data.
2. Identify the implications of this view for the passage you are studying.
3. Assess the extent of theological knowledge available to the original recipients of the letter.
4. Decide what meaning the passage possessed for its original recipients in light of the knowledge available to them.
5. Identify the additional knowledge about this topic that is available to us now because of later revelation.

Genre Analysis

1. Do a historical-cultural and contextual analysis.
2. Do a lexical-syntactical analysis.
3. Do a theological analysis.
4. Identify the literary genre and apply an appropriate analysis.
   a. Look for explicit references that show the author's intent regarding the method he was using.
   b. If the text does not explicitly identify the literary form of the passage, study the characteristics of the passage to ascertain its form.
   c. Apply the principles of genre analysis carefully but not rigidly.
      (1) Similes, metaphors and proverbs: look for the single point of comparison.
      (2) Parables: identify the focal teaching and the details of significance surrounding it.
      (3) Allegories: look for the multiple points of comparison intended by the author.
      (4) State your understanding of the meaning of the passage.
      (5) Check to see if your stated meaning "fits" into the immediate context and total context of the book. If it doesn't, recycle the process.
      (6) Compare your work with that of others.

Transculturation

1. Discern as accurately as possible the principle behind the given behavioral command.
2. Discern whether the principle is timeless or time-bound (transcultural or culture-bound).
3. If a principle is transcultural, study the nature of its behavioral expression within our culture.
4. If the behavioral expression of a principle should be changed, suggest a cultural equivalent that would adequately express the God-given principle behind the original command.

5. If after careful study the nature of the biblical principle and its attendant command remain in question, apply the biblical precept of humility.

EXERCISES

EX 11: A couple comes to you for counseling about a certain matter. The husband says that they need a new car. He wants to finance it through their local bank since they don't have the money to pay for it in cash. His wife, basing her argument on Romans 13:8 ("Owe no man any thing" KJV), believes it is wrong to borrow money to purchase the car. The husband says he doesn't think that the verse refers to their situation and wants to know what you think. What will you do?

EX 12: A married couple you have been counseling reveals that the husband has been having an affair. The husband professes to be a Christian, so you ask him how he reconciles his behavior with the biblical teaching on marital faithfulness. He replies that he loves both persons, and justifies his behavior based on 1 Corinthians 6:12 ("All things are lawful for me" RSV). What will you do?

EX 13: A sincere young Christian attended a teaching series about praying in faith. The series focused primarily on two verses. The first was Psalm 37:4 ("Delight yourself in the LORD and he will give you the desires of your heart"). The second was Mark 11:24 ("Whatever you ask for in prayer, believe that you have received it, and it will be yours"). Based on the teaching received in the series, he began to write checks "on faith," and they bounced, much to his dismay. How would you counsel him regarding the teaching he had received concerning these verses?

EX 14: Some writers have suggested that there is an inconsistency between the doctrine of Paul (as found in Gal. 2:15–16; Rom. 3:20, 28) and doctrine of James (as found in James 1:22–25; 2:8, 14–17, 21–24). Do you believe these can be reconciled? If so, how would you reconcile them?

EX 15: In Deuteronomy 19:21 God's command is "eye for eye, tooth for tooth." Jesus, claiming that He was fulfilling the law, said: "Do not resist an evil person. If someone strikes you on the right cheek, turn to him the other also" (Matt. 5:39). How do you reconcile these two statements?

EX 16: In 1 Timothy 2:12 Paul says that he does not allow a woman to teach or have authority over men. Using the model presented in this chapter, discuss these questions: (1) What was the meaning of this text for Timothy?; (2) What application should it have for us today?; (3) What implications does your view have for (a) female Sunday school teachers, (b) female hospital chaplains, (c) female seminary teachers, (d) female pastors, and (e) female missionaries?

EX 17: Some believers use Acts 4:32–35 as the basis for Christian communal living today. What hermeneutical considerations are relevant to such an application of this text?

EX 18: Basing his view on Ephesians 6:1–3, a noted Christian speaker teaches that children should never go against their parents' wishes. They are to allow God to direct them through their parents as long as they are unmarried. Is this a valid understanding of the text as Paul originally gave it? If it is, is it as valid to apply it in the same way today in our American culture? If you answered affirmatively to both of the above questions, does this obligation ever end?

EX 19: With the rising divorce rate in the twentieth century, many churches are being faced with the question of what roles, if any, divorced and remarried persons may play in the leadership/service functions of the church. How do you think the teaching of 1 Timothy 3:2, 12 applies to that question?

EX 20: As a preface to his exposition of a text a minister said, "I have gotten this message from no other man. I have consulted no other commentaries: it comes straight from the Book!" Comment on this method of expositional preparation.

Part Three

INTERPRETING GOD'S WORLD

CHAPTER 4

Principles of Experimental Design

INTRODUCTION

Development of the Scientific Method

To interpret information accurately from the world around us, we must have some method for determining whether there is a cause-and-effect relationship between two events. We generally employ an empirical research design and statistical analysis to make such a determination.

There are five basic steps to the scientific method. First, the researcher states a problem, sometimes in the form of a question. Second, he or she collects facts that relate to the question or problem. Third, the researcher forms a hypothesis that explains the known facts. Fourth, the investigator makes inferences (or predictions) that will be confirmed if his or her hypothesis is true. Fifth, the scientist conducts an experiment to verify his or her predictions. If the predictions hold true, one's hypothesis receives some confirmation. If the predictions are inaccurate, either the researcher must change the hypothesis or give an explanation why the experimental results were not as anticipated.

Definitions of Basic Terms

Because there is so much confusion about relativism and inability to know objective truth let's take a few moments to define several basic terms. *Belief* refers to a person's attitude toward a particular statement.[1] Thus I might believe that the Shroud of Turin is the actual burial cloth of Jesus. Or I might believe that the shroud is *not* the burial cloth of Jesus.

When we call a proposition (or statement) true, we mean that the statement describes an actual state of affairs. For example, the fact that Atlanta is the capital of Georgia is a true proposition. The fact that George Bush was President of the United States in 1991 is a true proposition. The statement that Alaska seceded from the Union in 1990 is not a true proposition.

There is an important distinction between belief and truth. Truth is not relative, but belief is. This is why it sometimes appears that truth changes, when it is our beliefs that have changed. People once believed that the earth was the center of our solar system. Only with great reluctance did some of them change their belief to accord with the actual state of affairs.

If a proposition is true, it remains true whether or not I believe it to be true. If a proposition is false, nothing I believe about the proposition will change that objective reality. Beliefs do not change objective reality, although they do change a person's subjective reality.

An *objective claim* is a proposition whose truth or falsity is independent of any specific individual's knowledge, beliefs, or experiences. A *subjective claim* is a proposition that a person believes is true based on his or her knowledge, beliefs, and experiences.

Empirical research enables us to formulate true empirical propositions, that is, make propositions that describe an actual state of affairs. Research can help us make accurate descriptions of the relationship between two variables. Empirical research also can help us investigate subjective claims to see whether they are true propositions.

Internal and External Validity

Whenever we conduct an experiment, we generally have two main goals. The first is to find whether there is a relationship between two or more variables. For example, an experimental psychologist named Ian may wish to see whether he can improve grade point averages (GPAs) of college students by having them take an eight-week course he has designed called "Developing Effective Study Habits." If Ian conducts this experiment, he wants to know (and be able to show) that the improvement in grades is due to his course and not to other factors. We call this ability to show that a change in grades is due to taking his course "internal validity." We call any factors that might compete with his course as an explanation for the increase in GPAs *threats to internal validity*.

Let us assume that after taking this course the average grade for students rose one letter grade (e.g., they went from a D− average to a C− average.) The second major thing Ian would want to do is to be able to predict whether his results could be generalized to students at other colleges. It is less significant for Ian to say that the program helped his students than if he can say that there is a reasonable likelihood that his program will help students at other colleges as well. We call the ability to generalize the results beyond those who took part in the experiment to a larger population "external validity." We call any factors that reduce Ian's ability to generalize from his experimental group to the larger population of college students *threats to external validity*.

We will examine the threats to internal validity in this chapter. In the process we will see why things such as control groups, double-blind studies, and well-validated assessment instruments are important to good research design. In the next chapter we will look at factors that are threats to external validity.

THREATS TO INTERNAL VALIDITY

Empirical research concerns itself with two sets of variables (a variable, reasonably enough, is anything that can vary up or down). *Independent variables* are the treatment variables, i.e., those variables that we believe cause changes in an organism. In older research, scientists usually tested only one treatment variable at a time. With modern statistical techniques it is now possible to evaluate more than one independent variable at a time. We can also examine the interaction between various variables (to be explained in a moment).

Dependent variables are those that measure the effect of the treatment (or independent variables). A researcher can examine scores on a single dependent variable, or can examine multiple dependent variables. Let's talk for a moment about multiple independent variables and interactions before going on.

Ian decided that he would like to use as independent variables (1) taking his study skills course, and (2) general intelligence. He will use scores on the Wechsler Adult Intelligence Scale-Revised (WAIS-R) as his measure of general intelligence. After completing the experiment he found that both independent variables were related to higher subsequent GPAs, and that there was an interaction between them. What do these results mean?

A statistically-significant relationship between IQ and GPA means the higher one's IQ, the higher one's GPA was likely to be. The statistically-significant relationship between taking the study skills course and subsequent GPA increase indicates that taking the study skills course generally led to higher GPAs. The interaction meant that taking the study skills course had different effects depending on one's IQ. Students with IQs of 90 or less showed little improvement in GPA after taking the course. As IQs increased, there was a corresponding increase in GPAs after the course.

We might hypothesize the following: those with IQs below 90 would have difficulty passing college courses with or without a study skills course, and thus they experienced little benefit. The more intellectual ability one has, the more that potential ability is available to be actualized after learning good study skills. Therefore a student with an IQ of 125 might, after taking the course, be able to raise her GPA to 4.0 (straight As), while a student with an IQ of 100 may only be able to raise his GPA to 2.5 (C+/B−).

It is possible to have multiple dependent variables as well. The dependent variable we have already mentioned is subsequent GPA. Ian also could measure changes in self-esteem, as assessed by some psychological test designed for that purpose. He also might decide to measure alcohol consumption, if this were a situation where students could give accurate information without fear of legal or academic reprisals. Ian might hypothesize that there would be increases in GPA and self-esteem after taking the study skills course, and decreases in weekly alcohol consumption. The rationale here would be that as students do better academically, they enjoy heightened self-esteem. They also have less need to drown their anxieties in alcohol. As a researcher, Ian probably can argue more persuasively that educators use his treatment widely if he can show positive changes on three culturally-desired variables rather than only one.

Let's return now to the issue of threats to internal validity. A *threat to internal validity* is any factor that could compete with the independent variable as a plausible explanation for the changes in the dependent variable. In Ian's experiment, are there any factors other than the study skills course that could cause the increased GPA? For simplicity's sake we'll focus primarily on one dependent variable, GPA, in our discussion.

There are, in any empirical research, several threats to internal validity. The exact number varies with different authors and researchers and the categories they use. In our discussion here I will describe eleven such threats. The better a researcher designs a project, the more threats to internal validity can be eliminated as possible explanations for changes in the dependent variable.

History

One variable that may confound the effect of the study skills course is history.[2] History includes any event or combination of events, other than the independent variable, that occurs during treatment and that may cause GPAs to rise. For example, Ian might have been conducting this experiment several years ago at the outbreak of the Vietnam war. Male students who "flunked out" of college at that time lost their educational waiver status. Fear of being drafted and going to Vietnam may have caused a significant increase in attention to studies. Fear, rather than Ian's study skills course, may have caused the rise in GPAs.

In this situation a control group would have helped. If the threat of Vietnam (or any other event than the study skills course) caused a significant increase in studying, this would have shown up in the control group as well. Thus Ian would be alerted that something other than his course was significantly affecting student grades.

Another example of how history could confound the experiment would be if colleges sent grades to each student's home. The members of Ian's study skills course were volunteers from among those students whose average grade was a D –. When those grades reached students' homes during their between-semester break, Dad, who was footing the bill for Junior's college, may have produced some major fireworks. Fear of the consequences Dad promised, rather than Ian's course, may have produced increased studying and improved GPAs (sorry about that, Ian).

Maturation

Maturation refers to any biological or psychological process that occurs because of the organism's growth. Such a process offers a competing explanation for the change in the dependent variable. Let's return to the situation with our college students. It is not uncommon for college freshmen to do poorly their first semester. There are many changes (living away from home for the first time, having to structure one's own time, not knowing how college professors test, etc.). Students' anxiety levels are often high and, therefore, they have reduced ability to study, integrate, and recall information on exams.

There is not usually a significant amount of biological maturation between the first and second semester of college life. However, there is likely to be significant psychological maturation. During the second semester the typical college student finds that being away from home is not such a foreign experience. Having to structure one's own time is beginning to feel like a positive challenge. Second-semester students generally have a better understanding of what college professors want on exams and term papers. As a result their anxiety levels are lower. They can study more effectively and their ability to retain information and integrate what they have learned on exams improves. It may be these maturational changes, rather than Ian's course, that produce the increase in GPAs. Again, a control group would help Ian know whether all freshmen's grades improved between the first and second semester as a result of psychological maturation, or whether the grades of students in his course improved significantly more than grades of freshmen in general.

Testing

Whenever we test someone on something, we change their life from that point on. For example, when Ian asks students in his experiment to estimate the amount of alcohol they are consuming per week, they may become sensitized to that fact. As a result, they may decide to cut down on drinking. If this were true, Ian's testing of them on this variable, rather than the study skills taught in his course, is primarily responsible for the decrease in alcohol consumption.

When we refer to testing in this context, we are usually referring to testing that the researcher does as part of his or her design. However, in this situation there is some testing that is occurring outside the research project itself that may be a severe threat to internal validity. This is the testing that occurs within each college class. As students get feedback on their papers and exams, this sensitizes them to what they need to do differently to improve their grades. It may be this feedback rather than Ian's course that causes their grades to improve.

Ian obviously cannot get the professors of students in his course to quit giving tests or term paper assignments. How could we eliminate this threat to internal validity? (Think about this question for a moment and see if you can answer it before reading further.)

By having a control group, Ian could rule in or rule out the possibility that something outside his course (such as feedback given by professors on tests) was the cause of improvement. If feedback by professors was the major contributor to increased performance the following semester, this would be present in the scores of control group subjects as well as in the experimental group subjects. If control group subjects' scores do not improve, or do not improve nearly as much as Ian's group does, then Ian has more justification for concluding that there is something in his group experience that is causing the improvement.

Instrumentation

Whenever there is measurement of something at two different times, there is the possibility that the measuring instrument will be less accurate at one time than another. *Reliability* refers to the consistency with which an instrument measures something accurately on repeated measurements.

For example, Ian's sister constantly watches her weight. She has found that her bathroom scales vary as much as five pounds depending on where she stands on the scales (front versus back) and on where in the bathroom she places the scales (the floor isn't level). From the standpoint of measurement, we would say that her scales are not very reliable.

Mechanical instrumentation can usually be improved to a point where it is very reliable. Researchers develop psychological assessment instruments and usually improve them to a point where they have reliabilities between the .70s and .90s (where 1.0 would be perfect reliability). It is harder to get assessments done by humans to have similar levels of reliability. For example, two psychologists are evaluating a new method of therapy. One psychologist is skeptical of the new method, the other is accepting. Each interviews a client who has been counseled using the new method and assesses the improvement he believes she has made. We would expect (and probably would be correct) that the two psychologists might have different assessments. In technical language, their *inter-rater reliability* would be low.

When humans assess subjects before and after treatment, changes in scores may occur because the raters (1) have gained experience, (2) are more tired or less tired, (3) have become bored, (4) have learned more about the purposes of the experiment, or (5) have become more relaxed or more stringent in their evaluations. Each of these possibilities could compete with the independent variable as the cause of changes in scores.

To make human assessments more reliable, researchers often develop very precise criteria that raters are to use in evaluating subjects. Raters can be trained, using common subjects, until their inter-rater reliability reaches a certain level before the researcher uses them to assess experimental subjects. Preferably the rating should be done by assistants who do not know the researcher's hypotheses so that these expectations or the desire to help the researcher obtain positive results do not contaminate the ratings.

Statistical Regression

Physicians and mental health professionals frequently place people in a treatment group because they are far from the average (or mean) in some way. For example, the students in Ian's study group were there because their average grade was $D-$. Teachers frequently place grade school and high school students in remedial or academic "treatment" groups because of extreme grades or extreme scores on IQ tests. (Extreme in this context means scores that are far from the mean.)

However, because of the properties of samples and populations, and because of the imperfect reliability of measuring instruments, any group whose mean is far from the population mean will, upon retesting, usually have a mean that is closer to the population mean. This happens whether or not the researcher performed a treatment, simply because of statistical factors.

Therefore, if Ian's group starts out far below the average grade for his college, and he retests the group at a later time (e.g., the end of the next semester), for statistical reasons alone their average grade is likely to be closer to the mean (higher). Unless the research design excludes this threat to internal validity, statistical regression toward the mean competes with the experimental treatment as an explanation for the improvement in grades. Here again a control group can help. If Ian randomly assigns students with $D-$ averages to his study skills group or to a control group, both groups should, at the time of retesting, show some regression toward the mean. If Ian's group shows significantly more improvement in grades than does the control group, there is reason to argue that their improvement is not due totally to statistical regression.

Mortality

Mortality refers to the fact that some people who begin an experimental treatment drop out for various reasons before its conclusion. If such people were a random sample of those in the treatment group, the scores of those remaining at the time of the posttest would still be representative of those exposed to the treatment. However, if those who dropped out of treatment scored primarily in the lower half of the sample on the pretest, then by removing their scores from the posttest the average score on the posttest will be elevated. In such a case, the change in average score from the pretest to the posttest may be partially or totally due to mortality rather than to the treatment.

For example, in Ian's study group the three subjects who received the lowest scores were three young men who, on the pretest (their first semester grades), received straight Fs. All three volunteered for Ian's group. A few weeks into the new semester one dropped out of the group and out of college to become a full-time bartender. A second dropped out because college interfered too much with his ability to smoke pot. A third dropped out because he didn't like to get up in the morning even though the college persisted in scheduling his courses then.

As you can see, removal of these three fellows from the posttest GPA average is likely to increase the group average, even if no one else's grades improve. For that reason researchers do their best to keep mortality to a minimum. If they have significant mortality, they realize they must report this as a competing explanation for the improvement found in posttest scores.

Selection

People who seek treatment for something, whether it is an academic problem, an interpersonal problem, or a medical problem, can usually be distinguished from people in the general population who do not seek help for that problem. Selection becomes a problem whenever a researcher compares subjects who seek treatment with subjects who do not seek treatment. Differences in posttest scores could be the result of nonequivalent groups rather than the treatment variable.

When random selection is impossible, researchers sometimes match subjects on selected traits to try to increase the equivalence of the treatment and control groups. There is now a consensus among statisticians and researchers that random assignment of people to treatment and control groups is preferable to matching. When a researcher matches people in two groups on several criteria, he or she is likely to be unaware of, and therefore not matching for, other criteria that could affect how persons respond to the treatment.

Experimenter Bias

Experimenter bias, or experimenter expectancy, refers to the fact that an experimenter's expectation often results in empirical data that confirm that expectation. We do not know exactly how researchers' expectations are translated into empirical data, but we can suggest some possibilities. Let's look first at some research that demonstrates this phenomenon.

Rosenthal has conducted several experiments that illustrate the effect of experimenter expectancy. In one he gave two groups of research assistants a set of pictures and asked them to obtain success or failure stories about the pictures. He told one group that they probably would be told success stories; he told the second group that they probably would be told failure stories. Those researchers told to expect success stories had more of them; those told to expect mostly failure stories received more of the latter.[3]

Rosenthal showed that experimenter bias could affect the results even when someone was working with planaria[4] or rats.[5] He randomly separated rats from the same gene pool into two groups. He told experimenters that one group of rats was "maze bright" and the other group was "maze dull." The rats whom the experimenters believed to be maze bright learned a maze more rapidly than those rats believed to be maze dull. Rosenthal also showed that an experimenter's bias affects not only the data that he collects, but may be communicated to his assistants and reflected in their data as well.[6]

Rosenhan confirmed Rosenthal's finding in an experiment that graphically illustrated the extent that experimenter bias can have on results. Rosenhan studied the relationship between hypnosis and conformity and found certain correlations. He confirmed these in a second experiment. He then reversed the correlations and presented these data to an assistant as the result of his experiment. She reran the experiment. Other assistants who had no knowledge of the original experiment scored her data twice. Her data yielded correlations that were significantly different from those actually obtained by Rosenhan and consistent with what she believed to be his results.[7]

As we can see, the impact of the experimenter's expectations on an experiment can be significant. They may, in some situations, be more important than the treatment itself in determining the research results. Thus experimenter bias is a severe threat to the internal validity of an experiment. We'll look at three ways experimenter expectancy may affect an experiment, and then discuss ways of reducing this threat.

Experimenter Expectancy and Demand Characteristics

Orne found that, although the experimenter's hypotheses are usually not stated explicitly in psychological experiments, subjects usually become aware of them through what Orne calls the "demand characteristics of the experimental situation."[8]

Experimental situations often emit cues that tell subjects how they are to behave in order to verify the experimenter's hypotheses. These cues are demand characteristics. (These may or may not be the actual hypotheses.)

An experiment has significant demand characteristics if, by its nature, most subjects are aware of how they are to behave if they are to verify the experimenter's hypothesis. "Muted awareness" refers to the phenomenon in which subjects sense what the experimenter expects of them, sense also that they are not supposed to have this awareness, and behave accordingly.[9] As good subjects, they (consciously or unconsciously) wish to further "progress in science," and since the experimenter is a scientist, they equate furthering progress in science with demonstrating the experimenter's hypothesis.

Orne hypothesized, and later showed, that the following

three things are true. First, the subject in an experiment usually can express some of the demand characteristics of the procedure. Second, most subjects perceive the same demand characteristics in an experiment and these may be the same as the hypothesis the researcher is testing. Third, these demand characteristics rather than the treatment variable(s) may be the major determinant of the subject's behavior.[10]

The subject's awareness of the demand characteristics of an experiment may come in at least three ways. First, the demand characteristics may be transmitted by the experiment itself. Second, demand characteristics may be transmitted through the experimenter's actions, responses and interrogations. Third, demand characteristics may be transmitted through phrasing of questions on surveys. We shall look at an example of each of these situations using cases from hypnosis literature. These same principles apply in other areas of psychological research as well.

Demand characteristics transmitted by the experiment itself. Ashley, Harper, and Runyon designed an experiment that would purportedly test whether a person's values alter his or her perception. In this experiment the researchers hypnotized subjects and suggested fictional life histories to them. In the life history, subjects were either rich or poor. The researchers then awakened the subjects and asked them to estimate the size of various coins. They found that those with hypnotically-suggested rich life histories estimated the coins to be smaller than those given poor life histories. They concluded:

> Even though we do not know fully what happens when we hypnotize a person, if we do hypnotize him and tell him he is rich and he behaves in one way in a coin-matching situation, and then, a few minutes later, we tell him he is now poor and he behaves in another way, *we can conclude that*

the observed difference is due to a change in his psychological organization (emphasis mine).[11]

Orne repeated the Ashley, Harper, and Runyon experiment but added an inquiry with the subjects afterward. From his inquiry he found that subjects in this experiment perceived the demand characteristics of the experiment. (The demand characteristics here were that rich and poor people should estimate the size of coins differently.) These demand characteristics, rather than the experimental variables (purported change of psychological orientation caused by hypnotic suggestion), may have been the major determinant of the subjects' behavior.[12]

Demand characteristics transmitted through the experimenter's actions, responses, and interrogations. Let's use the hypnosis literature one more time for an illustration. Within this literature there are two broad groups of investigators. One group, called the "credulous" school, believe that in hypnosis the potential exists for a person to enter an altered state of consciousness. In this state one's perceptions of reality can be modified by the hypnotist's suggestions. Thus, if a person, in response to hypnotic suggestions, says he or she feels no pain, there is the potential that the hypnotic state has changed the person's perceptions so that he or she is not feeling pain.

The "skeptical" school does not believe that a hypnotic state, *per se*, exists. They believe that "hypnotized" subjects are enacting a role, possibly at both a conscious and unconscious level, as the hypnotist prescribes this to them. It is of considerable significance that when credulous investigators do research, their research results usually corroborate the credulous view. Similarly, when skeptical investigators do research, their results usually corroborate their view. Why is this so?

The way that skeptical and credulous investigators conduct their research suggests an answer. There are definite, consistent differences in the way each group relates to their subjects. The credulous usually take more time with the hypnotic induction and tailor it to meet the personality of the subject. The skeptical usually give shorter, standardized inductions with little or no regard to the individual personality of the subject.

Although the above generalization does not always apply, it is apparent how these two different types of treatment may affect the hypnotic state attained. Since heterohypnosis (hypnotizing another person) involves an interpersonal relationship, many principles that characterize other interpersonal relationships also govern heterohypnosis. If someone treats you with respect, shows consideration to you as an individual, and earns your trust, you are more likely to be willing to enter a relationship with that person. On the other hand, if a person is cynical, short, and perfunctory with you, you are not likely to enter into a relationship, especially if you are somewhat anxious about the nature of that relationship, as most people are of hypnosis.

It could follow, then, that skeptical investigators may betray their skepticism about the reality of the hypnotic state by giving short, routine inductions. These inductions may be insufficient to build a relationship within which the subject feels comfortable and able to enter a hypnotic state with this researcher. (The same can occur if a skeptical researcher trains a research assistant to give inductions similarly.) Since most of these subjects never enter a hypnotic state, the skeptical investigator concludes that hypnosis is only role-playing or role-enactment.

Credulous investigators believe hypnosis is a genuine altered state of consciousness. However, they also believe that it is not usually entered unless a person feels comfortable and trusting of the person who is leading them into it. Accordingly, they spend more time in inductions, tailoring them to meet the specific needs of the subject. Many of their subjects do seem to enter a state similar to, but in important ways different from, their waking state.[13]

The point of this discussion is not to settle the issue of whether the credulous or the skeptical school is right, nor to decide whether Christians should be involved with hypnosis. The point for our discussion is that a researcher's hypotheses about an issue can, without his or her being consciously aware of it, affect how one conducts research with subjects, how one responds to their questions, and how one interrogates them afterward. There is a significant power differential between most researchers (usually Ph.D.s on the faculty of a university) and most subjects (usually anxious freshmen psychology majors). The subject may recognize, either through subtle or not-so-subtle behavior of the researcher, what kinds of answers the researcher wants and expects. In that situation the power differential or the desire to be a "good" subject will produce a powerful demand characteristic to respond in those ways. In this situation the demand characteristics transmitted through the experimenter's actions, rather than the treatment variable, may be the cause of the subject's behavior.

Experimenter bias transmitted in the phrasing of questions on surveys. By the careful choice of words, phrases and, especially modifiers—certain adverbs or adjectives—a researcher can easily manipulate the percentage of people who say they support or do not support a certain action, president, product, etc. The results can easily lead persons to false conclusions about support or lack of support for a person or issue if the researcher does not report the specific wording he or she uses.

Effect of Subject's Preconceptions and Expectations

We are familiar with the placebo effect. When people believe they are getting an effective medication they often report improvement and act in ways consistent with that self-report, although they are getting only a placebo. We now know that there is a biochemical basis to such reports. Hope appears to stimulate the brain to produce endorphins, a class of chemicals similar to morphine. These chemicals make people feel better and improves healing processes throughout their bodies.

There is another side to this. Patients on a placebo who believe they are getting a real drug often report noxious side effects from their medication. It is not uncommon for patients on placebos to report more side effects than those on therapeutic doses of the experimental medication![14]

In the above situations the subject or patient is in a situation where they have the following expectations: I am taking a medication prescribed to me by a caring, competent physician. Therefore I can expect to feel better. There is also the possibility that I may experience side effects from this medication, as I have from others.

When people taking sugar pills report that they are improving since starting on the medication, or that they are experiencing noxious side effects, it is clear that their expectations are producing changes that rival changes caused by the actual treatment. It is because both researcher and subject can bring expectations to the treatment situation, and these expectations can produce significant change, that careful research uses a double-blind method. Neither the doctor nor the patient knows who is receiving the real drug. Therefore the effects of expectations should be evenly distributed across treatment and control groups. Any differences between treatment and control groups should represent the actual difference that the new medication makes.

The Effect of Role Context

There are several research studies showing that in a scientific or experimental setting people will behave in ways that they would not if they were outside that setting. Perhaps the best-known example of this was an experiment done by Stanley Milgram.[15]

Subjects in Milgram's study believed that the study would attempt to measure the effect of punishment on learning. As each subject appeared at the laboratory, he met a second subject (an accomplice of the experimenter). The two then drew lots to see who would be the "learner" and the "teacher" in the experiment. Milgram had designed the drawing so that the accomplice would always be the "learner."

The researcher then strapped the "learner" into a realistic-appearing electric chair type of apparatus. Following this the researcher took the naive subject to an adjoining room. There the researcher showed him or her how to operate a switchboard that purportedly administered shocks to the "learner."

There were a series of thirty switches that could be used to deliver shocks ranging in intensity. The range was from 15 volts (labeled as "slight shock") to 300 volts ("intense shock"), 360 volts ("extreme intensity shock"), 420 volts ("danger: severe shock"), and finally 450 volts ("XXX").

The researcher told the subject to read lists of words with multiple-choice answers over a microphone. The "learner" would respond by pressing the button for one of four lights to indicate his reply. The researcher instructed the "teacher" to press a lever that would presumably shock the "learner" every time the latter made an error. Each shock was to be of a higher intensity than the previous one.

As the "learning" session progressed, many of the teacher-subjects became anxious or upset, particularly when the shock level reached 300 volts ("intense shock") and the "learner" pounded on the wall between the rooms. When this occurred, the subjects usually looked to the experimenter for guidance, only to be told that they must complete the experiment.

From this point on the learner made no further responses, and he did not even respond to the "teacher's" questions. The researcher then told the subject that failure to reply must be counted as a wrong answer. If there was no response they were to give the "learner" the next higher shock on the scale and go on with the list of words, continuing to increase the shock with each failure to respond.

No subject refused until the 300-volt level was reached (when the "learner" pounded on the wall). At that point five out of the forty subjects refused to continue. An additional nine subjects dropped out at the next succeeding shock levels. However, twenty-six (sixty-five percent) continued until they had pulled the last switch (450 volts). At that point, or at whatever point the subject refused to continue, the researcher explained the experiment to the subject. The "learner" also appeared and assured the subject that he or she had not been shocking him.

Other researchers have also shown that when people are in the role context of a scientific experiment, they voluntarily do things that they would not do under any other conditions. At the request of experimenters, subjects have thrown "nitric acid" at research assistants or handled "poisonous" snakes voluntarily.[16]

To test the limits of how far subjects would go in obeying a researcher's instructions Orne devised the following humorous research design (at least humorous in comparison to throwing acid at people or handling poisonous snakes or delivering 450-volt shocks to people). He gave subjects a sheet of random numbers that they were to add. When subjects finished the page, they were to pick up a card. The card instructed them to tear up the sheet they had just completed into a minimum of thirty-two pieces. They were then to return to their seats and add another sheet of numbers.

When subjects completed this sheet, they picked up another card that instructed them to repeat the process. The experimenter left the room at the beginning of the experiment and said he would return "eventually." To Orne's surprise, subjects remained at the task for several hours with few signs of overt hostility.[17]

The preceding experiments show that when subjects participate in what they understand to be a "scientific experiment," that context often affects their willingness to do requested tasks. They may commit serious antisocial acts or do exceedingly boring tasks that they would never do voluntarily outside a situation labeled as a scientific experiment. The effect of role context is so pervasive that it raises questions about whether subjects behave in certain ways because of the effect of the treatment variable, or because of the role context in which the research occurs.

The Effect of Doing Research on Human Subjects Using Natural Science Techniques

In the early part of the twentieth century there was a significant conflict within psychology about the proper way to study human beings. Freud had developed his theories of the unconscious mind, and Wundt and Titchener had developed an approach known as "introspection." Then J. B. Watson appeared and argued that the study of overt behavior was the appropriate and only scientific way to study humans. He derided those who were trying to study internal processes, saying that such studies were hopelessly subjective and unscientific. He argued that psychology should use physics as its model. The proper scientific study of humans should focus only on external, visible, measurable behavior.

Eventually many psychologists accepted this point of view, and, other than those psychologists who remained Freudian or neo-Freudian in their orientation, most psychology from 1920 until 1960 was affected by the strong influence of behavioral psychology. (This is not to say that no one besides analytic and neoanalytic practitioners discussed or studied internal processes during these years, but their work was strongly influenced by the behavioral bias.) Some underlying assumptions of this behavioral approach were:

1. *Empiricism:* The only data about humans that we can accept as true and as valid for scientific study are their external behaviors.

2. *Determinism:* Human behavior is not voluntary, even though humans may think so. One's unconscious processes (Freudians) or one's reinforcement history (behaviorists) determine one's behavior.

3. *Ratomorphism:* There is a basic continuity between animals and humans. By understanding animal behavior we can develop valid understandings of human behavior.

4. *Reductionism:* All behavior, human and otherwise, can be divided into smaller behavioral units that are easier to study scientifically. An understanding of smaller behavioral units can lead to a valid understanding of more complex behaviors.

These are not all the assumptions underlying behaviorism but are those most important for our present discussion.

Since the 1960s the group of psychologists who believe that neither Freudian nor behavioral psychology captures the fullness of what it means to be human has grown. Many of these psychologists have identified themselves as humanistic psychologists (not to be confused with secular humanism). They believe that we should view humans as beings who can choose. Unconscious processes and our reinforcement history influence, but do not determine, our behavior. They believe that the inner life of thoughts, feelings, and attitudes exists and is worthy of scientific study.

Some of these psychologists question whether the standard research laboratory and typical focus of experiments are valid ways of understanding human beings. Ulrich Neisser critiques contemporary psychological research in the following way:

> Most experimental cognitive psychology has taken a narrowly academic view of human abilities. The subjects of most experiments are given very artificial test-like tasks. They might be asked to report how many dots appeared, or classify characters, or say whether two forms are identical or not. They are not supposed to get bored, wonder whether the experiment is worth doing, respond for their own amusement, or quit. Yet often these would be intelligent courses of action....
>
> The prevailing view in [cognitive] psychology is usually one that is most convenient for us and least convenient for the people we theorize about. Psychologists rubricize people—put them into categories. They reduce mental processes to the simplest possible terms. They say, it's all association, or it's all conditioning, or it's all X, where X is whatever the current psychological fashion dictates. Whatever X may be, and whatever good experiments may originally have determined X, it does serious injustice to any person who is thinking and acting and moving and feeling in the real world.... [18]

Because of awarenesses such as Neisser's, several researchers are recommending that we radically change the way we do human research. Their proposals include some of the following ideas. First, we should remove research from the psychological laboratory so that we reduce the powerful effects of role context. Second, we should stop deceiving subjects. Third, we should treat subjects as co-investigators. They should be allowed to comment on the things that are significant to them in the experience, not have their responses reduced to those things that the investigator thinks are important and on which he or she wants data. Fourth, there should be a pre-experimental and postexperimental inquiry to identify the mind-set, expectations, and preconceptions of the subject before beginning the experiment, and their perceptions after completing it. (See Farnsworth, Georgi, Merleau-Ponty, and Kruger for further information about this movement, also known as phenomenological psychology.[19])

The main point of this section is: Researchers develop experiments based on their theory of human beings. If their theory says that internal processes such as thoughts, feelings, attitudes, and values are unimportant, they will design experiments that exclude focusing on such processes. The subjects are likely to sense what the researcher wants to hear based on the demand characteristics of the study. They will not talk about those things in which they sense the researcher has no interest.

Thus, our research results may be contaminated by our reductionistic view of human nature. Our research "results" are strongly affected by the effects of an unnatural setting (the laboratory) and the beliefs of the researcher about what is important and valid to study in human beings. These two factors may seriously contaminate the results the researcher thought were due to the treatment variable. As a result of the above issues, human research is now beginning to pay more attention to cognitive issues such as thoughts, beliefs, and attitudes.

RESEARCH DESIGNS: STRENGTHS
AND SHORTCOMINGS

Pseudo-Experimental or Pre-Experimental Designs

A research design has two basic purposes. The first purpose is to answer a research question; the second is to control other factors that might cause variation in the dependent variable. We want to know whether a change in X leads to a change in Y. We also want to be able to rule out the possibility that the change in Y is due to something other than the change in X. The following three designs are called pseudo-experimental or pre-experimental designs because, while they may give the initial appearance of being scientific, researchers who use them have very little control over threats to internal validity.[20]

One-Shot Case Study

This type of study may be diagrammed as shown in Figure 4-1, with the passage of time going from left to right.

The treatment occurs, followed by some activity that attempts to evaluate the result of the treatment. To understand why scientists call this a pseudo-experimental design, let us examine the example from chapter 1 of the pastor who developed a nine-week class for depressed parishioners in his congregation.

X	O
Treatment or	Observation or
Independent	Measurement of
Variable	Dependent Variable

FIGURE 4-1. One-shot case study.

After nine weeks the pastor passed out questionnaires that asked group members whether they felt their depression had decreased. He also asked what group members believed were the most helpful experiences in the class and what experiences were less helpful. Based on the feedback he received, he concluded that he had developed a program that reduced depression.

This design does not adequately control for history. We have no way of knowing whether another factor or combination of factors may have occurred during these nine weeks that contributed to, or even were, the primary cause in the reported decreases in depression. For example, the weather may have changed from dreary winter weather to pleasant spring weather, and this may have lifted everyone's spirits. It could have been that before the beginning of the group experience several members had lost their previous employment because of a lull in demand for their product. And then two weeks before the end of the group they all could have received recall notices and returned to work.

These and many other historical events could have caused the decrease in depression rather than the nine-week course. The only way to control for history is to have a control group of depressed people selected from the same population as the treatment group. These controls would, presumably, experience all of these other factors except the treatment.

The second possible source of invalidity is maturation. This refers to any biological or psychological maturation that occurs during the treatment period that might be the reason for the reported change in depression. Many people who experience depression recover from that depression without treatment in a period of anywhere from two to eighteen months. Thus we do not know whether the reported decrease in depression is due to this normal pattern of change or from the treatment. Again a control group would help us have some basis for comparison regarding how much of this decrease may be due to normal maturational factors.

A third possible source of invalidity is testing. This factor concerns the possible consequence of prior testing on the effect of the treatment on group members. You may remember that prior testing sometimes sensitizes people to the treatment. Thus the treatment following testing has a different effect than the treatment would have without prior testing. Since there was no prior testing, prior testing cannot be a possible source of internal validity.

This study is lacking in the area of instrumentation. Whenever we want to measure the effectiveness of a treatment we must have some means of measuring that factor. Preferably we need a measuring instrument that has proven validity and reliability. Validity, as you may remember from our earlier discussion, depends upon the measuring instrument being able to measure what it claims to be measuring. Reliability refers to whether it consistently gives the same reading when the factor remains constant.

In reviewing the matter of instrumentation, we find the study is extremely weak. There was no pretest of any kind. The posttest was an unvalidated questionnaire that asked people to rate their level of depression and compare it with the level of depression they thought they had nine weeks earlier. This is unfortunate, since there are several depression inventories available that researchers have validated. Most of these take only a few minutes to complete. The pastor then would have had some objective measures by which to judge whether group members' depression had decreased.

Statistical regression refers to the fact that if one has a group of subjects who score far from the mean, on retesting these members are likely to score closer to it. This factor is not applicable to this study, since the pastor did no pretesting.

Mortality is another factor that may affect the changes between pretreatment and posttreatment averages. If several subjects drop out, the posttreatment averages will not include their scores. The change between pretreatment and posttreatment averages may be due to missing scores because of dropouts rather than to the treatment.

The mortality factor relates to this research design only in some respects. It does not in a strict sense, since the pastor did no pretreatment testing. It does however, in that the questionnaires submitted after treatment came only from people who remained in the group until the end. If the pastor mailed questionnaires to those who dropped out of the group during the nine weeks, we might have found a more varied response pattern.

Selection is not a factor in this design because there is only one group. Selection becomes a factor only when subjects are not randomly assigned to the treatment and control group.

Experimenter bias or experimenter expectancy may have affected the results. Clearly this pastor believed that depression could be reduced and he believed that the experiences he had designed into the group experience would alleviate depression. His expectancies were probably transmitted through the demand characteristics of the experiment itself, as well as through his actions, responses, and questions. The group members probably had their own expectations of the group, and these also, rather than the treatment, may have caused feelings of reduced depression.

Role context also may have contaminated the results of the study. Most Christians do not want to disappoint their pastor. These Christians also wanted to help him receive his doctor of ministry degree. They knew that if they stated that their depression had decreased, not only would he be personally gratified, but also they might help him receive his degree. Thus the powerful effect of role context, rather than the treatment itself, may have been the reason for their reported decrease in depression.

The pastor treated his group members and evaluated them using a "human science" model rather than a natural science model. Therefore this factor probably did not enter as a possible contaminant of the internal validity of his research.

To summarize, it is unwarranted to conclude that this pastor's program reduces depression because his research design fails to protect against threats to internal validity caused by the following factors:

> history
> maturation
> instrumentation
> mortality
> experimenter expectancy transmitted by the experiment itself
> experimenter bias transmitted through the experimenter's actions, responses, and interrogations
> the effect of subjects' preconceptions and expectations, and
> the effect of role context.

One-Group Pretest-Posttest Design

In this type of design, a researcher administers a pretest, then the experimental treatment, then a posttest. Figure 4-2 describes this visually.

Let's assume that John Travers is an undergraduate psychology major and youth leader for the young teens (ages 13

$$O_1 \qquad X \qquad O_2$$
Pretest   Treatment   Posttest

FIGURE 4-2. One-group pretest-posttest design.

to 16) at a local church. He has concerns about the difficulty his young teens are having resisting pressure from their peers. With help from his faculty advisor he finds a validated inventory that measures teens' ability to resist peer pressure.

John administers the inventory to his young teens. He then has a six-session program where, for the first half hour, he presents a Bible study on some aspect of standing alone and resisting peer pressure. In the second half hour each young teen meets with an older teen of the same sex and the two of them discuss John's talk and how they might apply it. John has also encouraged the older teens that during this second half hour they may share their struggles regarding peer pressure and things that they have learned from that struggle. This format is used for six one-hour sessions. After six weeks John readministers the inventory and compares these scores with scores from before the six-week program. Let us look at the threats to internal validity and how well this research design controls them.

This design does not control history since we do not know what other events occur during these six weeks that might affect the young teens' ability to stand up to peer pressure. For example, the deaths of two peers from drunk driving during this six weeks, or any number of other events, could contribute to an unknown extent to the change in scores.

This design does not control for maturation, although because of the shortness of the interval and the continuity of the teens' setting, this factor probably represents less of a threat than it would if the treatment were longer or there were discontinuity in the teens' setting. If one were to use this design with a longer interval between testing or with situations that might cause significant biological or psychological maturation, this threat to internal validity would be greater. Therefore, although we think maturation would not be a significant threat in this experiment, from the standpoint of research rigor we would have to say that this design does not control adequately for it.

This design does not control the effect of testing. We have no way of measuring what effect the pretesting (and the knowledge that there would be a posttest) had on the teens exposed to the treatment. The teens had never had any personality inventory administered in their youth group, nor had they been part of a research study. The uniqueness of this experience may have caused them to be unusually attentive to the material John presented in that set of lessons. If so, the changes from pretest to posttest could be due to an unknown extent on the effect of pretesting and the knowledge of the future posttest.

Whether instrumentation is a threat to internal validity depends on the quality of research assessment instrument used. If the instrument John chose had high validity and reliability scores, and if he administered it in the same manner both times, then instrumentation would not be a threat to internal validity. If there were a change in the way he administered it, we would not know how much of any change in scores would be due to the treatment variable (the class) and how much might be due to the change in the administration.

Statistical regression is also a threat in this type of design. Teens in John's group may have been high on social conformity, and this was the reason he chose to teach on this issue. If his teens had extreme scores to begin with, we would expect some decrease in conformity scores because of statistical regression. Also, people usually score in a more healthy range on personality inventories the second time they take them. Since John has no control group, both of these sources of regression toward the mean are uncontrolled.

Mortality is also a threat to John's research design. During the period when John's experiment is in progress, two teens stop coming to the group, and a family containing one teen moves to another state. As a result of evangelism at school, two new teens enter the group. Thus the group who takes the posttest is missing three of the twelve members who took the pretest and has two new members who did not take the pretest. We simply cannot predict how much of the change in pretest-posttest scores is due to changes in group membership and how much is due to the treatment.

Since there was not a control group, the possibility of differences between the experimental group and control group because of nonrandom selection does not exist. On the remaining factors, there is little experimental control over threats to internal validity. John transmitted his experimenter expectancy (his desire to have the teens change in certain ways as a result of "treatment") through the experiment itself (his lessons), and through his actions, responses, and questions. The teens' preconceptions and expectations about how they should answer the posttest questions in light of the teaching series they had just finished affected their scores to an unknown extent. Their role context (Christian teens in a church youth program) affected the way they answered the posttest questions to an unknown extent. John did treat them as human beings using human science (rather than natural science) techniques.

Many factors mentioned above (such as expectations, preconceptions, role context) cannot be fully avoided in any research experiment. However, by using control groups and random selection we can often factor out how much of the change is due to these other factors, and how much is due to the treatment. Because the one-group pretest-posttest design fails to control so many threats to internal validity, it is also considered a pseudo-experimental or pre-experimental design.

Static-Group Comparison Design

The third type of research design that is considered pre-experimental is the static-group comparison design. In this design the researcher uses two static (intact) groups. He or she exposes one to a particular treatment. At some point after the exposure both groups are measured. Figure 4-3 shows this design.

$$X \qquad\qquad\qquad O_1$$
$$\text{- - - - - - - - - - - - - - - - -}$$
$$O_2$$

FIGURE 4-3. Static-group comparison design.

The dashed line indicates that subjects are not randomly assigned to the two groups. The experimenter uses groups that are already formed (therefore the name "static-group").

Let us suppose that in a large church the minister of adult education would like to assess the effectiveness of a new twelve-week program on marriage enrichment. Because of the size of this group, there are two classes for married adults ages 30 through 32. Both have good teachers who are popular with their respective classes. One teacher is primarily a lecturer. The other teacher acts primarily as a discussion leader, although he can lecture effectively when needed. Married couples are free to attend either class.

The minister of adult education decides to ask the teacher who is more of a discussion leader to lead the marriage enrichment course for a quarter. He will then have both classes anonymously complete a marriage intimacy inventory. The inventory has an objective grading system to evaluate the relative healthiness of couples' marriages. He then plans to compare the scores from the two groups to see if the course makes a difference.

Use the next few moments to identify what you think will be the threats to internal validity that this design does not control. Then compare your list with the list that follows. Since we have already discussed most of these threats, I will only comment on those threats that are present in this experiment.

Threats to Internal Validity Not Adequately Controlled in the Static-Group Comparison Design

There are six threats to internal validity in the research discussed above. Each of those is numbered below. Where a particular factor does not present a threat to internal validity, I have simply made a brief comment to that effect.

1. History: We have no way of controlling whether members have had similar histories. Dissimilarities in history may cause certain people to prefer lecture versus discussion. These same dissimilarities may affect the general level of communication, attitude to authority, and intimacy present in their marriages.

2. Maturation: Dissimilarities in maturation prior to the experiment may have caused some people to prefer lecture rather than discussion. These differences in maturation, rather than the marriage enrichment course, may be the cause of different scores on the marital intimacy inventory.

The effect of testing is not a threat because there is no testing before treatment. It would be a threat if anyone told either class that they would be taking marital intimacy inventory in a few weeks.

Instrumentation is not a threat since the minister of adult education used a standardized instrument with acceptable validity and reliability, and administered it in the same manner to both groups.

Statistical regression is not a threat because there are not two testings.

Mortality, likewise, is not a threat.

3. Nonrandom selection: This poses a very serious threat. We have no way of knowing the many ways the two groups differ and how those differences might be reflected in their marriage intimacy scores.

4. Experimenter bias: Bias was transmitted by the experiment itself and through the experimenter's actions, responses, and questions. Here the teacher of the class acts almost as a research assistant. Undoubtedly his bias, if he agrees to teach this class, is that it will improve the marriages of those who go through the process. He probably will communicate his hope several times during the quarter.

5. Effect of subject's preconceptions and expectations: Those who take the course probably will expect it to improve their marriage. As a result, they may work harder on their marriages. Their expectations and consequent work, rather than the class itself, could be a major determinant in their scores after it.

6. Effect of role context: People who have been members of a class studying marriage enrichment for twelve weeks are likely to feel some pressure to answer questions about the health of their marriage in positive ways. This factor, rather than the treatment, may be a determinant of their scores.

The minister of adult education conducted the treatment and testing using human science rather than natural science techniques as far as we know, so this factor would not be a threat to internal validity. However, even if he does find significant differences between the group who has gone through the marriage enrichment class and those who have not, he would not be justified in drawing a conclusion that the class material produced these results. The reason—the research design (static-group comparison) fails to control six threats to internal validity, and these factors, rather than the course, might be the source of the group differences.

True Experimental Designs

In the pseudo-experimental or pre-experimental designs we found that it was impossible to separate the differences caused by the treatment from differences caused by several other factors. There are three basic designs that are commonly known as true experimental designs. When an experiment uses one of these designs and reports finding significant differences, it is generally safe to assume that these differences are due to the treatment (the independent variable). These three designs control for most, if not all, of the threats to internal validity. These designs are the pretest-posttest control group design, the posttest-only control group design, and the Solomon four-group design.[21]

The Pretest-Posttest Control Group Design

These designs are more complex than those in the previous section of this chapter. In presenting them diagrammatically in Figure 4-4, X will continue to stand for application of the treatment and O will stand for observation or measurement. Movement from left to right will show the passage of time. R will indicate random assignment.

R   O   X   O

R   O   O

FIGURE 4-4. Pretest-posttest control group design.

At the beginning of the experiment the researcher randomly assigns half the subjects to one group, and half to the other. He or she measures both groups on the variable being studied. One group receives the treatment and is identified as the *experimental group* or *treatment group*. The group that does not receive the treatment is called the *control group*. The researcher then tests both groups again.

One variation of this design, shown in Figure 4-5, occurs when there are two different treatments (X and Y). The researcher then compares the two treatments with each other for effectiveness, rather than comparing treatment with no treatment.

$$R \qquad O \qquad X \qquad O$$
$$R \qquad O \qquad Y \qquad O$$

FIGURE 4-5. Pretest-posttest control group variation
using two treatments.

A common method used in pharmaceutical testing is to have a control group who receives a placebo and two experimental groups, each of whom receives a different level of the medication under study. This variation is shown in Figure 4-6.

$$R \quad O \quad X_{Placebo} \quad O$$
$$R \quad O \quad Y_{30mg.} \quad O$$
$$R \quad O \quad Y_{60mg.} \quad O$$

FIGURE 4-6. Pretest-posttest control group variation
using a placebo and two treatments.

Let us use the example of the two Sunday school groups, but modify the design so that it would be compatible with the pretest-posttest control group design. The purpose of the research would be to examine whether taking this twelve-week marriage enrichment course results in an improved marriage relationship as measured by a chosen marital intimacy inventory.

First the minister of adult education must enlist the cooperation of the two teachers and members of both classes. Then he or she must randomly assign couples to either the marriage enrichment class or to the adult elective usually offered to both classes. One teacher would lead each class. Both groups would be pretested on the inventory on the same date and would be posttested on the same date. Members of the treatment and control group would be asked not to discuss the content of the marriage enrichment class. If discussions did occur before posttesting, differences between the two experiences might be blurred.

This design considerably reduces the threats to internal validity present in the static-group comparison design. Both groups presumably have equivalent histories and maturation experiences because of random assignment. The minister pretests both groups, so that the pretest equally sensitizes everyone in whatever ways the pretest might affect couples. The measuring instrument is identical, and standardized instructions for administration of the marital inventory are used.

Since both groups probably include the same number of couples whose scores are far from the mean (either exceptionally good or exceptionally poor marriages), this controls for statistical regression to the mean. If the minister randomly assigns couples to both groups, and the teachers are experienced and well-liked, *mortality* should be equivalent. However, at the time of posttesting, mortality percentages should be checked to judge whether they are likely to alter the results for one group more than the other.

The effects of experimenter expectancy, subjects' expectations, and role context are a little more difficult to deal with at the level of research design. One way to minimize these effects is for both teachers at the time of the pretest and posttest to reassure couples that their responses are completely anonymous, and that Christian marriages are imperfect just as are non-Christian ones. For the treatment group at the time of posttesting the teacher should encourage couples to give their honest assessment of how their marriages are now, so that the minister of adult education will know whether this course has been helpful to them and whether to offer it to other couples in the future.

One way to minimize the effects of experimenter expectancy, which would be possible in some research but probably not in this study, is for those who conduct the actual treatment and for those who evaluate the results to be unaware of the research hypotheses. Another method of doing this, and one that pharmaceutical researchers often use, is double-blind studies. Here neither the prescribing doctor nor the patient knows who is receiving the experimental drug. While this method may seem cruel, it is the only way one can separate the effects of doctor and patient expectancy from the effects of the medication itself.

The Posttest-Only Group Design

This design is considerably simpler and less time-consuming both for researcher and subjects. The design is diagrammed in Figure 4-7.

```
R       X       O
R               O
```

FIGURE 4-7. Posttest-only control group design.

In this design the researcher randomly assigns subjects from the same population to either a treatment or a control group and, after treatment, measures both groups. This design controls for history, maturation, testing, and regression to the mean (since there is no pretesting). Without a pretest there is no chance for instrumentation deterioration between pretesting and posttesting.

The other factors (experimenter expectancy, subjects' expectations, and role context) can still affect the results, unless the researcher makes an effort to minimize them by his or her instructions. It is important to check level of mortality, but if mortality is nominal and there has been random assignment of subjects to groups, researchers consider this design as good as, if not better than, the pretest-posttest design.[22]

The Solomon Four-Group Design

One problem with the traditional pretest-posttest control group design is that we cannot tell how much the pretest sensitizes subjects to the treatment. If this factor is significant, it means that the results of the treatment may not generalize to a wider population unless the population also receives the pretest. A design that attempts to identify the effect pretesting has on subjects is the Solomon four-group design, diagrammed in Figure 4-8.

$$
\begin{array}{cccc}
R & O_1 & X & O_2 \\
R & O_3 &   & O_4 \\
R &   & X & O_5 \\
R &   &   & O_6 \\
\end{array}
$$

FIGURE 4-8. Solomon four-group design.

This research design is a combination of the two previous designs. The researcher randomly assigns subjects to one of four groups. Two of these groups receive pretesting, two do not. Two of the groups receive the treatment, two do not. By comparing O_2 with O_4 we can see the difference the treatment makes when both groups are pretested. By comparing O_5 with O_6 we can see what difference the treatment makes without pretesting. By comparing O_2 with O_5, we can see whether pretesting is necessary to get the treatment effect.

The Solomon four-group design controls for history, maturation, effect of testing, regression to the mean. With care, there need not be threats from instrumentation. As with all designs, the researcher must make certain that mortality has not become significant and must deal with experimenter expectancy, subjects' expectations, and role context in whatever ways seem most appropriate. While not widely used, the Solomon four-group design is the best design if one wants to know the difference pretesting makes on utilization of treatment.

An excellent discussion of extensions of the three true experimental designs can be found in *Reading Statistics and Research* by Huck, Cormier, and Bounds, pages 270–300.

Quasi-Experimental Designs

Some designs occupy the middle ground between pre-experimental and true experimental designs. They have both advantages and disadvantages when compared with true experimental designs. The major disadvantage is that they do not protect against internal threats to validity as well as the true experimental designs do. They have two basic advantages over the true experimental designs. The first is that they can sometimes be used in situations where a true experimental design would not be possible or feasible. The second is that they often reduce external threats to validity.

External validity deals with the likelihood that something will generalize from the experimental setting to the "real world." As you remember, a subject in a research laboratory is in a role context that can have powerful effects on his or her behavior. He or she may do things simply because of demand characteristics—experimenter expectancies that he or she senses from the research design or from the experimenter's instructions, responses, or interrogations. These factors, rather than the treatment itself, may be the cause of the "response to treatment."

In one's natural setting, surrounded by one's normal peer

group, these factors are likely to be less strong, and changed behavior following treatment is more likely to be the result of treatment. Also, it is more likely that the results found in one naturalistic setting are likely to generalize to other similar settings.

There are many kinds of quasi-experimental designs, far too many to discuss in a book of this nature. In this final section of the chapter we shall briefly examine four kinds of quasi-experimental designs.

The Nonequivalent Control Group Design

The nonequivalent control group design can be diagrammed as shown in Figure 4-9.

```
      O        X        O
   ---------------------------
      O                 O
```

FIGURE 4-9. Nonequivalent control group design.

In the world outside the laboratory it sometimes may be impossible to assign people randomly to treatment and control groups. A researcher may decide to use two intact groups that appear to be similar. Both receive a pretest, one receives the treatment, and then both receive a posttest. This design is similar to the first true experimental design we discussed—the pretest-posttest control group design, except that people are not randomly assigned to groups.

There are two versions of this design, the *intact nonequivalent group* and the *self-selected experimental group*. The intact nonequivalent group uses a group that is already present in a real-world setting, such as a church baseball team. A self-selected experimental group allows people to volunteer to be in a group for a specific purpose. The self-selected group is a much weaker experimental design because groups of volunteers usually have significant differences from non-volunteers.

Threats to the internal validity of this kind of group depend somewhat on the makeup of a specific group and the nature of the experiment. These general comments are usually true. First, nonrandom selection allows for the possibility that the experimental and control groups have significantly different histories and maturation experiences. If the researcher includes one group because of extreme scores on a variable (as sometimes happens with volunteers), statistical regression can be a factor. Mortality, as with all research designs, has to be watched.

Factors over which the researcher has some control include which group receives the treatment and the timing of the pretest and posttest. He or she also can control for the effect of pretesting (since he or she pretests both groups), and can ensure consistent instrumentation. The researcher has some control over the extent to which he or she exposes subjects to experimenter bias and may attempt to neutralize subjects' preconceptions and expectations so that treatment results are more likely to be the result of the treatment. Because of the naturalistic setting, the effects of role context may be less than in true experimental settings.

Separate-Sample Pretest-Posttest Design

Sometimes all subjects must receive a given treatment (therefore there is no group to serve as a control group). The researcher may still have some control over assigning people to treatment groups and to when he tests them and exposes them to the treatment. It may then be possible to assign subjects randomly to two groups, give one group a pretest and then the treatment, and give the second group the treatment and then a posttest (see Figure 4-10).

R   O   (X)

R   X   O

This design has many advantages over one in which the researcher treats then tests the entire group, or where he pretests, then treats, then posttests the entire group. (These options would be the first two pseudo-experimental designs discussed earlier.)

This design can control for testing, statistical regression, and selection. There is always the possibility that some significant historical event or maturation could occur between observation of the first group and the second group. Mortality should always be watched, as in every experimental design. With care a researcher can control for instrumentation, experimenter bias, subject preconceptions and expectations, and role context.

Single-Group Time-Series Designs

In this design the researcher takes repeated measures for a period before and after treatment. There are a variety of applications in which this can be useful. Let us use a hypothetical example of a medical patient who is having large fluctuations in his blood pressure. There is a treatment available that could possibly help his condition. The attending physician would like a way of documenting the change in this patient's condition before and after treatment.

The time-series design might include having the patient's blood pressure monitored hourly for six hours before the procedure. The treatment could be performed, and then the patient's blood pressure could be monitored hourly for six hours following the procedure. If we represent the hourly observations by Os and the treatment by X, the diagram might look like Figure 4-11.

$$O_1 \ O_2 \ O_3 \ O_4 \ O_5 \ O_6 \quad X \quad O_7 \ O_8 \ O_9 \ O_{10} \ O_{11} \ O_{12}$$

FIGURE 4-11. Single-group time-series design.

If a researcher wanted to picture a treatment that continues for a certain period, this can be done by drawing lines over the observations that occurred while the treatment was also occurring. For example, Figure 4-12 shows that the researcher made four observations, and then initiated a treatment that continued while he made two more observations. He discontinued the treatment (or completed it) as he made the last three observations.

$$O \ O \ O \ O \ X \ \overline{O \ O} \ O \ O \ O$$

FIGURE 4-12. Single-group time-series design variation.

There are many applications of this design that could be used in a Christian context. For example, a youth minister might want to find the most interesting Sunday school format for teens. He has three possible teaching formats that he feels comfortable using. He might try one for fall quarter, using X_1 to designate the first format he is using, and O_1 through O_{12} to designate attendance for the twelve Sundays in the fall quarter. X_2 could designate the method used in winter quarter, and X_3 the method in spring quarter, with both followed by twelve observations. By graphing this data this youth minister could get a clear visual picture of teens' responses to each method.

There are several threats to the internal validity of this design. History may affect these data. For example, a church split could drastically reduce the number of subjects and not allow for a clear measure of youth response to a particular style of teaching. Maturation could affect the data. Threats from testing and instrumentation should be small because the teens in his youth group are unaware that he is charting their attendance, and it is relatively easy to set up a reliable way of taking attendance. The teens of his church this year are not a random selection of teens from all churches all years. Thus it would be invalid to generalize his results to all youth groups and churches elsewhere. Effects of experimenter bias and subjects' preconceptions can be minimized by not letting students know that he is conducting the experiment. The effect of role context may not be able to be removed. Many teens (especially younger teens) will be in Sunday school because of their parents. Their preference for or aversion to a given teaching method will not be a factor in their attendance. If this (parental) factor seems to be heavily contaminating or blurring his results, he may want to use a different kind of observation that might be more sensitive to teens' interest level.

Multiple-Group Time-Series Designs

This is similar to the last design, except that the researcher treats and evaluates more than one group. For example, someone who wanted to make a case for raising the legal drinking age to twenty-one could assemble statistics for the number of people killed in teen drunk driving accidents for cities that have raised the legal drinking age. He or she could try to find the number of people killed per month in such accidents for six months before the new law and twelve months after its initiation. If it can be shown that there has been a similar trend in several cities, this increases the argument that such a law could benefit one's own community. Some researchers consider this design to be one of the best quasi-experimental designs.[23]

With the multiple-group time-series design, history and maturation can be a threat to internal validity. So can statistical regression if there are many extreme scores within the groups. As in others, mortality should be monitored.

CHAPTER SUMMARY

In this chapter we have discussed the various things (besides a treatment variable) that may cause changes in dependent variables. We have identified eleven such factors. When we do not control these factors, the change we observe may be due to one of them and not to the treatment, but we have no way of knowing the size of their effect. For that reason we call them threats to the internal validity of a research project.

There are three categories of research design. Pre-experimental or pseudo-experimental designs have very few controls over threats to internal validity. Thus, although they give a semblance of being scientific and may show significant differences between pre- and posttesting or between control and experimental groups, we do not know what those differences mean.

True experimental designs have a high degree of control over threats to internal validity. If one of these research designs shows significant differences between a control and experimental group, this generally means that the difference is due to the treatment variable.

Quasi-experimental designs can sometimes be used in situations where true experimental designs are impossible or unfeasible. They do not possess as much control over threats to internal validity as true experimental designs. However, they may be subject to fewer threats to external validity, i.e., their results may more readily generalize to real-life situations outside the laboratory.

EXERCISES

EX 21: Sigmund Freud viewed himself as a scientific researcher. His books recount his conclusions about the human psyche and about psychotherapy based on his observations as he counseled people. Discuss his style of research in light of the eleven threats to internal validity identified in this chapter. What general conclusions, if any, do you make about this style of research?

EX 22: If you can remember anyone around you who has tried to do some research, either formal or informal, try to recall what they were trying to investigate. Assess their research in light of the eleven threats to internal validity.

EX 23: This exercise has several subparts that are given below:

(a) Identify some question that you have an interest in investigating (this does not mean that you would investigate it, but that you have an interest in investigating it).

(b) Think of how you might have tried to investigate it before reading this chapter. Then identify weaknesses in that design.

(c) Try to develop a method using a true experimental design. You do not have to have specific measures in your plan (such as the name of a specific psychological test or the appropriate statistical technique), but complete the rest of your design.

(d) Critique this from the standpoint of threats to internal validity.

EX 24: Chapter 1 mentioned that in 1987 Shere Hite reported in her survey of several thousand women that 75 percent of women married five years or longer said they had had or were having an affair. Andrew Greeley reported in 1990 that 90 percent of those women he had contacted through telephone surveys said they had been faithful during their present marriage. Based on what you know about research design, what explanations can you give for this significant discrepancy?

EX 25: Several years ago there were many advertisements on radio and television that said that researchers had shown that, with the aid of their particular antihistamine, people with colds usually recovered within a week. As a result, sales of antihistamines for treatment of colds increased dramatically. Comment on this research.

CHAPTER 5

Principles of
Statistical Analysis

Statistics and statisticians have often been the focus of sarcasm-tinged humor. Pirie defined a statistician as "someone who draws a mathematically precise line from an unwarranted assumption to a foregone conclusion."[1]

About the misuse of statistics by politicians one writer noted: "It has . . . been said that a politician uses statistics in much the same way that a drunk uses a lamppost—more for support than illumination."[2] Even Mark Twain jested about statistics, in this case the statistical procedure called extrapolation:

In the space of one hundred and seventy-six years the Lower Mississippi has shortened itself two hundred and forty-two miles. That is an average of a trifle over one mile and a third per year. Therefore any calm person, who is not blind or idiotic, can see that in the Old Oolitic Silurian Period, just a million years ago next November, the Lower Mississippi River was upward of one million three hundred thousand miles long, and stuck out over the Gulf of Mexico like a fishing rod. And by the same token any person can see that seven hundred and forty-two years from now the Lower Mississippi will only be a mile and three-quarters long, and Cairo and New Orleans will have joined their streets together, and be plodding comfortably along under a single mayor and a mutual board of aldermen. There is something fascinating about science. One gets such wholesale returns of conjecture out of such a trifling investment of fact.[3]

Richard Runyon put this in perspective when he said, "Figures don't lie, but liars figure. . . . [W]hen statistics are used to beguile and to deceive, the fault lies within us rather than in the statistics."[4]

This chapter has several purposes: These include the following:

1. to help you understand the difference between descriptive and inferential statistics,
2. to help you understand the meaning of terms such as .05 and .01 levels of significance, the null hypothesis, one-tailed versus two-tailed tests, the power of a test, and parametric versus nonparametric tests,
3. to help you understand the difference between correlation and causation,
4. to help you understand what t-tests, multiple analysis of variance, and multiple regression analysis do,
5. to help you understand the common ways people try to mislead us using statistics, and
6. to help you understand why scientific researchers get different results although they seemingly are conducting the same test.

In this chapter you will not learn everything you need to know to develop a research design or do a statistical analysis on your own. That task would take two or three graduate courses. What this chapter will do will be to make you a more intelligent consumer of statistical information. Also, if you want to do an experiment and have a consultant help you with the research design, selection, processing, and interpreting of appropriate statistical tests, this chapter will help you understand why certain things need to be done, and what the results mean.

UNDERSTANDING DESCRIPTIVE STATISTICS

Descriptive and Inferential Statistics

Before describing the difference between descriptive and inferential statistics it will be helpful to have common definitions of two terms, population and sample. A *population* refers to any group of living organisms, whether plant, animal, or human. For example, a population could be all third-graders in Evansville, Indiana, or all third-graders in the United States. A *sample* refers to a group chosen from a larger population. Thus a sample from each previously mentioned population might be one-third of the third-graders in Evansville, or one-tenth of the third-graders in the United States.

Descriptive statistics are statistical procedures that describe or summarize groups of numbers. We cannot use them to guess about larger groups than the group which they describe. *Inferential statistics* include statistical procedures that allow us to make inferences (scientific guesses) about a population based on information derived from a sample of that population. Let us turn our attention first to descriptive statistics.

Descriptive Statistics

If we have a group of 500 numbers, we are likely to have some difficulty comprehending each of them. Descriptive statistics give us ways of summarizing those 500 numbers in a more comprehensible fashion. There are three kinds of descriptive statistics. We call them measures of central tendency, measures of variability, and measures of relationship.

Measures of Central Tendency

The measures of central tendency give us ways to characterize the middle score in a group of scores. We calculate the *mean* by adding up all the scores in a distribution and dividing that total by the number of scores in the group. The *mode* is the most commonly-recurring score in the distribution. The *median* is the score that divides the upper 50 percent of scores in a distribution from the lower 50 percent of scores.

In the normal bell-shaped distribution the mean, median, and mode are identical (see Figure 5-1). In a *positively-skewed distribution* the tail goes in a positive direction. The mean will be farthest to the right, the mode farthest to the left, and the median between them. In a *negatively-skewed distribution* the tail goes in a negative direction. The mean will be farthest to the left, the mode farthest to the right, and the median will be between them.

One little-known fact that deceptive persuaders often use to their advantage is that the word "average" can legitimately be used for any of these measures of central tendency. Most people believe that "average" is a synonym for "mean" only, but this is untrue. Therefore, whenever a distribution is skewed, a deceptive persuader can choose whichever of the three measures of central tendency best fits his needs. Since the meaning of the word "average" is ambiguous, we will use the word "mean" rather than "average" throughout the remainder of this book.

Measures of Variability

The scores in a population usually vary. Measures of *variability* simply measure the degree of dispersion. Tightlyclustered distributions have little variability or variance: distributions that spread over a considerable range of numbers have larger variances.

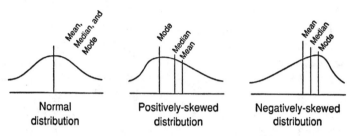

Normal distribution   Positively-skewed distribution   Negatively-skewed distribution

FIGURE 5-1. **Measures of central tendency.**

There are three commonly used measures of dispersion. The *range* is simply the difference between the highest and lowest score. It tells us little about how much dispersion there is, but only about two scores—the highest and lowest ones.

The *variance* gives us more information. We can calculate the variance by finding the difference between each score and the mean, squaring each of these differences, adding them, then dividing that total by the number of scores. The further that scores are from the mean (the more dispersed the scores are), the larger the variance will be.

The *standard deviation* is simply the square root of the variance. As with the variance, the greater the dispersion in a distribution of scores, the larger the standard deviation.

Measures of Relationship

A *correlation* describes the degree to which there is a co-relationship between two variables. It can vary from −1 to +1. A correlation of +1 indicates that two variables have a strong co-relationship. When one variable increases, so does the other (see graph below). When two variables have a correlation of −1 we say they are inversely (or negatively) correlated. This means that as one increases, the other decreases. When there is no systematic relationship between two variables, (that is, a change in one variable is unrelated to a change in the other), they have a co-relationship of 0.

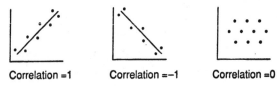

Correlation =1   Correlation =−1   Correlation =0

FIGURE 5-2. Measures of relationship.

There are several types of correlation formulas, depending on the kind of data with which we are dealing.[5] The *Pearson product-moment correlation* uses continuous data on both axes, such as height and weight. The *point-biserial correlation* can be used when one variable is dichotomous (that is, has only two categories), and the other variable is continuous. For example, plotting sex as one variable and IQ as a second might use this correlational method.

The *biserial correlation* correlates the relationship between a dichotomous variable and a continuous one. We use it when an artificial dichotomy is imposed on one variable. For example, if one were to dichotomize subjects' annual incomes into incomes below $25,000 and those above $25,000, and plot this against IQ, the biserial correlation would be appropriate to use.

We can use the *phi correlation* to correlate two truly dichotomous variables (such as sex and "handedness"). The *tetrachoric correlation* is used to correlate two artificially-dichotomous variables. Researchers use *multiple correlation* or *multiple regression* to correlate two or more predictor variables with a single criterion variable. For example, with this method one could correlate high-school GPA and SAT scores with college GPA. Researchers use *canonical correlation* to correlate two or more predictor variables with two or more criterion variables. There are other correlation formulas available to compute correlations for situations not covered by one of the above.

Correlations and Causation

You may already be convinced that correlation does not prove causation. If you are not sure, the following paragraphs are for you. Co-relationships, that is, correlations significantly different from zero, abound in nature and in contemporary life. Some of these occur by chance only, and disappear upon retesting. Some of these remain significant upon retesting, but do not mean that a change in one variable causes the change in the other.

For example, there is a significant negative correlation between the amount of space in sequential pieces of sidewalk concrete and the crime rate for any given day. Second, the New Hebrides islanders have observed that people there who are in good health usually had lice. Those in poor health usually didn't. Therefore they concluded that lice made a person healthy.

We can explain the negative correlation between the amount of space between sequential sidewalk blocks and crime rate in the following way. As the temperature goes down, the concrete in sidewalks shrinks by a small amount. As temperature goes down, people who commit crimes tend to postpone their plans until more pleasant weather. Therefore the negative correlation between distance between sidewalk spaces and crimes committed.

The explanation for the New Hebrides islanders took researchers a while to understand. On investigation they found that nearly everyone there has lice—it is a normal condition. But if a person became sick and developed a fever, the high temperature made it uncomfortable for the lice, and they left.[6] Therefore, the observations on which they based their correlation were correct. Their error was to attribute causation because of that correlation.

If we find a significant positive or negative correlation between two variables, what are possible conclusions we can legitimately draw? First, as mentioned before, it may be a chance correlation. Second, there may be another factor that causes changes in both A and B. This occurred in the first example above. Cold weather caused both the concrete sidewalk to shrink and criminals to decide to stay inside until a more comfortable working day.

Third, rather than A causing changes in B, B may be causing changes in A. The New Hebrides islanders thought that lice (A) brought good health (B). The reality was that poor health (−B) caused the lice to flee (−A). Last, we have the possibility that the covariation is real, but the cause and effect nature of the relationship is purely speculative.

Logicians call the fallacy of believing correlation proves causation the *post hoc propter hoc fallacy*, meaning that someone assumes that because B follows A, A causes B. In the next section of this book we'll discuss this issue again.

Ways People Try to Mislead Others Using Descriptive Statistics

Using "Average" to Mislead

Mr. Adams owns a small business that employs nine full-time workers and himself. He becomes aware of some discontent about wages, and calls the group together to discuss the issue. He says he wants to be fair to all employees. He cannot tell salaries of individuals to anyone else in the company. However, he has tallied the average hourly wage for employees (adding in the amount spent for benefits), and says that the average amount spent on employees per hour worked is $12.90. (Mr. Adams included the amount spent for benefits, since he knew this figure would be difficult for employees to find, and would make any counter-calculations difficult.) He said that the company would be unable to raise salaries much above their present levels and still meet all other expenses.

This figure astonished the employees, for it certainly seemed like a reasonable level of compensation. It did not seem consistent with the amount they were receiving in their paychecks. However, they lacked data to disprove Mr. Adams's statement, so the meeting adjourned.

One of Mr. Adams's employees, John, was not willing to let the matter end so quickly. With the cooperation of the other employees, he found out each employee's hourly wage. From payment stubs and W-2 information he estimated that employees received an average of $3.00 per hour of benefits. With these pieces of information, he calculated the average salary of the nine employees. The employees asked for a second meeting with Mr. Adams. In this meeting, John stated that he had figured the average salaries of the nine employees, and his figure was $5.00 per hour (plus benefits) rather than $12.90 per hour. Was he or Mr. Adams correct?

Both were, because of the ambiguous definition of the word "average." The hourly salaries of Mr. Adams and the nine other employees are shown below:

```
$    4.00
$    4.00
$    5.00
$    5.00
$    5.00
$    5.50
$    5.50
$  10.00
$  10.00
$  45.00   (Mr. Adams)
─────────
$  99.00
+ $ 30.00  ($3.00 per hour for benefits for ten employees)
─────────
$129.00
```

Mr. Adams arrived at his "average" hourly cost to the company by dividing $129.00 by 10, arriving at an average cost of $12.90 per employee per hour, which is a legitimate way to use the word "average."

John used as his definition for "average" the modal salary (the one that occurs most often), which is also a legitimate usage. The modal salary in this case turned out to be $5.00. Thus both John and Mr. Adams were using this term correctly, but arriving at very different figures. You can see how the ambiguity in this word has allowed management and employee leaders to develop very different figures to justify their arguments. Television advertisers often present consumers with similar kinds of confusing statistical claims for a product.

The Semi-Attached Figure

Darrell Huff defines and illustrates the semi-attached figure in a way that is difficult to duplicate or improve upon. Here is his description:

> If you can't prove what you want to prove, demonstrate something else and pretend that they are the same thing. In the daze that follows the collision of statistics with the human mind, hardly anybody will notice the difference. The semi-attached figure is a device guaranteed to stand you in good stead. It always has.
>
> You can't prove that your nostrum cures colds, but you can publish (in large type) a sworn laboratory report that half an ounce of the stuff killed 31,108 germs in a test tube in eleven seconds.[7]

Most advertisers who use a semi-attached figure like the above conveniently neglect to mention that a human exposed to a similar level of the nostrum would die in seven seconds.

Misleading Graphs

The most common and most unrecognized way that people try to deceive us is with graphs. There are at least six ways to do this. After reading this section I would encourage you to pick up any available newspaper or magazine. Look for graphs used as part of advertising, and see how frequently these methods appear.[8]

The first method is to leave one or both axes unlabeled. This gives the viewer no ability to assess the magnitude of the improvement produced by the advertised product. This method is particularly useful on television, where the advertiser presents the graph so briefly that one has no time to notice unlabeled axes.

As an alternative, collapse the space along one axis to make the change resulting from treatment look more impressive. Think for a moment about how this works. If you have a scale for something that potentially ranges from zero to 100, movement from 74 to 76 isn't anything to make someone sit up and take notice. However, on a bar graph you can collapse the scale from zero to 70 by putting a jagged line crossways through the graph. This shows that you're removing part of the graph, allegedly for space considerations. You then decide (again for reasons of space), to top the graph at 80. Therefore your graph focuses entirely on the portion of the scale from 70 to 80. Your insignificant change of 2 points on a 100 point scale now looks like something! By using only the methods described in this paragraph you have made the 2 point gain look ten times as impressive as it really is. Since the scale now covers only a 10-point series, any change will look 10 times larger than if the scale covered a 100-point series.

Third, if the response to treatment has been less than overwhelming, you can increase the visual impact of a graph by changing the category of measurement used on that axis. For example, you may want to persuade people to buy your fertilizer to put on corn they are growing in their garden. (Please note that my use of the word "you" in this section is purely a literary device. I, of course, know that you would never really use such dastardly methods: it would always be someone else.)

Getting back to your venture, you plant some corn to serve as a control. You then plant other corn, which you fertilize with various concentrations to find the optimal level of fertilization. Unfortunately, at three concentrations your fertilized corn only grew an average of one, two, and three centimeters higher than the control group. Since corn in your area usually grows to an average of 160 centimeters, results of one, two, and three centimeters are somewhat less than astounding.

At this point you can do three things to persuade people to buy your fertilizer. First, change the measure from centimeters to millimeters. Now you have increases of 10, 20, and 30 to talk about. Second, publish these results through a medium where people are unlikely to recognize that you've changed the measuring scale from centimeters to millimeters. Again, television is very helpful, since you control how long anyone is able to look at the "proof." Third, take some pictures of the control and treated corn from an angle that causes the treated corn to look much taller than the control corn.

A fourth way to exaggerate the rise and fall of some variable over time is to start the vertical axis at some numerical value other than zero. The number you choose depends on two things—how unscrupulous you are and how much you think you can get away with.

A fifth way to use graphs to deceive is through what Runyon has called the "double-whammy" graph. Here you plot two things, such as cost of living and purchasing power, on the same graph, without telling people that these are reciprocal measures of the same thing. By including them both on the graph it makes the situation look twice as bad as it really is.

Sixth, cumulative graphs can be used to deceive quite nicely. Let us suppose you wanted to present evidence of the productivity of a certain person in its most positive light, but there is a problem. About half the time this person is not producing anything. If you were to graph his or her productivity each hour, the graph would not be very positive. Many hours would be zero, and those that were nonzero would not be far above it.

A cumulative graph may be the answer. As long as the subject is producing anything, the graph will rise. Even on the hours when the person produces nothing, the graph will only level off, but at a point comfortably away from zero on the y-axis. Since the line on a cumulative graph never decreases, it always gives the impression of growth.

UNDERSTANDING INFERENTIAL STATISTICS

As we saw in the last section, descriptive statistics are procedures that we can use to describe or summarize groups of numbers. *Inferential statistics* include statistical procedures that allow us to make inferences (scientific guesses) about a population based on information derived from a sample of that population.

When we use correlational research designs (such as surveys), we can affirm only that a co-relationship does or does not exist. When we use true research designs, we can begin to make inferences about the cause-and-effect relationship between two variables. Thus, to do empirical research that we hope will generalize beyond the group with whom we conducted the research, we must understand the principles of both research design and inferential statistics.

Sampling

Sampling is at the heart of inferential statistics. It is too expensive and time-consuming to conduct trials of a medication or teaching approach on everyone in a population. The goal in inferential statistics is to conduct an experiment on a sample, and be able to generalize those results to a population.

Biased Samples

The test of a random sample is this: Does every subject in the population have an equal chance to be in the sample? If we select a true random sample from a population, then generalizations of our results to that population have a high likelihood of being accurate. If our sample is not truly random, (i.e., is biased in some way), then our generalizations to the population will be inaccurate to an unknown degree.

It is important that samples include everyone to whom we wish to generalize. In the latter part of 1990 women created a furor when they learned that many animal research studies funded by the federal government were using only male animals. They made the point that male and female members of many species have significantly different biochemistries. Research, if it is to be useful in developing treatments for women, should include equal numbers of both males and females, or else should include two groups—males and females—in each study. Women had a right to be angry. It seems hard to believe that researchers and those who select which research projects are funded overlooked this point for so long.

Even when we do our best to make a human sample completely random, it is very easy for some unrecognized source of bias to enter the selection process. Huff states: "Most polls are biased toward the person with more money, more education, more information and alertness, better appearance, more conventional behavior, and more settled habits than the average of the populations he is chosen to represent."[9]

A famous example of a sample designed to be random that turned out to be biased was the *Literary Digest* poll of 1936. Surveyers chose people at random from telephone directories and automobile registrations, and asked them whether they were going to vote for Alf Landon or FDR for president. The poll predicted that Landon would win the presidential election, a prediction that turned out to be inaccurate.

We now can understand the reason for this poll's lack of predictive validity. The reason it was not representative was that in 1936, in the midst of the Great Depression, anyone with a car or a telephone was well-to-do. Then, as now, the affluent tended to vote Republican. The method of sampling was biased, that is, it was not a true random sample of the U.S. voting public. The poll included a larger percentage of Republicans than were in the general population, and erroneously predicted a Republican win.

Even after developing a sampling procedure that removes all sources of known bias, it probably is well to treat our results with a degree of humility. There can always be a hidden source of bias somewhere, and usually is.[10]

Error Variance and Standard Error

Let us assume that we have a population of 100 marbles in a pan, numbered 1 through 100. We take a sample of 10 marbles out of the pan without looking, record their numbers, and then return them to the pan. (There will be slight differences depending on whether we replace each marble in the pan before choosing the next. Since this chapter is trying to give the basics of inferential statistics I've chosen not to include this complexity.) We repeat this process several times. We could then calculate the mean for each sample of ten marbles. These means will obviously differ depending on which of the 100 marbles are in that sample.

Just as we computed a variance score in the section on descriptive statistics, we can now compute a variance score on the means of the various samples we have drawn. The highest mean we could get would be 95.5, which would occur if we drew the marbles numbered 91 through 100. The lowest mean we could get would be 5.5, which would occur if we drew the marbles numbered 1 through 10.

We could continue to take samples of 10 from this population and compute their means. If we then plot those means on a graph, we would eventually have a distribution of means that looks like a normal (or bell) curve. We could calculate the variance of those mean scores using the formula discussed in the section on descriptive statistics. That variance would be called the *error variance.*

In the section on descriptive statistics we said that we can compute the standard deviation by taking the square root of the variance. Here also we can compute the standard deviation of our sample of means by taking the square root of the variance. In this context we call this term the *standard error.*

We've seen how to calculate the standard error, but what does the standard error mean? If we were to take many samples from this population, we could then compute the standard deviation of those means. We do not do that, but we can calculate an estimate of that number by taking the square root of the error variance. We call this estimate the standard error.

From statistical procedures we have not discussed in this book, we know that if we were to take additional samples from that same population, 68 percent of the time the mean of those samples would lie within one standard deviation (one standard error) of the population mean. Ninety-five percent of the time they would lie within approximately two standard deviations of the mean.

The standard error will be used in many subsequent calculations to decide whether a difference between two sets of scores suggests that a treatment did make a measurable difference (and therefore we are drawing from two different populations), or whether the variation in scores is what one would expect from a single population because of random sampling (and therefore the treatment did not make a difference).

The standard error is often used to compute a *confidence interval*. Pollsters use confidence intervals when they make statements such as "65 plus or minus 5 percent favor candidate A."

A confidence interval is ±2 (actually 1.96) standard deviations from the mean. What pollsters mean when they say "based on our survey, 65 ± 5 percent favor candidate A" is that if they were to take repeated samples, 95 percent of the time the percentage of people favoring candidate A would lie between 60 percent and 70 percent. This figure will be correct if the population is normally distributed on the variable being measured. To the degree that a particular population differs from a normal distribution, these estimates will be inexact.

The Scientific Method and the Null Hypothesis

Much modern research is based on sampling and probabilities. Let us take a moment to integrate this into the classical scientific method that we discussed in the last chapter. The first few steps are the same. They are:

1. The researcher states a problem, sometimes as a question.
2. He or she collects facts that relate to the question or problem.
3. The researcher forms a hypothesis that explains the known facts.
4. The investigator makes inferences or predictions that will be confirmed if his or her hypothesis is true.

5. The scientist conducts an experiment to verify his or her predictions.

It is in steps four and five that modern probability theory modifies the way we do these steps and discuss them. After we conduct an experiment and expose one group to a treatment and not the other, we measure them in some way and tabulate the results. We use statistical methods, not to prove that our treatment worked, but to decide whether the null hypothesis can be rejected.

You might be tempted to ask two questions: "What is the null hypothesis?" and "Doesn't this seem like a convoluted way to prove that the treatment was effective?" We shall start with the first question.

The *null hypothesis* is the hypothesis that the scores of the treatment group are not significantly different from the scores of the control group. The null hypothesis suggests that these two samples come from the same population. If a researcher finds any differences between the two means, these are due to sampling error and do not reflect differences due to the treatment. Since researchers hope that their treatments did make a difference, they hope they can reject the null hypothesis.

Sometimes researchers talk about null hypotheses and *alternative hypotheses*. Alternative hypotheses are the logical opposites of null hypotheses. Researchers hope that the alternative hypotheses are true. However, the way scientific research is conducted, researchers do not prove that their alternative hypotheses are true. Instead, they try to prove that null hypotheses should be rejected. How do they go about doing that?

We use the methods of inferential statistics, as you remember, to make inferences about the population from which a sample is selected. This sample will have variance within itself, which we call error variance. The question we are asking with t-tests and analysis of variance tests is, "Is the difference between the mean of the treatment and control group large enough to be considered a significant difference, or is there a reasonable likelihood that the differences are probably due to error variance alone?" Another way of asking this question is, "Is it likely that these two groups are samples of the same population (that is, the treatment did not cause a significant difference), or that they are samples of different populations (that is, the treatment did make a significant difference)?"

Before answering that question researchers have to answer another question. That question is, "How large a difference does there have to be in order for us to say it is a significant one?" Statisticians have agreed on an answer to this one.

If we are drawing samples from the same population and measuring them on some variable, frequently the average of any two samples will be close together. However, there is the possibility that we will draw one sample totally from the higher scores in the population, and the second sample totally from lower scores in the population. (This would not happen very frequently, but it would happen once in awhile.)

We might believe, based on the large difference between the two means, that we were drawing from two different populations, even though we were drawing from only one. In statistical language, we might reject the null hypothesis even though it was true. (That is, although we are drawing both samples from one population, we might conclude that we were drawing them from different ones.)

Now back to determining what to consider a significant difference. Statisticians by convention have agreed to call a *significant difference* any difference between the two samples that is large enough that the probability of a difference that size coming from the same population by chance is less than .05 (in research articles and statistics texts they denote this as $p < .05$).

To say it another way, statisticians consider a difference between two samples significant when that difference is large enough that the possibility of rejecting a true null hypothesis is less than .05. Rejecting the null hypothesis when it is true means concluding that there is a difference between the populations from which we drew these samples, when there really is not a difference—both samples are from the same population. Thus, a significant difference is one that is large enough that the probability that we are rejecting a true null hypothesis is less than .05.

Statisticians have adopted a second convention as well. If the difference between the treatment and control group is large enough that the probability that we are rejecting a true null hypothesis is less than .01 ($p < .01$), statisticians call this a *very significant difference.*

The other question that we asked several paragraphs ago was this: "Isn't this process of stating a null hypothesis and then rejecting it a convoluted way of proving something?" Would it not be simpler to state the researcher's hypothesis (the alternative hypothesis), and prove it true? Why would it not be valid to do it this way? Try to answer this yourself before reading the next paragraph.

The reason this would not be valid is that we do not have enough data to say that we have proven the alternative hypothesis to be true. We are working only with a sample. Even if we reject the null hypothesis with that sample, we have not proven that the treatment would work with the entire population. There are threats to internal validity and external validity that we may not have recognized, even if we have carefully constructed an experiment using a true experimental design. Therefore, rejecting the null hypothesis with a sample in an experimental setting is not equivalent to proving the alternative hypothesis will work with the entire population in a nonexperimental (natural) setting. That is why we do not use the more straightforward statement saying that "the researcher proved that his or her treatment worked."

Type 1 and Type 2 Errors

It is possible to reject a null hypothesis when it is true. That is, it is possible to say that there is a significant difference between our treatment and control groups when the difference is due to sampling error or error variance. Researchers call this kind of error a *Type 1* error. The level of significance we choose determines the frequency with which it occurs. If we choose the .05 level of significance, then probably one time in twenty we will say incorrectly that two groups are different when they are not. If we choose the .01 level of significance, then the likelihood is that one time in one hundred we will say incorrectly that the two groups are different when they are not.

A Type 2 error is the mirror image of a Type 1 error. A *Type 2* error is the likelihood of accepting the null hypothesis when it is not true. In a Type 2 error we say there is no difference between two groups when there really is. The likelihood of committing a Type 2 error does not depend on a single factor as does the Type 1 error. However, as you might have recognized, the more stringent we make our criteria so that we do not make a Type 1 error, the more likely we are to make a Type 2 error.

One-Tailed and Two-Tailed Tests

If you read research articles you will undoubtedly hear references to another concept—one-tailed and two-tailed tests. Think again of the normal curve. We want to set our cutoff points so that if two sample means are far enough apart that they have less than a .05 probability of coming from the same population by chance, we will say there is a significant difference between them.

We need to decide whether we want to test only whether our treatment improved subjects' scores, or whether it improved or worsened subjects' scores. If we want to test only whether it improved scores, then we should use a one-tailed test. If we want to measure a significant change in either direction, we should use a two-tailed test. (You can find the cutoff scores for one-tailed and two-tailed tests in the back of most statistics textbooks.)

T-Tests

T-tests can be used in a variety of ways. The most common way is to compare the means of two groups. If the means of the two groups (e.g., two samples) are far enough apart, a researcher can conclude that they come from different populations. A *t-test* is an inferential statistic because it allows a researcher to make predictions about a population, although he or she probably will never see the entire population.

The procedure is straightforward. The researcher states the null hypothesis, sets a level of significance (usually .05 or .01, occasionally .001), and selects either a one-tailed test or a two-tailed test. From these and the size of the sample, using tables for t-tests, the researcher obtains a critical value. The *critical value* is the value that must be exceeded by the calculated value of the t-test for differences between the means to be considered significant. If the calculated value exceeds the critical value, the researcher can reject the null hypothesis and say that he or she found significant differences. If the calculated value does not exceed the critical value, the researcher does not reject the null hypothesis. Here he states that "he found no significant differences."

Analysis of Variance Procedures

When more than two groups are compared, researchers use another statistical procedure, commonly called *analysis of variance* (and abbreviated ANOVA). As with the t-test, the researcher must decide what significance level he or she will use and whether to use a one-tailed or two-tailed test. From this a critical value can be found, and then compared with the calculated value.

When investigators use two or more independent variables the statistical analysis is called *factorial analysis of variance* or *multiple analysis of variance* (sometimes abbreviated MANOVA). Some researchers use another kind of statistical analysis, called *multiple regression analysis,* rather than analysis of variance. When there are two or more independent variables, a researcher may find that there is a significant interaction between them. This means that the effect of one variable changes depending on the level of the other variable.

Multiple analysis of variance or multiple regression analysis is especially helpful as we recognize that most variables do not act in isolation. For example, one given style of teaching may not be best for all students at all age levels. It may be interesting to compare a new style of teaching (first independent variable) at different IQ levels (second independent variable) and at different grade levels (third independent variable). In so doing we may find that the new teaching method results in increased academic scores for students with above average IQs who are grades 4 and above, but that there are no significant improvements when used with students of average IQ or less or students below the fourth grade. By using these more complex procedures we can answer more specific research questions.

Analysis of Covariance

Sometimes when researchers work with a sample, the influence of one variable (perhaps one they are not interested in testing) is so strong that it would obscure the effects of the treatment variable. In this case the researchers might want to control the effects of the unwanted variable so that they could clearly see the effects of the treatment. This can be done through analysis of covariance.

For example, let us assume that Dr. Armstrong has developed a ten-hour program called "Introduction to the Collegiate Environment." He would like to assess whether his program will improve GPAs during the first year of college. He randomly assigns forty students to either a control group or a treatment group. Fortunately for Dr. Armstrong, all twenty of those assigned to the treatment group agree to go through the ten-hour program.

However, after a few weeks teaching the class, Dr. Armstrong starts to believe that, although he used random assignment to select students to be in his treatment and control groups, the students in his treatment group are not representative of the college population. He fears that his treatment group has a general ability somewhat lower than that of the college as a whole, and that this may affect the research results.

One way that Dr. Armstrong could correct for this bias, if there is such, is to use general ability level as a covariate. He has scores on the Scholastic Aptitude Test (SAT) available to him for all students. He can statistically adjust the scores on his dependent variable (first year GPA), using the scores on a general intelligence measure on the SAT as a covariate. In this way he can determine whether his program did make a difference in freshmen GPA after the variance caused by unequal ability level has been controlled for (or removed) using analysis of covariance.

Analysis of covariance allows researchers to increase the power of a given statistical test. Power refers to the "sensitivity of a statistical test to differences among the groups the researcher is comparing." If there was a difference between the general ability of the average student in Dr. Armstrong's control and treatment group (e.g., students in the treatment group generally had somewhat lower abilities), then, even though Dr. Armstrong's program did increase the treatment group's first year GPA over what it would have been without his treatment, there may not be a significant difference between scores of his treatment group and those of the control group. He may have brought the treatment group's scores up to a point where they were about equal to those of the control group. Though his treatment did make a difference, analysis of variance of GPA scores would not be sensitive enough to show that it did. However, if Dr. Armstrong did an analysis of covariance in which he used a measure of intelligence as a covariate and adjusted group means based on this, he might very well find that his treatment did make a difference. Thus, analysis of covariance may be used to increase the sensitivity of a statistical test.

Analysis of covariance can be used to help a researcher separate the effects of several interrelated factors that may have significant theoretical or practical interest. For example, a sociologist named Steve King may be interested in looking at the factors that cause a child to be aggressive. He believes that the most important factor is whether a child is physically abused by his or her parents. Others within Dr. King's department believe social class is the most important determinant (i.e., that aggressive behavior is more acceptable in some social classes than in others). Others in his department argue that the emotional effect of divorce or separation on children is the major cause of aggressiveness. Still others might argue that when a child sees repeated violence between father and mother, this causes childhood aggression.

By using analysis of covariance, Dr. King could control for

the effects of social class, family disruption, and spousal violence. After statistically controlling for these three factors, he could then find whether those factors accounted for (explained) most of the variance regarding children's aggressiveness or whether there is still a significant amount of variance explained by whether a child is physically abused. Other techniques can be used to clarify the relative amounts of variance contributed by each of these factors.

Parametric and Nonparametric Statistics

The statistics we have discussed until now are called *parametric statistics*. There are two basic assumptions that should be met before using parametric statistics. First, the samples should be normally distributed, and second, the variances of the samples should be similar. If our treatment and control groups do not meet these two assumptions, some researchers believe *nonparametric* (or distribution-free) *statistics* should be used.

However, there are differences of opinion about this issue. Some statisticians argue that parametric statistics are "robust" to violations of sample normality and variance heterogeneity. These researchers believe that parametric statistics produce valid results even when samples are not normally distributed or do not have equal variances.

There is agreement among researchers that nonparametric statistics should be used when working with nominal scale data. An example of nominal scale data occurs when a researcher assigns an arbitrary number to a particular category, as when he or she designates Roman Catholics as 01, Southern Baptists as 02, United Church of Christ members as 03, etc. The researcher is using the various numbers only for categorization, and not because they have any relationship to one another or to the group they designate.

When we turn to ordinal scale data, numbers show the

relative order of individuals, but there may be unequal distances between the numbers 1, 2, and 3. The ranking of soccer teams within a league would be an example of ordinal scale data. Some researchers believe nonparametric statistics should be used with this level of data; others believe that parametric statistics can be validly used.

When we get to interval scale data, where the intervals between adjacent numbers are equal, there is general agreement that it is valid to use parametric statistics.

One other area that researchers do not agree on regards small samples. Some believe that with small samples nonparametric statistics should be used, others believe parametric statistics can still be used validly. When in doubt, consult whoever will be evaluating your research project. When possible, most researchers prefer to use parametric statistics because of their greater power.[11]

THREATS TO EXTERNAL VALIDITY

External validity refers to the researcher's ability to generalize his or her findings from the research setting and sample to some broader population. Clearly research will have little practical use unless the findings will generalize into some "real world" setting. We will find that some things that are threats to the internal validity of an experiment are also threats to its external validity.[12]

Experimentally-Accessible Population and Target Population Are Different

One threat to generalizability is that the population sampled by the researcher is different from the population to which he or she wishes to generalize. Frequently the population from which a researcher samples contains freshmen and sophomore college students fulfilling a requirement for

Psychology 101 or 102. The research results can legitimately be generalized to other freshmen and sophomore college students fulfilling requirements of Psychology 101 and 102 courses. Whether the results generalize to the general adult population of the United States remains unproven.

Interaction Between Treatment and Specific Subjects

A second threat to external validity is the possibility of an interaction between the treatment and specific subjects. For example, suppose a Christian counselor develops a method for dealing with fear using inner healing (sometimes called "healing of memories"). For the next six months he randomly assigns incoming clients who have problems with fear either to a control group (treating them with secular behavioral methods) or to a group dealing with healing of memories. However, he finds that approximately half his Christian clients are unwilling to try healing of memories. He does the research with the remaining clients and calculates his results.

This Christian counselor cannot validly generalize his findings to all Christian clients since his research group is not a random sample from all Christian clients. At most he could generalize his findings to Christian clients who have fears and are open to the use of inner healing in their therapy.

Inadequate Description of the Treatment Variable

In order for those in the applied professions (e.g., physicians, psychiatrists, psychologists, and counselors) to use a method, it must be described in enough detail that they can repeat what the researcher did. In order for researchers to replicate a finding to discover whether it reoccurs in a variety of settings, the method must be described in detail. The details should include specifics of the treatment, duration of the treatment and any other information necessary for someone to replicate the subjects' experiences in their treatment or research setting. Specific interpersonal characteristics of the researcher may not be included but may be a very important factor from the subjects' perspectives. Failure of a researcher to give a thorough description of the entire procedure may result in failure of other researchers or applied professionals to receive the same results.

Inaccurate Methods of Measuring the Dependent Variable

When dealing with the phenomena of change in the physical world, operational definitions can be very appropriate and helpful. However, when human beings change, some of those changes can occur without any behavioral expression, or without the same behavioral expression in all subjects. The challenge in these human science experiments is to develop a method of measurement that is not limited to overt behavioral expressions but one that is still valid and reliable. In addition, when describing a situation for other researchers or clinicians, it also must be able to be communicated so that others can measure the same variable validly and reliably. An unreliable or invalid method of measurement can obscure true treatment effects.

Multiple-Treatment Interference

Often those who are subjects of research, such as college students, have been subjects in several experiments. Thus the expectations, attitudes, and history they bring to a new experiment are likely to be different from the average person in the population to whom the researcher would like to generalize his or her results. Whenever a subject has participated in previous experiments this affects his or her response to a particular treatment to an unknown extent, and therefore affects the generalizability of the treatment results to an unknown extent.

Interaction of History and Treatment Effects

Whenever research is conducted, there is the possibility that some historical event will occur that will make subjects' responses to treatment different from people's responses when that historical event is not present. For example, suppose a researcher wished to test the effectiveness of a new weight-loss method he had developed. For the next sixteen applicants to a weight-loss clinic he randomly assigned eight to the clinic's standard program and (with their informed consent) eight to the experimental treatment. He began the research project in mid-March.

Something the researcher did not know at the time of assignment was that four of the eight members of his treatment group were to be brides in June weddings. None of the members of the control group were. These four subjects entered the treatment with extremely high motivation to lose weight. Their successes during the early weeks of the program motivated others in their group to try as hard, so that in the end all eight lost weight, and lost significantly more weight than the control group.

In such a situation we do not know whether the treatment will generalize to other groups where 50 percent of the subjects are not brides-to-be. This interaction between the specific historical situation and the treatment produced a result that may not generalize to a population who are not as highly motivated.

Interaction of Time of Measurement and Treatment Effects

Let us consider another hypothetical situation. A graduate student wishes to compare the results of two different kinds of marital enrichment groups on marital satisfaction as measured by the Marital Satisfaction Inventory. One of these approaches (Group A) emphasizes building communication skills and meets for two to three hours per week for several weeks. The other approach (Group B) involves a weekend encounter that emphasizes developing a very intense, positive experience through a series of carefully structured exercises.

Our graduate student researcher has access to two groups that have been through the communication skills-building experience and two groups that have been through the weekend encounter. Everyone in both groups agrees to take the Marital Satisfaction Inventory and returns it as requested (this only happens in hypothetical experiments).

Of the two groups who had gone through the experience three months ago, Group A scored significantly higher on marital satisfaction than Group B. Of the two groups that had completed the experiences within the last two weeks, Group B scored significantly higher than Group A. How do we explain the differences?

It is plausible to assume that people in a communication skills-building setting usually do not experience the emotional high that couples do who go through an intense, positive weekend experience. If an investigator tests couples shortly after the completion of their experience, couples in Group B will rate their marital satisfaction higher than those in Group A. It is also plausible to assume that couples who learn skills that they can continue to use for months and years after their group ends may have higher marital satisfaction scores three months after the end of their experience than those who had an intense weekend encounter that did not focus on learning skills.

Thus the results on the dependent variable may be different depending on the timing of the measurement. For research results to be generalizable to other populations, the timing of the measurement of the dependent variable should be included in the description of the study. Also, for situations where it is important not only to gain a certain level of functioning but also to maintain that level, a research design that continues to follow subjects for a reasonable period after the completion of the treatment is helpful.

Pretest Sensitization

In the last chapter we discussed how a pretest may sensitize subjects to specific kinds of information or experiences. As a result the pretest sensitization rather than the treatment itself may be the cause of the differences between treatment and control subjects' scores. Sensitization also may threaten generalizability. Treatment results may not generalize beyond the treatment sample unless the population also has a pretest to sensitize them.

The Hawthorne Effect

The Hawthorne Effect received its name from a series of experiments done with a group of workers at the Western Electric Plant in Hawthorne, Illinois, in the late 1920s and early 1930s. There are several factors that may have entered this situation and affected workers' production, but a chief one, according to them, was simply the knowledge that they were part of an experiment. Thus factors such as role context, the desire to make a positive contribution to science, demand characteristics, and knowledge that one is participating in an experiment may affect how subjects respond to a treatment. It may be these other factors, rather than the treatment itself, that are causing the change. If the researcher moves the treatment from its experimental setting to a natural, nonexperimental setting, it may not produce the same results.

Novelty and Disruption Effects

Whenever a researcher introduces a treatment it usually has the benefit of being considered a new, novel treatment. New treatments generally produce hope in subjects, which may activate the placebo effect. Raised expectations and the activity of endorphins may produce the treatment effect, rather than the treatment itself.

Disruption effects refer to the fact that when researchers, therapists, doctors, and patients have to learn to use a new procedure or treatment, they may fail to use it effectively at first. After a time they become more comfortable and skilled with the new treatment, which may be more effective than previous treatments. However, if the researcher measured the results during the initial usage of the treatment, the measured effectiveness of the treatment may be lower than warranted.

Experimenter Bias or Experimenter Expectancy

Experimenter effects, as discussed in the last chapter, are those cues that researchers or their assistants give, that show subjects how to respond if they are to confirm the researcher's hypothesis. Experimenter effects are threats to both the internal validity and external validity of a study.[13]

SOME CONCLUSIONS

It is possible to use a valid statistical method with a poor experimental design, such as the pseudo-experimental designs identified in the last chapter. No statistical method can make up for an invalid design. To verify that a treatment result is valid, we must assess both the research design and the statistical method used to process the results. If either of these are deficient, the conclusions may be invalid.

When advertisers or politicians present statistics, it is probably well to use that as an opportunity to review the ways that research designs and statistics can be used to mislead or deceive. Rarely are such reports intended to be an objective analysis of the facts of the situation.

However, when you hear that scientific researchers have

come to differing conclusions, this is probably not reason to become cynical about the validity of all research. As you can see from the discussions in the last two chapters, there are many threats to internal and external validity. Researchers, working in good faith, often unwittingly fail to control for one or more of these threats. Often the way that science progresses is that one researcher fails to replicate the results of another, and in the resulting inquiry to discover why, researchers become aware of an important factor that neither of them had considered before.

SUMMARY OF PARTS OF CHAPTERS 4 AND 5

Internal and External Threats to Validity

Internal Threats

1. History
2. Maturation
3. Effect of testing
4. Reliability of instrumentation
5. Statistical regression to the mean
6. Mortality
7. Nonrandom selection
8. Experimenter bias or expectancy transmitted by the experiment itself
9. Experimenter bias transmitted by the experimenter's actions, responses, and interrogations
10. Experimenter bias transmitted in the phrasing of questions on surveys
11. Subjects' preconceptions and expectations
12. Effect of role context
13. Effect of natural science techniques

External Threats

1. Experimentally-accessible population and target population are different
2. Interaction between treatment and specific subjects
3. Inadequate description of the treatment variable
4. Inaccurate methods of measuring the dependent variable
5. Multiple-treatment interference
6. Interaction of history and treatment effects
7. Interaction of time of measurement and treatment effects
8. Pretest sensitization
9. The Hawthorne Effect
10. Novelty and disruption effects
11. Experimenter bias or expectancy

EXERCISES

EX 26: In his dissertation research, a doctoral student recently studied the response of newlywed couples to three marriage enrichment programs. He randomly assigned 99 newlywed couples (couples married an average of 13 months) to one of three marital enrichment programs or a control group. The three treatment programs were *Growing Together, Training in Marriage Enrichment,* and *Learning to Live Together.* The four groups received a pretest and posttest using *Enrich,* a validated marital assessment instrument that gives scores on marital satisfaction in fourteen different areas. Figure 5-3 summarizes the improvements for the three treatment groups with this caption.

EX 27: In a Christian counseling center are three therapists with differing theoretical orientations. One day at lunch they are discussing how they deal with clients suffering from phobias. They decide to try the following experiment.

All clients with the presenting problem of one clearly defined phobia will be randomly assigned to one of these therapists or to a waiting list control. One therapist is a behaviorist and will use behavioral methods primarily to treat his phobic clients. One therapist is a cognitive psychologist, and will use cognitive methods primarily to treat his phobic clients. One therapist is a Christian humanistic psychologist, and will use healing of memories and other experiential methods primarily to treat his clients.

Those clients presenting with more than one phobia will also be counseled. They will not be part of the experiment because of the differences among clients with one phobia and those who have more. All clients will be tested at the beginning and then every fourth session using a validated phobia survey upon which all three therapists agree. They also agree that the purpose of their research is not to see who can cure client phobias most quickly. The focus of their research will

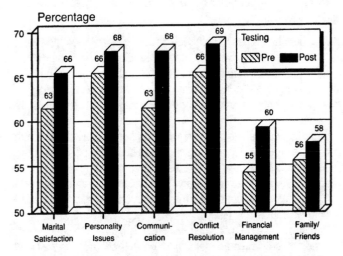

FIGURE 5-3. Significant changes on *Enrich* of newlywed couples in enrichment programs.

(From *Prepare/Enrich* Newsletter, Winter 1991 (6:1), 1.

Examine this table in light of what you have learned in this chapter and write out your response.

be to try to understand the process of healing and how this is similar or different among their three approaches.

Evaluate their research plan with regard to the internal and external threats to validity covered in these last two chapters.

EX 28: A threat to external validity is the difference between the experimentally-accessible population and the target population. If a researcher randomly assigns his subjects to the relevant comparison groups, does he eliminate this threat to external validity? (This is taken from Huck, Cormier, and Bounds, *Reading Statistics and Research*, p. 268.)

EX 29: The class attendance for your Sunday school class for the last quarter has been: 32, 29, 31, 27, 33, 24, 28, 30, 35, 31, 30, 31, 34. What are the mean, median, and mode of these attendance figures? Is the distribution of your class attendance totals positively-skewed or negatively skewed?

EX 30: Your church has been slowly declining in membership over the past four years. The governing body of the church has designated an *ad hoc* committee to study the issue of church growth and bring recommendations back to it regarding how to help the church begin to grow again. The governing body elected you to be part of that committee.

At the first committee meeting one member voices his opinion that three of the most rapidly-growing churches in the county are Southern Baptist churches. He said that all three have two things in common—dynamic pastors and excellent home visitation programs to follow up first-time visitors. He concludes that if your church had these two ingredients it would grow also.

From the above data do you think it would be valid to conclude that if you add these two components your church will grow as well? Why or why not? If you disagree, what principles found in these last two chapters would you cite for support? Can you suggest an approach, from the standpoint of a scientific researcher, to help your committee fulfill its responsibilities?

Part Four

DISCOVERING FALLACIES IN REASONING

CHAPTER 6

Logical Fallacies I

Many people will never take a formal course in logic. However, the following statements show that logic provides a necessary, though usually unconscious, background for all life, and particularly for the maintenance of a democracy.

Logical principles... are inescapable, because any attempt to disregard them reduces our thoughts to confusion and gibberish.

Marvin Cohen and Ernest Nagel[1]

In a republican nation, whose citizens are to be led by reason and persuasion and not by force, the art of reasoning becomes of first importance.

Thomas Jefferson

Civilized life depends upon the success of reason in social intercourse, the prevalence of logic over violence in interpersonal conflict.

Juliana Geran Pilon

Democratic institutions require that citizens think for themselves, discuss problems freely with one another, and decide issues on the basis of deliberation and the weighing of evidence. Through the study of logic we can acquire not only practice in reasoning, but also respect for reason, and thus reinforce and secure the values we prize.

Irving M. Copi[2]

BASIC DEFINITIONS AND ISSUES

Logic is the study of the rules of correct argument. Its goal is to help people learn to reason correctly, or argue reasonably. Formally, logic is the study of the methods and principles used to distinguish good (or correct) from bad (or incorrect) reasoning. The logician wants people to know the criteria by which they can test arguments for correctness.[3]

An *argument* is a group of statements. A *premise* is a statement whose truthfulness is assumed to have been established already. A *conclusion* is a statement that allegedly follows from one or more premises with logical certainty. The classical way of stating an argument is to state a major premise, a minor premise, then a conclusion. For example:

Major premise: All Baptists are human beings.
Minor premise: John is a Baptist.
Conclusion: John is a human being.

However, logical arguments vary a great deal in their structure. Sometimes they contain only a single premise and a conclusion. Sometimes an argument contains two premises of equal weight, rather than having one major and one minor premise. Sometimes the conclusion comes first, followed by the supporting premises.

In logic an *inference* is a statement that logically follows from another statement or set of statements. Note that statisticians use this word in a related sense. In research an inferential statistic is one that allows a researcher to make inferences (scientific guesses) about a population based on data from a sample.

Logical arguments may err in either of two ways. First, one or more of the premises may be untrue. Second, the logic that joins the premises to the conclusion, the form, may be faulty. We say that premises or propositions are either true or false. We say that arguments—the logical processes that relate premises to conclusions, are correct or incorrect (or valid or invalid).[4] We describe a deductive argument whose premises are true and whose conclusion validly follows from them as sound. We describe a deductive argument lacking one or both ingredients as unsound. It is possible for an argument to be valid (the form of the argument is correct) and yet reach an unsound conclusion because one or more of the premises are untrue.

In logic, arguments are divided into two broad categories— deductive and inductive. *Deductive arguments* are those in which the conclusion follows necessarily from the premises, provided that the argument has valid form. *Inductive arguments* are those arguments in which the conclusion probably but not necessarily follows from the premises. An example will clarify this difference.

Deductive argument:
   John has washed all the apples in that container.
   These apples are from that container.
   Therefore John has washed all these apples.

Inductive argument:
   These apples are from that container.
   These apples have been washed.
   Therefore probably all the apples in that container have
      been washed.

In a valid deductive argument, if the premises are true, the conclusion follows unquestionably. In an inductive argument, if the premises are true, the conclusion probably, but not necessarily, follows.

Generalizations, such as generalizing from a sample to a population, are one type of inductive argument. The empirical researcher's argument might be articulated in this way:

First premise: Treatment X caused a significant change in those who experienced it.

Second premise: The sample used in this experiment was a random sample drawn from population A.

Conclusion: Other members of population A who experience treatment X probably will have similar results.

Notice that as an inductive argument or inductive generalization, we can say only that the conclusion probably will occur. Logicians sometimes describe inductive generalizations on a continuum from strong to weak. A strong, or universal, generalization is one that is true of all members of a class, such as the statement "All humans are mammals." A weak, or particular, generalization is one that is true of certain members of a class. You can see that as researchers control for threats to internal and external validity, they can make stronger inductive generalizations.

In logic we sometimes differentiate between verbal and real disputes. *Verbal disputes* may arise because people are using the same terms but with different denotations. *Real disputes* occur when, even after people have carefully defined their terms, they disagree with each other regarding the truthfulness or accuracy of one or more premises or conclusions.

Aristotle, Classical Logic, and Modern Symbolic Logic

Aristotle developed what was to become the scholarly discipline of formal logic. His system operates through the well-known classical syllogism, which includes a major premise, minor premise, and conclusion. Aristotle's students formulated three laws that they believed summarized the basis for Aristotle's system of logic. These were the law of identity, the law of contradiction, and the law of the excluded middle. Medieval philosophers developed logic into a fine, detailed science and philosophical weapon. Most educated people of the Middle Ages believed that it was through study of syllogisms that new knowledge would be gained. Galileo and others demonstrated that new information also could be gained through empirical investigation. When scholars introduced this empirically-derived information as premises in a syllogism, the growth of knowledge proceeded much faster than when scholars depended on the discovery of new information through logic alone.

The standard-form categorical syllogisms continue to be taught today, and the rules governing them continue to be refined.[5] Syllogistic (or Aristotelian) logic, however, has been largely superseded today by what is called modern symbolic logic. This type of logic is more mathematical in nature than syllogistic logic. It requires that a person become acquainted with a unique form of notation and language. It is generally agreed that modern symbolic logic is superior to syllogistic logic because it includes all the valid argument forms of syllogistic logic and can deal with several argument forms that cannot be "handled" by syllogistic logic.

There is value in understanding both syllogistic logic and modern symbolic logic. However, I am not convinced that mastery of this material is the best way to help contemporary Christians learn to spot fallacies in their own and others' thinking. We need the ability to identify fallacies within the context of a conversation or argument and introduce that knowledge in a way that can change the conversation or argument. To use classical syllogisms or modern symbolic logic in a conversation requires that we spend considerable time educating the other person or persons in that method of analysis. Everyday conversation or debate usually does not allow the time necessary for that kind of education.

For that reason I am choosing to use the space I have available to clarify logical fallacies in ways that can be explained easily and used in the context of an ongoing conversation. For those who wish to learn more about classical syllogisms and modern symbolic logic, most college textbooks and courses will include this information.

Logic in Human Life

Stuart Chase has listed seven areas of life in which people use logic (or claim to use it). His first area, interestingly, is *common sense.* When we use common sense we are attempting to reason correctly, or make valid arguments. We do not have formal names for the processes we use or the fallacies we try to refute. We had said in an earlier section that hermeneutics is a codification of the processes we use every day at an unconscious level to understand what people mean. In an analogous way, logic is a codification of the common sense that we use every day to reason correctly.

Formal logic developed out of the work of Aristotle and his students. Since the development of classical syllogistic logic and modern symbolic logic was discussed briefly in the previous section, we will not repeat that discussion here.

According to Chase, a third way in which logic affects our contemporary life is through *mathematics.* Mathematics is primarily systematized logic. You may remember that we said that measures of central tendency were ways in which we could summarize large groups of numbers that would be difficult to comprehend individually. In a somewhat analogous way, mathematics, and the rules that govern mathematical procedures from algebra to calculus, enable us to comprehend processes and discover relationships that we could not comprehend without it.

A fourth way in which logic pervades modern life is through *modern science*. Scientists use logic, not just in mathematics, but also while examining relationships, making hypotheses, checking hypotheses and facts, and when using modern symbolic logic.

Fifth, logic supposedly controls the *courtroom process*. Attorneys present facts and arguments that help the jury make a decision whether those facts best fit the hypothesis of the prosecution or the defense. In reality, many attorneys try to create the illusion that the facts best support their position, whether or not that illusion is true. There is much showmanship and psychology involved in trials, especially those presented to a jury. The judge's role is to keep the arguments undistorted.

Sixth, logic is used *to win arguments, votes, and customers*. In reality we all know that while people in these situations try to convince others that they are basing what they say on logic, it is wise to be skeptical of many of their conclusions. Chase says, "Advertising campaigns . . . [s]ometimes give us useful information about new products, but mostly they are a verbal stew of half truths, reiteration, snob appeal, and *non-sequiturs,* reinforced with bathing beauties and jingles. . . ."[6]

Last, *propagandists* allegedly use, but primarily abuse, logic. Demagogues, dictators, and fanatical ideologists all try to convince audiences that their reasoning is logical and sound. In reality, they twist, slant, and distort the reasoning process in whatever ways they believe they can without detection. Some of these speakers believe that the bigger the misrepresentation they can get away with, the greater the triumph. Propagandists are not really searching for truth. They have already made up their minds. Such speakers do not attempt to use logic in an honest search for truth, but only with the intent to deceive more effectively.

LOGICAL FALLACIES

Arguments, like men, are often pretenders.

Plato

It would be a very good thing if every trick could receive some short and obviously appropriate name, so that when a man used this or that particular trick, he could at once be reproved for it.

Arthur Schopenhauer

A fallacy can be defined as an error in reasoning or argument. But a fallacy is more than a poor line of reasoning. Copi explains:

> Some arguments . . . are so obviously incorrect [that they] deceive no one. It is customary in the study of logic to reserve the term "fallacy" for arguments that may be psychologically persuasive, though incorrect. We therefore define a fallacy as a type of argument that may seem . . . correct but that proves, upon examination, not to be so.[7]

After that statement, consensus ends. There are significant differences among writers and logicians on the number of fallacies, their names, and the best way of organizing them. Aristotle, in his book *Sophistical Refutations,* identified thirteen. Chase, 2500 years later, also listed thirteen.[8] Barry and Socio discuss forty-five.[9] Fearnside and Holther list fifty-one.[10] Pirie lists eighty-three.[11] David Fische gives the most extensive list, identifying more than 112 types of fallacies.[12]

Fallacies also differ in the names by which logicians identify them. A few well-known fallacies have names that have stood the test of time and are used almost universally. Writers have given a variety of names to the less well-known fallacies. Some writers have attempted to give fallacies names that they believed were particularly meaningful or memorable. For the most part others have not adopted these personally-given names. Writers identify a few fallacies most often by their Latin names, some by either Latin or English names, and some only by their English names.

Logicians have also tried to find ways of categorizing fallacies, but no one system has attracted widespread support. Some writers use no system. Others differentiate between formal and informal fallacies or between deductive and inductive fallacies. Others differentiate fallacies of ambiguity, relevance, knowledge, generalization, and causation. The early modern logician, De Morgan, has said, "There is no such thing as a classification of [all] the ways in which men may arrive at an error: it is much to be doubted whether there ever can be."[13]

In deciding on a way to present the various fallacies, I think we should ask ourselves what goals we have. These are my goals for you as readers: (1) that you clearly understand as many ways that people can reason incorrectly as possible, (2) that you can explain what is wrong with an argument in everyday English, so that you can introduce this information into a conversation or argument in a way that flows naturally, (3) that you can recognize the common Latin names for fallacies, in the event that a speaker or writer alludes to a fallacy in these terms, (4) that you not have to learn more things about each of these fallacies than is necessary for you to use them effectively, and (5) that you can find them quickly in this book when you need to refer to them.

I have organized the fallacies discussed in this chapter and the next in alphabetical order by their English names (with two exceptions).

One of those exceptions is when a Latin phrase has entered the English language so thoroughly that people know it by that name, and where no English translation of the phrase has attracted wide support. In the cases of *ad hominem* arguments, *non sequiturs,* and *post hoc* arguments, I have brought these phrases into the list in Latin.

The second exception to strict English alphabetical order occurs with two groups: classical syllogism fallacies, and statistical fallacies. I have grouped several specific fallacies under these two categories. There are a few fallacies that could be placed either under one of these categories or by themselves, and either choice could be defended or disputed.

There are differences in the importance of the following fallacies and in the frequency with which you will encounter them. For those reasons more space will be given to some than to others. When people use the Latin name with some frequency, that will be given. I will usually give the literal translation of the Latin term, followed by a more idiomatic translation, if there is a difference between them. As you read about these fallacies, focus on understanding the error in the thought process. If you can understand this and explain it to others in a conversation or argument, that ability is more important than remembering the technical name of the fallacy, especially since there is so much variation among writers regarding names. Lastly, in the following headings I will not repeat the words "The Fallacy of...." each time. "The Fallacy of Amphiboly" will be simply "Amphiboly."

Accent. The faulty reasoning here is that it is possible to misrepresent someone else's meaning, or transform a valid statement into an invalid one, by the way we accent the statement. This commonly occurs in one of three ways. First, a statement may be spoken in a different tone of voice than the original speaker used. Through this the second speaker may convey a different meaning than the original speaker intended. Second, a speaker or writer may quote someone and put that person's words in a different context. Through this the speaker or writer may suggest the original speaker was advocating something he or she was not.

A third way that accent occurs is when a sentence is constructed so that by accenting different parts of it a logical and accurate statement may be transformed into an untrue statement. For example, most people would agree with the validity of the statement, "We should not speak ill of our friends." However, by accenting the last three words of the statement it might seem that we are implying that it is fine to speak ill of people if they are not one's friends. Or by accenting the word "speak," a listener might infer that we were suggesting that we could work ill on our friends if we do it nonverbally.[14]

You may be wondering why "accent" is considered a fallacy, since there are no premises, no argument, and no conclusion, whether sound or unsound. There are probably many people who would say that accent seems more like a hermeneutical error (misrepresenting the author's intended meaning) rather than a logical fallacy. I agree with that point of view. Nevertheless, many consider accent to be a logical fallacy, so I include it here.

Accident. Life contains many general rules and statements that are true in most circumstances. However, there are rare situations, which because of their special (or accidental) features, make applying that generally-valid rule unwise or unsound.

An example of this might be the following: Normally when someone lends you something, it is proper for you to return it when the owner asks for it. Suppose a friend, however, lent you his pistol so that you could learn how to use it. You have kept it and practiced with it for several weeks. During this time your friend experienced several setbacks, losing both his job and his girlfriend. He becomes despondent. He asks for his gun back.

Normally the rule of returning the property you borrowed when the owner requests it back would apply. However, because of the accidental (unique) circumstances of this situation, most people would say that, if you are a friend, you should not return the gun. It would be committing the fallacy of accident to insist that someone obey a generally-valid rule when there is a reasonable justification for making an exception to that rule.

If we become rigid in our thinking we are more likely to commit this fallacy. One biblical example of this was where the Pharisees criticized Jesus for healing on the Sabbath. The rule of resting on the Sabbath was a valid expression of God's will for the Israelites. However, Jesus maintained that it was legitimate to break that good rule on one Sabbath to show God's love and make this man whole again.

***Ad hominem* argument** [*argumentum ad hominem:* argument directed to the man]. If you cannot attack the argument, attack the arguer. In this fallacy a debater, rather than focus on the merits and demerits of a proposition, tries to persuade the audience to reject his opponent's view by attacking his opponent's character, life situation, or other beliefs. The fallacy of this is that the character, life situation, or other beliefs a person holds does not affect the validity or lack of validity of his or her argument. Even the most wicked men sometimes tell the truth or reason correctly.[15]

Morris Cohen has said:

If the premises are sufficient, they are so no matter by whom stated. A person's unreliable character may weaken his credibility as a witness when he is reporting what he himself has observed. But in an objective argument his character, and even his motives, should be ignored.[16]

One (probably fictitious) example of the use of *ad hominem* occurred between two attorneys who were defending a particular man. One attorney, who had done the most preparation for the trial slipped a note to the other. It said simply, "No case. Abuse the plaintiff's attorney."

The most effective *ad hominem* arguments arouse strong emotions and transfer those feelings to the opponent and his argument. Pirie cites the following example: "Dr. Green argues very plausibly for fluoridation. What he does not tell us is that he is the same Dr. Green who ten years ago published articles in favour of both euthanasia and infanticide."[17]

Because of the strong emotional reaction most people have to infanticide, anything that Dr. Green says, despite its logic or reasonableness, probably will be rejected by them. Logically, the validity of Dr. Green's arguments is not affected by positions he took ten years ago. But the powerful transference produced by the *ad hominem* argument is likely to cause his audience to scorn anything else he has to say.

There are valid arguments raised against people that are not *ad hominem* arguments. For example, it was valid to raise the question of whether Franklin D. Roosevelt was well enough in 1944 to serve another term. The same was true of Eisenhower in 1956. It was an *ad hominem* argument of a very vicious kind when Roosevelt's enemies charged that a certain government policy was wrong because it originated with "that cripple in the White House."[18]

Another way that an *ad hominem* argument may work is for a debater to claim that his opponent is a member of a group whom the audience dislikes. Here again, when a debater does this successfully, the audience turns all the antipathy it has toward that group onto the speaker and what he is saying. In liberal Christian circles some people have effectively destroyed the credibility of others by labeling them "Fundamentalists." In conservative circles some people have done the same to others by labeling a person a "liberal."

Amphiboly. Some sentences have an ambiguous meaning because the author constructed them poorly. Such a sentence may be a valid premise when interpreted one way, and be invalid when interpreted another. When a speaker uses a poorly constructed statement as a premise in a way that makes it true, but then draws a conclusion from it based on a different interpretation of that same statement, he or she commits the fallacy of amphiboly.

Amphiboly forms the basis of more humor than invalid argumentation, and for that reason I will use the rest of this paragraph to give you a sampling.

With her enormous nose aimed at the sky, my mother rushed toward the plane.

Clean and decent dancing, every night except Sunday (roadhouse sign).

If you don't go to other people's funerals, they won't come to yours.

Just received. A new stock of sports shirts for men with 15 to 19 necks (advertisement).

Dog for sale. Eats anything. Very fond of children.

The marriage of Miss Anna Black and Mr. Willis Dash, which was announced in this paper a few weeks ago, was a mistake and we wish to correct it.

Police authorities are finding the solution of murders more and more difficult because the victims are unwilling to cooperate with the police.[19]

Appeal to Antiquity [*argumentum ad antiquitam:* appeal to antiquity]. This fallacy is based on the notion that something is right or some practice should be continued because it has been an accepted belief or practice for many years. "We've always done it that way. . . ." Conservatives of all kinds, including conservative Christians, tend to use this inadequate argument. For its logical opposite, see Appeal to Newness.

Appeal to Authority [*argumentum ad verecundiam:* appeal to (false) authority]. When we are dealing with a complex issue, it is proper and valid to consult people who are experts in that area. It is also proper and valid in a subsequent discussion or debate to identify the source of your information and his or her credentials. A person commits the fallacy of appeal to authority when he or she consults an expert in one field about his views in another field where he has no more expertise than anyone else. Sometimes, by virtue of the expert's reputation in his or her field, people will give greater credence than is warranted to his or her views on other topics.

Advertisers frequently commit this fallacy. They employ people whose expertise is on the football field to educate you on the most nutritious breakfast cereal for your children, the dog food that is best for your dog's coat, or the best way to invest your money and become rich (even though many athletes, after years of enormous salaries, have little left to show for them). Other (self-appointed) examples of this are people who have won an Oscar for some movie or other and who believe this qualifies them to make pronouncements on nuclear power or foreign policy.[20]

Even when an authority who has expertise in some field speaks on that subject, this is still not a reason for us to suspend our own critical judgment. There are several reasons for this. First, the authority may be misquoted, either intentionally or unintentionally. Second, in an age when knowledge is growing so rapidly, even competent people are not always well-informed on all matters within their general area of expertise. Third, there are often significant differences of opinion among experts on various issues. Therefore quoting only one authority while not admitting that there are other points of view may lead to the inaccurate conclusion that there is a consensus on issues when there is not.

Writers sometimes commit the fallacy of appeal to false authority through the misuse of footnotes. Chase says:

> A book loaded with footnotes seems to show that the author has consulted everybody since Confucius. What the author has to say, accordingly, must be so. Sometimes, however—as I have learned by experience in many libraries—he has only laid down a barrage of references to cover the thinness of his thoughts. F. C. S. Shiller remarks ironically that "nothing has a greater hold on the human mind than nonsense fortified with technicalities."[21]

There is another expression of the appeal to false authority that is somewhat widespread among conservative Christians. This is the practice of some speakers to make statements that are sometimes unique to them, use an overhead projector, and put Bible verses after each statement. The same thing may appear in handouts, booklets, or books they produce.

The typical assumption that one makes in such a setting is that the Bible verse listed substantiates the point they are making. In a sense, this is a Christian analogue of footnoting. Most conservative Christians believe that if God said something in His Word, it is true. The speaker appears to be saying that God makes this point in this passage of Scripture. It is an ultimate appeal to authority.

If you take the time to research some of these assumed references, you may be surprised. While some speakers are very careful to use good hermeneutics in their Scripture references, some, including a few nationally prominent speakers, do not do so. You may find that some referenced passages address the same general topic the speaker was mentioning, but not the specific teaching he was advocating in his presentation. Sometimes you will find that the referenced verse only supports the speaker's teaching when interpreted without its context. Sometimes you will be unable to find any link between the speaker's thought and the Bible verse that allegedly supports it. So, whenever anyone appeals to authority, no matter who he or she is or to whom he or she is appealing, do not disengage your critical faculties!

Appeal to the Crowd [*argumentum ad populum:* appeal to the crowd or appeal to the mob]. This fallacy occurs when a speaker attempts to move a crowd to action by inciting their emotions rather than appealing to facts. Such speakers often attempt to inflame passions by appealing to deeply-held prejudices or fears, and by using emotion-laden words and phrases. Propagandists, demagogues, and reactionary groups frequently employ these methods.

An appeal to the crowd encourages peoples' unthinking acceptance of ideas by presenting them in a strong theatrical manner, with intentional pauses that manipulate the crowd into responding with verbal affirmation. The logical error in this appeal is not that people should not experience emotions, but that they should not be encouraged to let emotions replace or substitute for reason.

Appeal to Moderation [*argumentum ad temperantiam:* appeal to moderation]. Sometimes, when there is much disagreement about an issue, political expediency requires finding some workable compromise. Sometimes two groups have each staked out differing viewpoints and each is making some legitimate points. Finding a compromise solution that considers the valid points of both groups can reduce the conflict. Some people, influenced by the relativism of our age, believe that none of us see reality clearly. It is best if we develop ways of including everyone's perceptions in our models and plans. All these factors support the appeal to moderation.

The appeal to moderation is the belief that where there are differences of opinion, the moderate viewpoint is the correct one. The fallacy of this lies in the fact that truth is not necessarily found in the middle. There is a very strong possibility that at least sometimes people argue for a position, not because it is correct, but because it is in their best interests. It is also very possible that in some situations some people's perspective is distorted more than others. In either of these situations a moderate proposal, while perhaps the best political solution, is not necessarily the solution that is closest to the truth.

Appeal to Newness [*argumentum ad novitam:* appeal to newness]. The logical opposite of appeal to antiquity. This fallacy argues that something is best because it is newest. It is widely used in advertising.

Appeal to Pity [*argumentum ad misericordiam:* appeal to mercy]. Speakers use the appeal to pity whenever they attempt to use human sympathy, rather than facts, to move a person or group of people toward a conclusion. Criminal lawyers sometimes use this approach to persuade a jury to disregard the facts in a case and acquit their client. Clarence Darrow, a famous trial lawyer, used the appeal to pity in his summary to the jury regarding Thomas Kidd, a union officer accused of criminal conspiracy:

> I appeal to you not for Thomas Kidd, but I appeal to you for the long line—the long, long line reaching back through the ages and forward to the years to come—the long line of

despoiled and downtrodden people of the earth. I appeal to
you for those men who rise in the morning before daylight
comes and who go home at night when the light has faded
from the sky and give their life, their strength, their toil to
make others rich and great. I appeal to you in the name of
those women who are offering up their lives to this modern
god of gold, and I appeal to you in the name of those little
children, the living and the unborn. . . .

Could you convict Thomas Kidd after that? Would you, as a
member of the jury, even remember that your job was to
make a judgment based on the facts of the case? If not, then
you've experienced the power of an appeal to pity.

Appeal to Popularity [*argumentum ad numeram:* appeal to
numbers]. The appeal to popularity is a fallacy based on the
notion that if many people believe something is right, that
notion must be right. This appeal has a very important psychological motivator. We all want to be like others, based on
the largely unconscious fear that if we are different, others
may not accept us or may laugh at us behind our back. How
many of us are willing to wear a piece of clothing that is
clearly out of style, even if the article is still usable? If wide
lapels are no longer in, how many of us are willing to wear
something with wide lapels? For men, if narrow ties are in,
what do you do with your wide ties? The appeal to what is
popular now is a very powerful appeal, and one that influences
us all.

Appeal of the Poor [*argumentum ad lazarum:* the appeal of
Lazarus]. This argument, not widely used today, gets its
Latin name from Lazarus, the poor man of Luke 16. It involves the idea that the poverty of the arguer enhances the
case he or she is making. Think for a moment of the respect
we have for Gandhi or for Mother Teresa. Their willingness

to live a life of poverty has engaged the respect of an entire world. However, from a logical standpoint, an argument that either of these people make should be judged on its own merits, and not on the life-style of its maker, noble as that life-style has been. For its logical opposite, see Appeal to Wealth.

Appeal to the Stone [*argumentum ad lapidem:* appeal to the stone]. This fallacy does not involve much sophistication to use. It consists of ignoring the argument altogether, refusing to discuss either its premises, inference, or conclusion, that is, being as responsive as a stone. People in power use it most frequently when their subordinates raise issues that those in power do not want to change, but for which they have no adequate rebuttal.

Appeal to Wealth [*argumentum ad crumenam:* argument of the moneypouch]. This fallacy assumes that money is a measure of rightness, and that those with money are more likely to be correct.[22] It is used frequently in advertising, again at a subconscious level. The audience sees people of obvious means choosing a certain product, vacationing at a certain place, and subconsciously assume that they will be viewed as people of substance and good judgment if they do the same.

Apriorism. In the scientific method we derive our conclusions from facts. As we become aware of more facts, we may modify or even discard earlier conclusions. To start out with conclusions first *(a priori)* and use them to decide whether to accept certain facts is the wrong way around. This is the fallacy of apriorism.

One example of apriorism from history would be the alleged conversation that went something like this: "We don't need to look through your telescope, Mr. Galileo. We know that there cannot be more than seven heavenly bodies."[23]

We all can be guilty of apriorism. Whenever we adopt a certain theory, whether dispensationalism or covenantal theology, Calvinism, or Arminianism, we are likely to read the Bible in light of the conclusion we've already drawn. Only when we "hold our conclusions lightly," being willing to modify them if we receive new information, can we avoid the fallacy of apriorism.

Argument from Ignorance [*argumentum ad ignorantiam:* argument to ignorance]. See Shifting the Burden of Proof.

Begging the Question [*petitio principii:* begging the principle]. Begging the question occurs when a speaker or writer, in attempting to prove a conclusion, uses as his premise part or all the information in his conclusion. It might seem that such a logical error would be immediately obvious to listeners or readers. It is less obvious when a person customarily uses long sentences with many ambiguous and vague referents. Listening to such a speaker often lulls us into a state of drowsiness where we may not recognize such question-begging when it occurs. Here are some examples:

> To allow every man unbounded freedom of speech must always be, on the whole, advantageous to the state; for it is highly conducive to the interests of the community that each individual should enjoy a liberty, perfectly unlimited, of expressing his sentiments.[24]

> Free trade will be good for this country. The reason is patently clear. Isn't it obvious that unrestricted commercial relations will bestow on all sections of this nation the benefits which result when there is an unimpeded flow to goods between countries?[25]

The fallacy that occurs in begging the question is that unproven propositions in the conclusion are used in the premises to "prove" the conclusion. There is no argument, for the process begins with the same material with which it ends. This is the same process that occurs in circular arguments [*circulus in probando*], more informally called arguing in circles.

Bifurcation. Bifurcate means to divide something into two parts. The fallacy of bifurcation occurs when someone asserts that there are only two options open to someone when there are in reality more. In 1948 Bertrand Russell was guilty of bifurcation when he said, "Either we must have war against Russia before she has the atom bomb, or we will have to lie down and let them govern us."

Another example of bifurcation was forcing people to decide whether fluorine was poison or not. The truth is that while in large doses fluorine is a poison, in small doses it does not appear to have any negative effect, and significantly reduces cavities. During Senator McCarthy's ill-famed career in the Senate, he tried to bifurcate the entire country. Everyone was either a Communist (or Communist sympathizer) or a patriot. This is sometimes called the fallacy of false dilemma or the fallacy of black and white thinking.

Blinding with Science. Speakers commit the fallacy of blinding with science when they use technical jargon to deceive an audience into believing that propositions of a scientific nature are being discussed when the propositions are derived more from personal bias than scientific data. It also applies when people claim that objective scientific evidence supports them when it does not.

Catastrophizing. This name does not appear in logic textbooks, but I think it should. It is a carryover from the field of psychology, specifically the field of cognitive psychology. Catastrophizing is a fallacy that can occur in one of two ways. The first way involves predicting, either mentally or verbally, that something with a very low likelihood of happening, but that would be truly catastrophic if it did, will surely occur. The second way involves predicting that something (which may have a reasonable chance of happening) will happen, and it will be catastrophic (when it really will not).

An example of the first might be a mother, whose son is a careful driver who has never had an accident, worrying every time he goes out in the evening that he will be involved in a terrible car crash and that the next telephone call will be the police asking her to come to the morgue to identify his charred remains.

An example of the second kind of catastrophizing might occur when a freshman in college has to make his first presentation before a class. He worries that his nervousness will be evident to all, and that the reaction to him will be uniformly negative.

Circular Argument. See Begging the Question.

Classical Syllogism Fallacies. The following six fallacies are related to the classical syllogism. The fallacy in this group you are most likely to read about is the fallacy of the undistributed middle. This is, unfortunately, the most complicated one to understand. It is discussed as the last fallacy in this section.

   1. **Contradictory Premises.** One premise contradicts the other, thus making a valid conclusion impossible.

   2. **Exclusive Premises.** If both premises in a syllogism are negative, no conclusion can be drawn from them. Example:

> Premise A: No starfish has wings.
> Premise B: This is not a starfish.
> Conclusion: ????

3. Positive Conclusion from a Negative Premise. A syllogism may contain one negative premise, but if it does, the conclusion must be negative. If someone draws a positive conclusion, it is invalid.

4. The Fallacy of Four Terms *[quaternio terminorum]*. The classic syllogism works by having one term repeated in the first two lines and then eliminated from the conclusion. You relate each of two things to a middle term, and then the middle term disappears in the conclusion (see below). However, if you have four terms in the first two lines rather than three, you cannot validly draw a standard syllogistic conclusion.

5. Illicit Process. If a person draws a conclusion that refers to everything in a class, the premises upon which it was built also must refer to everything in that class. For example, a conclusion that "All schoolteachers are..." cannot be legitimately made if the premises only refer to some schoolteachers. To make such a conclusion would be to commit the fallacy of illicit process.

6. The Fallacy of the Undistributed Middle. Consider the following standard syllogism:

> My son has a pet dog.
> All dogs have four legs.
> My son's pet has four legs.

The standard syllogism works, as shown above, by relating two things to a middle term, and then the middle term drops out in the conclusion. Only if one of those statements refers to everything in a class will the syllogism work. Consider the following syllogism:

> All dogs have four legs.
> All cows have four legs.
> All dogs are cows.

This syllogism does not work because neither of the premises contains everything in a class. While it is true that dogs have four legs and so do cows, neither of these groups contains all the four-legged creatures that exist. Thus cows and dogs can both have four legs and not be identical.

Here is a commonsense way of understanding the fallacy of the undistributed middle. Classic syllogisms work by having two categories in the first two lines, each of which relates to a third category. We cannot tell what relationship these two will have to each other unless one of the first two lines contains everything in a category. Unless it does this we cannot "distribute" (eliminate) the middle term from the conclusion.

Cliche Thinking. A person commits the fallacy of cliche thinking whenever he or she uses a cliche uncritically as a premise in an argument or as a substitute for an argument.[26] Cliches often reflect personal prejudices that we may be unaware we hold. Consider the following:

> "Never send a boy to do a man's job."
> "You can never trust a. . . ."

Complex Question. The fallacy of a complex question occurs when someone asks a question that implies that the respondent has given a positive answer to a prior question. "Have you stopped using drugs?" implies that someone has already admitted he or she used drugs at one time, a fact which may or may not have been true. The time-worn question, "Have you stopped beating your wife?" falls into the same category.

The fallacy of complex question is known by a number of names. It has been called the "loaded question," "leading question," "trick question," and "multiple questions." Attorneys sometimes use complex questions in legal proceedings to try to get a defendant to incriminate himself or herself.

Speakers or leaders sometimes use them to move an audience in a certain direction. An executive of a private company might ask his audience, "Why is private development of resources so much more efficient than public development?" The unstated question is, "Is private development of resources more efficient than public development?" However, if he can move his audience's attention to the second question, they may not even be aware that he never answered the first question, but instead based his discussion of the second question on the assumption that private development of resources is more efficient.

An intelligent way to deal with complex questions is to identify the multiple questions the speaker is asking, and answer them in order. When one does this, the second question may not even need to be answered. If, for example, a person replies that he or she has never used illegal drugs, there is no need to answer the question of whether it is continuing. An approach to use against this method, and one used both in legal and parliamentary proceedings, is to ask that the speaker "divide the question."

You may be wondering what the fallacy is in a complex question. The fallacy lies in assuming an answer to the hidden question without a factual basis. In a sense the speaker or questioner is begging the question, for he is assuming as true a premise that he has never proven.

Composition. The fallacy of composition occurs when someone assumes that what is true of the individual members of a class is true of the entire class. A simple example would be that if each part of a machine was light in weight, the entire machine would be light in weight. Another example would be the assumption that if everyone on an athletic team were exceptional players, the team as a whole would be exceptional. See Division for the opposite fallacy.

Concealed Evidence. A person commits the fallacy of concealed evidence whenever he or she presents only that evidence favorable to his or her position, and suppresses relevant but unfavorable evidence.

Converse Accident. As we said in the discussion of the fallacy of accident, life contains general rules and statements that are true in most circumstances. However, there are rare situations which because of their special (or accidental) features, make applying that generally-valid rule unwise or unsound. In those situations we should recognize that a legitimate exception exists.

In the fallacy of converse accident, a person examines a few atypical cases and then generalizes from them. For example, a person might see several beautiful strawberries on the top of a box of strawberries. He might assume that all the berries in the box were that beautiful and only realize he had committed the fallacy of converse accident when he got home and emptied the box.

Similarly, a person may know of two people who were on a beneficial medication who developed serious side effects from it. He or she would be committing the fallacy of converse accident to conclude that everyone who takes that medication will develop those side effects. Compare with the fallacy of accident.

Damning the Alternatives. Sometimes a person argues for a certain position by trying to show that all the other alternatives would be bad. For example, pro-choice advocates sometimes assert that abortion should continue to be available on demand by attempting to show that all the other alternatives would be tragic and harmful. Women would seek unsafe abortions, careers would be interrupted, and couples would be saddled with children whom they do not want. From a logical standpoint, one cannot prove that Position A is right by showing that there are difficulties with the other positions. There may be as great or even greater difficulties with Position A.

Dismissal. The fallacy of dismissal can occur in at least two ways. One way, often seen in politics, occurs when someone accuses a candidate of some sort of misconduct or bad judgment. Such candidates sometimes adopt an attitude of superiority and say something like the following: "I cannot believe that anyone takes these charges seriously. I will not dignify these charges with a response." Such an action, while sometimes effective politically, does nothing to change or challenge the facts. As such, it is a logical fallacy.

A second type of dismissal occurs when a person claims that the situation under discussion is "an exception that proves the rule." In this event, we need to examine the situation more closely to decide whether this is an atypical case. If it is, we would be committing the fallacy of accident if we applied the general rule. If it is not, the other person is committing the fallacy of dismissal by trying to remove the situation from examination without presenting appropriate facts to justify such a removal.

Division. One commits the fallacy of composition when he or she says that what is true of the individual members of a group is true of the entire group. For example, if an engine contains many light parts, a person would be committing the fallacy of composition if he or she concluded that the entire engine is light.

The fallacy of division is the opposite of the fallacy of composition. A person commits the fallacy of division when he or she says that what is true of a group is also true of the individual members of a group. For example, if someone says that the United States is a rich nation, it does not thereby follow that everyone in the United States is also rich (that is also the fallacy of wishful thinking). The following syllogism is an example of the fallacy of division.

> American Indians are disappearing.
> That man is an American Indian.
> Therefore that man is disappearing.[27]

Emotional Appeals. A person commits the fallacy of an emotional appeal whenever he or she attempts to persuade by emotions (fear, envy, hatred, superstition, pride, etc.) rather than by reason, when reason would be the appropriate means to use. This does not mean that emotional appeals are always improper. If a proposition has been proven true by reason, it may be appropriate to encourage people to act on that truth by an appeal to their emotions.

Equivocation. Ambiguity of sentence structure can lead to the fallacy of amphiboly. Changes in which words a speaker emphasizes can lead to the fallacy of accent. The fallacy of equivocation occurs because words, as you recall from the hermeneutics section of this book, can have a variety of denotations (or meanings). If a person constructs one premise of a syllogism using one denotation of a word, and constructs the second premise or conclusion using a different denotation of the same word, he or she commits the fallacy of equivocation. Here is a syllogism designed to illustrate the fallacy of equivocation and get the adrenaline of all feminists flowing:

> Only man is rational.
> No woman is a man.
> Therefore no woman is rational.[28]

Engel, the author of this syllogism, equivocates, for in the first premise he uses the word "man" in the generic sense referring to all human beings. In the second premise he uses the word "man" to refer to male human beings only. Therefore his conclusion is invalid because it commits the fallacy of equivocation.

We shall conclude on a lighter note with one more equivocating syllogism:

> Some dogs have fuzzy ears.
> My dog has fuzzy ears.
> Therefore my dog is some dog![30]

Every Schoolboy Knows. Sometimes a speaker is making a controversial proposition and wants to stifle any disagreement with his position. One method for doing this is to state that every schoolboy knows the truth of what he is saying. Since most people in the audience do not want to betray their ignorance of something that every schoolchild allegedly knows, this method often is effective in stifling debate and allowing propositions to be accepted with few or no facts to support them. This is sometimes called the fallacy of self-evident truths, for the speaker claims that "everybody knows that this is true."

One way to illustrate the invalidity of self-evident truths is to show that many self-evident truths contradict one another. For example:

> "Look before you leap" but
> "He who hesitates is lost."

> "Leave well enough alone" but
> "Progress never stands still."

> "A man gets what he pays for" but
> "The best things in life are free."[30]

> "Absence makes the heart grow fonder" but
> "Out of sight, out of mind."

> "A penny saved is a penny earned" but
> "Penny wise and pound foolish."

False Analogies. Analogies are like parables. Speakers or writers use them to help us understand some difficult idea by relating it to something we understand better. When a speaker or writer uses analogies well, we grasp what they are saying in terms of something we already know.

A speaker or writer can use analogies fallaciously in at least three ways. First, he or she can fail to recognize that, while two situations may be alike in one or more respects, they are not alike in all respects. Second, he or she can say that two things are alike in a certain way when they are not. Third, he or she may believe that an analogy proves something to be true. An analogy never proves anything. Its purpose is to illuminate something that people do not understand by comparing it with something they do.

A frequently abused analogy is, "History teaches...." Nothing in the flow of human history exactly repeats itself. The speaker in Hyde Park committed a false analogy when he asked: "How does Winston Churchill propose to build three hundred thousand houses a year in his postwar housing program, when it took him five years to build one brick wall at his country place?"

Churchill built the wall with his own hands as a hobby. The housing program was to be developed by the British government and built by thousands of craftsmen and laborers. The two situations compared were different on so many counts that the analogy between them was fallacious.[31]

Fear or Force [*argumentum ad baculum*: argument of the walking stick]. The fallacy of appeal to fear or force occurs when someone abandons the use of reason for persuasion and threatens the use of force or unpleasant consequences if the other party does not agree to one's proposal. Writers sometimes call this fallacy "Carry the big stick." The statement "Might makes right," epitomizes those who use this approach. That statement, of course, is fallacious.

Harry Hopkins' account of a meeting of the "Big Three" at Yalta shortly before the end of World War II contains an historical example of an important world leader who "reasoned" along these lines. Churchill reportedly told the others that the Pope had suggested that a particular course of action would be the morally correct thing to do. Stalin reportedly expressed his disagreement by asking, "And how many divisions did you say the Pope has?"

Communist leaders are not the only ones who use an appeal to fear to press an argument. The lobbyist who says to a politician, "The best reason for supporting my position is that I represent two million of your constituents," is using fear to persuade. The number of people the lobbyist represents is logically irrelevant to the merits of a position. However, the fear that his constituents may not re-elect him or her is psychologically very relevant to the politician. Because of this the lobbyist, though he has not convinced the politician by reason, may influence him or her through fear.

This chapter has discussed thirty-eight fallacies. Use the following exercises to develop your ability to identify these fallacies and explain the incorrect reasoning in each one.

SUMMARY OF CHAPTER 6

List of Logical Fallacies

Accent	Appeal to Pity
Accident	Appeal to Popularity
Ad hominem	Appeal of the Poor
Amphiboly	Appeal to the Stone
Appeal to Antiquity	Appeal to Wealth
Appeal to Authority	Apriorism
Appeal to the Crowd	Begging the Question
Appeal to Moderation	Bifurcation
Appeal to Newness	Blinding with Science

Catastrophizing
Classical Syllogism Fallacies
   Contradictory Premises
   Exclusive Premises
   Positive Conclusion from
     Negative Premises
   Fallacy of Four Terms
   Illicit Process
   Undistributed Middle
Cliche Thinking
Complex Question

Composition
Concealed Evidence
Converse Accident
Damning the Alternatives
Dismissal
Division
Emotional Appeals
Equivocation
Every Schoolboy Knows
False Analogies
Fear or Force

EXERCISES

For each situation below, identify the fallacy involved if there is one, and explain the faulty reasoning. Sometimes more than one fallacy could be named, since the fallacies do overlap. Suggested answers are included in the back of the book.

EX 31: A sixteen-year-old Christian asked a middle-aged person in his church why the church conducted a certain activity in a particular way. The teen argued that it was boring and not meaningful to him or his peers. The older man explained that this is the way the church had done it for many years and that this was the way almost all the other churches in the denomination did it. Are there one or more fallacies involved in this discussion? If so, what are they?

EX 32: A Christian mother is trying to persuade her daughter not to continue her experimentation with drugs, citing the dangers involved. The daughter angrily replies that all her friends do, and besides, the mother takes tranquilizers, so why should the mother be pointing at her use? What fallacies are involved in this argument?

EX 33: When government officials released Nelson Mandela from prison in 1990 he achieved almost instant worldwide celebrity status. He conducted an international tour and was honored by ticker-tape parades in New York City and elsewhere. Hundreds of thousands listened to him speak, though few had known his philosophy before that time. Does this instant celebrity status remind you of any fallacy? If so, what is it?

EX 34: If one or both premises of an argument are false, what can you say about the truthfulness of the conclusion? If both premises are true but the argument is invalid, what can you say about the truthfulness of the conclusion?

EX 35: Early in the history of the Christian church a group developed a belief that could be transformed into the following syllogism:

> *Premise:* Christ is the Vine.
> *Premise:* Vines are part of the created order.
> *Conclusion:* Therefore Christ is part of the created order.

What is the logical error in this argument?

EX 36: Two seminarians were discussing a theology textbook that three theologians had coauthored. One student remarked that one of the three authors had a moral lapse and had lost his faculty position at a seminary. His unspoken inference was that because of this the parts of the book written by this person had decreased value and validity. What logical fallacy was he committing?

EX 37: A noted Christian speaker was discussing spiritual gifts. Using 1 Corinthians 12 and 14 as a basis, he identified several gifts. However, his definitions were descriptions of natural talents that God can use when they are dedicated to Him, rather than supernatural manifestations of the Holy Spirit coming upon a person for a brief or extended period to enable that person to do something that would edify that person and the church.

(a) Do you think it was hermeneutically valid for this speaker to do this? If not, what hermeneutical principle was he violating?

(b) Do you think he was committing any logical fallacies? If so, what?

EX 38: In the abortion debate, the basic issue that must be settled is whether abortion involves the termination of an innocent human life. Some abortion rights activists have argued that if women are denied legal abortions, only rich women could have them safely, since only they could travel to countries where abortion is still legal. Therefore, abortion on demand should remain legal in the United States. Without attempting to address the entire abortion issue, are there any logical fallacies in this argument?

EX 39: Jonathan Edwards preached a sermon in 1741 that has long been remembered. A portion of that sermon goes as follows:

> The God that holds you over the pit of hell, much as one holds a spider or some loathsome insect over the fire, abhors you, and is dreadfully provoked; His wrath towards you burns like fire; He looks upon you as worthy of nothing else, but to be cast into the fire; you are ten thousand times so abominable in His eyes as the most hateful and venomous serpent is in ours. You have offended Him infinitely more than a stubborn rebel did His prince; and yet it is nothing but His hand that holds you from falling into the fire every moment.

Comment on this portion of sermon logically and hermeneutically.

EX 40: A billboard reads, "Come to us for unwanted pregnancies." What logical fallacy does this statement most closely resemble?

CHAPTER 7

Logical Fallacies II

If you have not yet spent some time doing the exercises at the end of chapter 6, please do so. To be able to identify and explain fallacies effectively in a conversation or discussion depends on your ability to identify these same fallacies in a less pressured setting, such as reading this book and having time to think about what is wrong with an argument. You will also find that doing these exercises will prepare you well for the fallacies you are likely to hear in the coming six months, for the same kinds of fallacies tend to be repeated regularly in Christian circles. In this chapter we will continue our discussion of logical fallacies, beginning with the gambler's fallacy.

The Gambler's Fallacy. Suppose you decided to flip a coin fifty times, keeping record of the number of heads and tails. Assume that no one had tampered with this coin in order to cause it to land more often on one side than the other. On the first forty flips, you have a total of thirty heads and ten tails. What is the likelihood of flipping either heads or tails on the next ten attempts?

The likelihood of either heads or tails on these final ten

tosses is exactly what it has been throughout the first forty flips—50:50. If the coin is "true," the fact that it has landed many more times on heads than tails will not affect the final ten tosses. The belief that the next toss (or spin of the wheel or hand of cards) will be influenced by the last one is called "the gambler's fallacy."

The Genetic Fallacy. The genetic fallacy occurs whenever someone dismisses an argument because he or she does not like its source. It is common for conservative Christians to refuse to seriously consider an idea because it was developed by theologically liberal Christians or by non-Christians. It is equally common for members of these latter two groups to refuse to seriously consider an idea because it was developed or promoted by conservative Christians. The source of an argument in no way affects its validity. See *ad hominem* arguments.

Guilt by Association. A person commits the fallacy of guilt by association when he or she judges someone guilty, without any evidence of complicity in wrongdoing, based on an association with someone else who is guilty of wrongdoing.

Guilt by association can occur in any of several ways. Sometimes people assume that someone is guilty because that person associates with a particular person, that is, he or she is seen in the company of a person who is accused of or is guilty of wrongdoing.

People sometimes assume someone is guilty because that person is kin to someone who is guilty. People who are kin to a wrongdoer sometimes do commit wrong themselves, either by personal involvement or by failing to report what they know to be a serious violation of the law. When a person assumes that someone is guilty because that person is kin to someone who is guilty, he or she commits a fallacy when the assumption is based on kinship alone, with no other evidence of complicity.

A third way in which some people fallaciously assume guilt by association is through verbal association. These people assume that if a person uses a few of the same phrases as a guilty person, or if that person supports some of the same ideas, he or she is in complicity with the guilty person.

There is a relationship between the fallacy of guilt by association and the fallacy of false analogies. The logical error here is that simply because two people have one thing in common, it does not follow that they are alike in all other ways.

The reverse of guilt by association is the fallacy of innocence by association. When a person tries to prove he is innocent by showing that he associates with various important and respected people, he is committing the fallacy of innocence by association. People often use this approach in legal proceedings, when the minister, the mayor, and other respected community leaders testify about the character of the defendant. All this testimony is beside the point. The question in a court of law is whether the defendant committed the crime of which he is accused. His friendship with civic leaders is irrelevant to this question. Also, because a person is moral in most areas of his or her life does not prove innocence in the area under examination.

As in the fallacy of guilt by association, because a person has some connection with another person neither proves that he is guilty of wrongdoing nor innocent of it. Rogues have associated with good people and good people have had to associate with rogues from the beginning of time.

Humor and Ridicule. A speaker commits the fallacy of humor and ridicule when he or she changes from using logical argument to substantiate his or her conclusions to humor or ridicule either to distract the audience's attention or to ridicule the person or the argument of another. This fallacy often overlaps with *ad hominem* arguments and appeals to the mob.

Humor and ridicule can be extremely effective ploys when one is arguing in front of an audience, often derailing a superior argument. But as Graham Greene's Monsignor Quixote reminds us, "Laughter is not an argument. It can be stupid abuse."[1]

A sad example of the effectiveness of sarcastic humor occurred at the post-World War I conference in Versailles. Woodrow Wilson proposed his peace plan called the "Fourteen Points." The French leader Clemenceau allegedly retorted, "Fourteen Points! God Almighty only had ten!" While humor and ridicule may draw a positive response from one's audience, it is not a substitute for reasoned analysis and argument. For that reason it is considered a fallacy.[2]

Intuition. One possible way that we can apprehend truth is through intuition. While intuition may be a source of true propositions, it is not a sound basis for validating such propositions. Intuition may lead us to the subjective belief that a certain proposition is true, but we must substantiate our intuitional hypothesis with facts before we have objectively proven it to be true.

Invincible Ignorance. The fallacy of invincible ignorance occurs when someone adopts a particular point of view, and then rigidly maintains that point of view despite all evidence to the contrary. In appeal to the stone the person makes no response. In this fallacy a person keeps making the same response, despite mounting evidence to the contrary.

Irrelevant Thesis or Irrelevant Conclusion. A person commits this fallacy when one's premises, persuasive though they may be, do not lead to the conclusion one is trying to prove. For example, a legislator may be trying to have his housing proposal accepted by the legislature. He may argue at length about the benefits of housing over homelessness and over the rights of citizens to be accorded some minimum level of decent housing. These arguments are examples of irrelevant thesis.

The relevant thesis that he should be arguing, from a logical standpoint, is whether his proposal is financially realistic and is the best way to address the problem of decent housing for all citizens. That is the specific question the legislature is considering.

Similarly, prosecuting attorneys in their closing statements will sometimes argue about the terribleness of the crime of murder to motivate the jury to return a guilty verdict. The terribleness of the crime of murder is irrelevant to the question of whether this defendant committed the murder with which the court has charged him or her.

A defending attorney also may commit the fallacy of irrelevant thesis by trying to appeal to the sympathy of the jury because of the difficulty of the defendant's home life or to other factors. These arguments are irrelevant to the question of whether the defendant committed the crime as charged. While these other factors might play a role in the sentencing phase of the legal process, they are irrelevant to the purpose of deciding guilt or innocence. In this regard one sympathetic judge reportedly complimented a young lawyer on his excellent speech and expressed hope that he would some day find a case to which it applied.[3] See also *non sequitur*.

Loaded Words and Name-Calling. Sometimes people, rather than producing logical arguments for their position, resort to the use of loaded words or name-calling. Think for a moment of the attitude and feelings produced in yourself when a person says that someone is a "welfare cheat," a "slum landlord," or a "hard-working citizen." The speaker is aware that the use of certain names often evokes powerful feelings within us. He can use these feelings, rather than logical argument, to propel us toward the conclusion he wants us to accept. Whether these terms accurately fit a person or not becomes a side issue: with the emotion the name-caller has produced in us we often move forward without questioning whether he has produced adequate evidence to justify his use of that particular epithet. When a person uses loaded words to produce a more negative or positive attitude toward someone than the facts justify, he or she is guilty of using loaded words.

Magical Thinking. The most usual description of this fallacy is that it occurs when someone attributes causal power to thoughts and words. It is not uncommon for children to wish some evil on their playmates or parents in a moment of temporary anger. If the playmate or parent then experiences some misfortune, these children may believe that they, through their words or thoughts, caused the misfortune to happen.

Occasionally adults may make the same attribution. Usually this does not suggest anything more than that the person feels guilty for what he or she said, and it may be helpful to clarify this difference. In rare circumstances it may suggest the presence of schizophrenia or of severe depression with delusions.

Meaningless Claim. The fallacy of meaningless claim occurs whenever a person makes claims that, by their nature, are impossible to verify or refute. For example, an automobile dealership that claims they have "the best deal in town" is making a meaningless claim. Does this mean that their cars are the best line of automobiles available within the city? If so, what criteria are they using? Best for whom?

Does this mean they have the lowest priced cars in town? Does it mean the best cost-to-benefit ratio if a car is kept five years? Ten years? This claim, and many of those made in advertising, become meaningless claims upon careful examination.

There is a related fallacy called the fallacy of unknowable fact. Meaningless claims occur because someone uses vague, ambiguous, or amphibolous language, as in the above example. The fallacy of unknowable fact occurs when a proposition is clear in what it states, but what it states is untestable. One example of an unknowable fact was a statement by a Bible teacher some years ago that one particular place in the universe that has no astronomical bodies in it is probably where heaven is located—it is just that we cannot see it.

Non Sequitur [that which does not follow]. A *non sequitur* is equivalent to the fallacy of irrelevant thesis or the fallacy of irrelevant conclusion. In a *non sequitur* the conclusion simply does not follow from the premise or premises. Runyon humorously shares one of his favorites.

> My nominee for the all-time champion of the *non sequitur* is the late David Janssen, who solemnly informed us that studies made by a leading university showed that Excedrin is more effective for *"pain other than headache"* (italics mine). He then concluded with cherubic innocence and sincerity, "So the next time you have a headache, try Excedrin."[4]

One-Sided Assessment. Often, when we have to make a complicated decision, there are advantages and disadvantages for each alternative. For example, if we have two alternatives, A and B, there would be four categories to consider— the advantages and disadvantages of A, and the advantages and disadvantages of B. A one-sided assessment would occur if we were only to examine two of these alternatives, such as the advantages of A and the disadvantages of B.

Oversimplification. Someone has said, "There is a simple solution to every complex problem, and it's usually wrong." The fallacy of oversimplification occurs when we treat a situation as if it contained only a few relevant factors, when, in reality, it contains many. Part of the problem of oversimplifying a situation is that we deprive ourselves of important information necessary to fully understand it, and by that we substantially reduce our chances of finding a solution that will truly solve it.[5]

Poisoning the Well. Poisoning the well occurs whenever a person, without logical justification for doing so, lays down an insult and says that it applies to anyone who would be so foolish as to disagree with him or her. For example, if someone were to say during a debate about national appropriations that "Everyone except an idiot knows that we are not spending enough money on education" he or she would be poisoning the well. When someone stands up to argue the point, he identifies himself as the idiot about whom the person is speaking. People poison the well whenever they summarily discount everything that comes from a certain source (the "well").[6] The fallacy is that they arbitrarily label all evidence from a different position as unsound, but with no logical basis for doing so.

Poisoning the well is similar to, but not identical with, *ad hominem* arguments. In both a person discredits someone else or his or her position on fallacious grounds. However, in an *ad hominem* argument a specific person is abused; in poisoning the well the poisoner throws open the invitation to be abused to whomever is willing to disagree.

Provincialism. The fallacy of provincialism is an argument that sees things strictly from the perspective of one's own group. Behavior that people abhor when others do it is acceptable if their group does it. For example, we may think it terrible that Libya has spies in our country, but have a much reduced emotional reaction at the thought of the United States having spies in that country.

Red Herring. The fallacy of the red herring gets its name from a technique used to train some hunting dogs. In the evening the trainer drags a fresh carcass of a rabbit, bird, squirrel, or other prey through the field. This trail grows "cold" overnight.

The next morning the trainer drags a smoked red herring, tied to a string, diagonally across the path he had made the former evening. He then lets the dog in training out on the original trail. When the dog gets to the point where the path of the red herring crosses the older trail, he will usually be distracted by the fresher, stronger scent of the red herring. The trainer then pulls him back and puts him on the original trail, helping him learn to stay on the trail of his original quarry.

In an argument, a skillful debater who is losing will sometimes throw out a red herring. A red herring in this instance is an irrelevant but interesting side topic. It often is successful in causing the discussion to move in a totally different direction, and the audience may never recognize the weakness of the skillful debater's argument.

Within a situation such as that described above, it is important for the disputants to remain alert to the possibility that their opponent will throw out a red herring. If he or she does, the best recourse is to recognize that he or she has introduced an irrelevant issue, and return the discussion to its original course.

Refuting the Example. When people discuss or debate an issue, they may include an example as a way of clarifying a concept or making the discussion more meaningful to the audience. Sometimes opponents will seize upon the example and find a way to expose some weakness in it. If they do so, and then try to imply that they have therefore defeated the other position, they are committing the fallacy of refuting the example.

Shifting the Burden of Proof [*argumentum ad ignoratiam:* appeal to ignorance]. This fallacy uses a person's inability to disprove a proposition as an argument for the validity of that proposition. For example, since no one has proved that ghosts don't exist, it must mean that they do. Conversely, someone using this fallacy may claim that a person's inability to prove a proposition as an argument against its validity. Since the Soviet cosmonauts were unable to see God anywhere in the universe, He must not exist.

Normally, when someone proposes a new position it is up to them to offer proof for that position. Shifting the burden of proof is a fallacy because one's inability to prove or disprove something establishes neither the truth nor the falsity of the opposite position.[7]

Slippery Slope. Someone commits the fallacy of the slippery slope when he or she claims that we must not take a certain position, not based on facts that can be shown, but because taking that position will put us on a slippery slope that will lead to destructive ends. There are many examples of people predicting the end of America, and even Western civilization, if people would act in certain ways that would put us all on a "slippery slope." Some examples that met with dire predictions include:

- the abolition of slavery,
- giving women the right to vote,
- the introduction of machines that would do work formerly done manually, and

• the introduction of computers that would speed up or replace work originally done by people.

As we now know, none of the above have led to the end of Western civilization. This does not mean that there are not actions or positions that do place us as a nation or as a civilization at risk of moving further in an unhealthy direction. Each situation must be looked at in its historical context. We must be willing to differentiate between changes that we do not like because we are afraid of change (e.g., introducing machines into factories), or because the status quo is more in our self-interest than the proposed change (slave-owners in the mid-1800s), or because it really does place our nation at risk.

Special Pleading. A person commits the fallacy of special pleading when he asks or demands that we apply a different set of criteria (usually more liberal) to him and his ideas or desires than we apply to others. Historically special pleading sometimes was called "benefit of clergy." It had its roots in medieval Europe. Special pleading referred to the right of church offenders to be tried in a church court rather than a civil court, even for civil offenses. This is primarily what the pleader asks for—that he be tried in a different court.

Sometimes Christians resort to special pleading after they have developed theological theories, but then find that certain scriptural passages, as normally interpreted, contradict their theories. It has not been uncommon for Christians, when faced with this predicament, to develop new denotations of one or more of the words in that passage. Thus the "new" meaning of the passage no longer disagrees with their theory. If there is no linguistic evidence from other sources to justify the newly-created denotation, and if the only justification for creating it was to make the passage compatible with one's theological theory, this change is an example of special pleading.

Statistical Fallacies. This section will cover several statistical fallacies. You have already read about them in the statistics and research section of this book. The benefit of going over them in this section again is that logicians have often developed succinct names for the fallacies. These short names allow us to use them more easily in discussion or debate.

Biased Question. A person commits the fallacy of the biased question when he or she frames a question so that the interviewee answers it in a certain direction. The interviewer usually reports the results of the poll without information of the possible bias created by the slanted question. Notice the very different results that probably would occur if one were to ask either Question A or B to 1,000 Americans.

Question A: "Do you think that the United States should continue to help poorer countries through gifts of foreign aid?"

Question B: "In light of growing budget deficits and urgent domestic needs that are not being funded, do you think that the United States should continue to help poorer countries through gifts of foreign aid?"

Obviously you would expect to get far more "No's" in response to Question B than to Question A. However, an unethical pollster could ask 1,000 people Question B, and then report that 75 percent of those polled believe we should discontinue foreign aid, without revealing the biased question he used to obtain those results.

Biased Sample. People commit this fallacy when they use a sample that is not representative of the population to which they are generalizing the results.

Concealed Quantification. When a person speaks about a group, he or she can speak either about the whole group or about certain members of that group (subgroups). The fallacy of concealed quantification occurs when a person speaks or writes so ambiguously that it is unclear whether he or she is speaking of the entire group or of some subgroup within it.

False Precision. People commit the fallacy of false precision when they include a figure in their presentation that is far more precise than the level of measurement warrants. For example, if they measure the sample data to the nearest whole number, it is improper to present the mean as 46.57. Most people unconsciously equate more specific numerical results with greater scientific adequacy of research design. A representation such as this conveys to the audience a much higher level of precision and accuracy than one's measurements justify.

Figures Prove. As you have seen in chapters four and five, there are many ways in which figures can be used to mislead or deceive. There are many ways in which a research design can be developed that does not yield valid results. Whenever people use the phrase "Figures prove..." and the results are important to you, ask them to explain how they arrived at those figures.

Hasty Generalization [*secundum quid:* following which]. Also known as Hasty Conclusion, Overgeneralization or Unwarranted Extrapolation. "One swallow doesn't make a summer." A person commits this fallacy when he or she constructs a generalized rule based on too few cases. Note that the conclusion itself may turn out to be correct: it is in the process that the error occurs. The person drew a conclusion before he or she had sufficient evidence to warrant it.

From a statistical standpoint you may remember that the magnitude of one's sampling error is larger the smaller the sample. In practical terms this means that when we have very small samples, the risk increases that the individuals in our sample may not be a good representation of the population. Therefore our generalizations may not be accurate.

Unwarranted Extrapolation is another form of overgeneralization. It is possible to take two or three points, plot them on a graph, and then extend the line indefinitely. Extrapolation can be done backward or forward, as Mark Twain did regarding the Mississippi river. Forward extrapolations are more common. Extrapolation is a legitimate scientific tool. Scientists frequently extrapolate based on their theories, and then do experiments to see whether the data confirm their hypotheses. Two important differences between fallacious and valid extrapolations are these:

1. When a person extrapolates based on only two or three data points, those extrapolations are more likely to be in error. Scientists do extrapolate, but only after they have obtained enough data points to see the shape of the curve clearly.

2. Reporting an extrapolation before testing it is unwise. Scientists generally use research to confirm or disconfirm their predictions before reporting them.

Another important factor to consider when making generalizations or extrapolations is whether the period or situation we are examining is unusual for some reason. If it is, then generalizations made from it will very likely turn out to be inaccurate. For example, in the five years between 1947 and 1952, television sets in American homes increased by 10,000 percent. If we project this rate of growth for the next five years, we would soon be having 40 sets per family. If we use 1946 as a base year rather than 1947, it is possible to "prove" that every American family will soon have 40,000 TV sets.[8]

Post Hoc *Fallacy* [*post hoc ergo propter hoc:* after this therefore because of this]. This fallacy argues that because A precedes B, A causes B. Chantecler, the rooster in Rostand's famous play, realized that every day after he crowed the sun came up. Therefore, he reasoned, his crowing caused the sun to rise.[9]

This is a well-known fallacy. We have already discussed it in the section on statistics and research design, showing that correlation does not prove causation. Writers have also called this the fallacy of false cause and the fallacy of questionable causation.

Pirie recounts a story that illustrates *post hoc* reasoning. Several years ago a tourist met a Spanish peasant and his wife on a train. They had never seen bananas before, so he offered one to each of them. As the farmer bit into his, the train entered a tunnel. "Don't eat it, Carmen" he shouted. "They make you blind!"[10]

Post hoc fallacies often appear in advertising. Young women of exceptional natural beauty are pictured using a certain product, and fifteen seconds later, being escorted on a date by a handsome man. The clear inference advertisers wish young women to make is that if they use this product, they will soon be the object of male attention and affection.

Chase offers the following observation:

> There are thousands of phenomena that are gradually ascending. Using *post hoc* reasoning, one could speculate that any number of possible things cause any number of other things. We might even be able to offer plausible explanations connecting the phenomena chosen, e.g., number of college graduates, number of people receiving psychological counseling, number of people addicted to alcohol or drugs, number of people declaring personal bankruptcy. . . . In order for a presumed relationship to be valid and not *post hoc*, there must be clear evidence of linkage besides simply correlation.[11]

Sweeping Generalization [*dicto simpliciter:* said simply]. The fallacy of sweeping generalization occurs when a person attempts to use a generalized rule to apply to every subgroup or situation, disregarding diversity. For example, the statements "All Baptists believe...." or "All Presbyterians believe...." would undoubtedly be a sweeping generalization because of the wide diversities in these groups.

Compare this with the fallacy of accident. Accident usually refers to a single instance or person that is an exception to the rule. Sweeping generalization usually refers to a subgroup of people or situations that are exceptions to the rule. However, just to keep life interesting, some writers treat them as synonyms.

Note also the difference between hasty generalization and sweeping generalization. In hasty generalization a person constructs a generalized rule based on too few cases. In sweeping generalization he attempts to apply a generalized rule to a group that has much diversity.

[This concludes the section on statistical fallacies.]

Straw Man. The straw man fallacy occurs when a person distorts an opposing position in some way, then attacks and demolishes this distorted position. By demolishing the distorted position, he or she claims to have demolished the entire position.

The straw man fallacy is related to the irrelevant thesis or irrelevant conclusion fallacy. His conclusion (that he has destroyed the opposing viewpoint) does not logically follow from his action of demolishing a distortion of the opposition.

Traditional Wisdom. The fallacy of traditional wisdom tries to apply conclusions from the past to the present. It can often be identified by statements such as "the founding fathers," "tried and true," and "the lessons of history." Writers have also called it appeal to antiquity.

Sometimes there is wisdom that can be gained from looking at the past. Hayakawa was famous for his statement to the effect that "Those who fail to learn from the mistakes of the past are doomed to repeat them." However, an appeal to the past can be a fallacy in at least two ways. First, history is always more complex than we understand. There were always more forces at work than we have the time to study or the mental capacity to comprehend. Therefore the models we or others tend to apply to the past are always partial and sometimes are in error. Second, there is always the possibility, even the likelihood, that our present situation differs in one or more important ways from the historical situation to which we are comparing it. Therefore, to maintain that it is so much alike that conclusions drawn from that situation can apply to our own may sometimes result in committing the fallacy of false analogy.

Trivial Objections. A person commits the fallacy of trivial objections when he or she attacks a minor part of a position, expending an inordinate amount of time and energy focused on those objections. People who raise trivial objections may believe that they are adequately refuting the entire position, but they are not. This fallacy has also been called hairsplitting.

Two Wrongs Make a Right. People commit this fallacy when they attempt to justify wrong behavior done by them by pointing to similar wrong behavior that the opposing position has done. Children of all ages use this fallacy.

Unaccepted Enthymemes. This fallacy probably deserves wider recognition than it has now. An enthymeme is an argument in which one of its stages (premises) is understood rather than stated. There is not a problem if all parties in the argument accept the tacit, or unstated, premise. However, if one side does not accept the unstated premise, the next stage in the argument seems to them to be a *non sequitur* or an irrelevant conclusion. We can resolve this kind of situation best by making the unstated premise explicit, and then arguing either for or against its acceptance based on relevant evidence.

Unknowable Fact. See Meaningless Claims.

Unobtainable Perfection. Sometimes people will criticize the alternatives that are available to them because each option is imperfect in some way. Unless one option is perfect, it is fallacious to reject other alternatives just because they do not represent a perfect solution.

Unwarranted Extrapolation. See Hasty Generalization in the Statistics section.

Wishful Thinking. If we accept a proposition because we wish that it were true rather than because there is evidence that shows that it is true, we commit the fallacy of wishful thinking. Or if we reject something solely because we wish it were not true, rather than because there is evidence that it is untrue, we commit this fallacy. For example, when we recognize our deepest motivations and become aware of how selfish and self-serving some of our behavior is, we commit the fallacy of wishful thinking if we dismiss this recognition out of hand because it is an uncomfortable one with which to deal.

You Too! [*tu quoque:* you also]. The fallacy of you too! occurs when, during an argument, one opponent stops presenting facts to bolster his or her argument and points to something negative about the opponent or the opponent's position, as if that proved the validity of his own. This is a fallacy because, as you know by this time, it is impossible to prove the validity of one position by showing weaknesses in the character or arguments of an opponent.

This fallacy probably occurs with greater frequency in

daily relationships than any other. Children who are quarreling frequently use you too arguments. Married couples who are quarreling do the same. Bar fights, I am told, frequently start the same way.

One humorous example of you too! to conclude our discussion of fallacies occurred in Moscow in the 1930s. According to the story, when Moscow first opened the underground to visitors, officials invited an American tourist to inspect a station. Officials showed him the technically-advanced (for that time) turnstiles and the gleaming washrooms. He was impressed, and after expressing his admiration asked, "How about the trains?" His guide then showed him the safety features and beautiful frescoes that adorned the tunnel walls. He again expressed his admiration, and then asked, "But where are the trains?"

"How about the trains?" snapped his guide. "How about the trains? How about the sharecroppers in Alabama?"[12]

SUMMARY OF CHAPTERS 6 AND 7

List of Logical Fallacies

Accent

Accident

Ad hominem

Amphiboly

Appeal to Antiquity

Appeal to Authority

Appeal to the Crowd

Appeal to Moderation

Appeal to Newness

Appeal to Pity

Appeal to Popularity

Appeal of the Poor

Appeal to the Stone

Appeal to Wealth

Apriorism

Begging the Question

Bifurcation

Blinding with Science

Catastrophizing

Classical Syllogism
   Fallacies
   • Contradictory Premises
   • Exclusive Premises
   • Positive Conclusion from
       Negative Premises
   • Fallacy of Four Terms

- Illicit Process
- Undistributed Middle

Cliche Thinking
Complex Question
Composition
Concealed Evidence
Converse Accident
Damning the Alternatives
Dismissal
Division
Emotional Appeals
Equivocation
Every Schoolboy Knows
False Analogies
Fear or Force
Gambler's Fallacy
Genetic Fallacy
Guilt by Association
Humor and Ridicule
Intuition
Invincible Ignorance
Irrelevant Thesis or
    Irrelevant Conclusion
Loaded Words or
    Name-Calling
Magical Thinking
Meaningless Claim

Non Sequitur
One-Sided Assessment
Oversimplification
Poisoning the Well
Provincialism
Red Herring
Refuting the Example
Shifting the Burden of Proof
Slippery Slope
Special Pleading
Statistical Fallacies
- Biased Question
- Biased Sample
- Concealed Quantification
- False Precision
- Figures Prove
- Hasty Generalization
- *Post Hoc* Fallacy
- Sweeping Generalization

Straw Man
Traditional Wisdom
Trivial Objections
Two Wrongs Make a Right
Unaccepted Enthymemes
Unobtainable Perfection
Wishful Thinking
You Too!

EXERCISES

For each situation, identify the fallacy involved, if there is one, and explain the faulty reasoning. Sometimes more than one fallacy could be named, since the fallacies do overlap. Suggested answers are included in the back of the book.

EX 41: A hunter said, "I fail to see why hunting should be considered cruel when it gives tremendous pleasure to many people and employment to many more."[13] Are there any fallacies in this argument? If so, what are they?

EX 42: During the Persian Gulf War of 1991 the Soviet Union moved repressively against the Baltic States, killing and wounding many innocent citizens. President Bush sent State Department officials to the Soviet Union to express his concern. These officials found that all the Soviets were willing to talk about was their concern regarding Allied Forces' conduct in the Iraqi war. Does this remind you of any logical fallacy?

EX 43: In his seminars one well-known Christian speaker will often state a point (frequently one that is unique to him), and follow this with an interesting anecdote that illustrates the point. Often he offers no other argument to prove his point than the anecdote, although the anecdotes are so interesting that many people are unaware of this fact. Are any logical fallacies involved here?

EX 44: A Christian recently argued that we shouldn't use our minds (referring to our mental and critical capacities) to study the Bible and develop our theology. He noted that we already have 2300 denominations, conflicts within those denominations, and even conflicts within individual churches. He concluded that this continuing conflict shows that use of our mental and critical capacities is not the proper way to build our theology. Do you agree or disagree with this conclusion? Why?

EX 45: Some Christians believe that while the Bible is God's Word and is trustworthy in spiritual matters, it may contain errors concerning facts of history, science, and sociological matters (especially the roles of men and women). Other believers argue that since God inspired the Bible and since God is trustworthy, then we should trust all that He says. They further argue that by taking the position that the Bible has errors in certain parts, we place ourselves on the "slippery slope" where we will soon be believing that it has errors in more parts. We will eventually be like certain denominations that have very little regard for the Word of God. Do you believe this latter argument is an example of the fallacy of slippery slope or is it a valid concern?

EX 46: The Pharisees criticized Jesus for not being a good man or a true prophet because He ate with tax collectors and sinners (Matt. 9:10). They assumed that if He were a truly godly man, He would not associate with such groups, for in so doing He risked ceremonial defilement. Of what fallacy is this an example?

EX 47: Two world-renowned scientists, writing a book about life, stated the following: "Life began somewhere else in the universe and was sent here by rocket ships in the form of micro-organisms by a higher civilization....I know this sounds ridiculous, and maybe it isn't true, but you can't prove that it isn't." Do you have any comments about the logic used by these two distinguished scientists?

EX 48: G. K. Chesterton once said, "If Americans can be divorced for 'incompatibility,' I cannot conceive why they are not all divorced. I have known many happy marriages, but never a compatible one. For a man and a woman, as such, are incompatible." What logical fallacy is present in this statement?

EX 49: A certain Christian college has not taken any direct government aid in over 100 years of its existence. Insisting on the constitutional separation of church and state, the college has ignored a multitude of decrees and directives that the federal government has sent to it. The federal government has insisted that the college must state that it is complying with Title IX of the Education Amendments of 1972, which bans discrimination against women. College officials say they have no quarrel with women's rights. They will not sign the form as a matter of principle, since the college receives no federal funds. The president of the college suggested that he feared that to do so would put them on a slippery slope that would soon lead to further government intrusion. He stated the following: "Once the nose of the camel gets in the tent, the whole camel moves in. If we signed this, we'd be expected to sign compliance forms for everything under the sun."[14]

Do you think that this is an example of legitimate fear of slippery slope or is this an example of a fallacious use of it? Discuss how you would go about making such a decision. Are there any other aspects of this situation that remind you of a possible fallacy?

EX 50: John Strachey, in *The Coming Struggle for Power*, stated the following: "In that melancholy book *The Future of An Illusion*, Dr. Freud, himself one of the last great theorists of the European capitalist class, has stated with simple clarity the impossibility of religious belief for the educated man of today."[15] Do you see any problem with the logic of Mr. Strachey's statement? If so, what is it?

EX 51: Of what logical fallacy does the following statement remind you? "I've looked everywhere in this area for an instruction book on how to play the concertina without success."[16]

EX 52: During the Revolutionary period, Thomas Paine strongly argued against reconciliation with England. In his book *Common Sense* he included the following statement.

> Though I would carefully avoid giving unnecessary offence, yet I am inclined to believe, that all those who espouse the doctrine of reconciliation, may be included within the following descriptions.
> Interested men, who are not to be trusted, weak men who cannot see, prejudiced men who will not see, and a certain set of moderate men who think better of the European world than it deserves; and this last class, by an ill-judged deliberation, will be the cause of more calamities to this Continent than all the other three.

Does he commit a logical fallacy here? If he does, what is it?

EX 53: In his famous debate with Thomas Huxley on the subject of evolution, Bishop Wilberforce scored several debating points with the audience when he asked Huxley if he descended from the monkey on his mother's side or his father's side of the family.[17] In argumentation, this is an example of what?

Part Five

CONCLUDING QUESTIONS AND CONCEPTS

CHAPTER 8

Is There a Fourth Way of Gaining Knowledge?

A BRIEF REVIEW

Developmentally we go through a series of changes in the process by which we assimilate truth. As children we often accept propositions uncritically from parents and teachers whom we trust. During our adolescent years we often move into a position where we trust authority figures less, or even actively distrust them ("Don't trust anyone over 30!"). During our early adult life most of us move toward a position between these former two, where we become intentionally critical or intentionally careful as we hear or read propositions that claim to be true.

As we have seen in this book, there are three primary sources of truth. For the Christian, Scripture is an important source of true propositions. Hermeneutics is the science and art by which we accurately uncover the truths found in Scripture.

Experience is the second source of truth. Simple truths may be discovered through normal observation (e.g., red skies in the morning mean increased chances of stormy weather). More complex truths can be discovered through empirical investigation (scientific research) and through statistical analysis of the resulting data. The true propositions discovered through either of these two processes may be elaborated with inductive and deductive logic.

While people could insist that they would accept as true only those things they had personally researched and verified, most of us have neither the time nor the expertise to independently research and verify the multitude of truths on which we base our everyday lives. We must depend on the trustworthiness of others who have researched those truths personally, expecting that they will use the same level of careful analysis as we would if we were in their place. If we find they are not doing so, we may decide that we will no longer use them as credible sources of information.

All people have elementary systems of hermeneutics, empirical investigation, and logical analysis that they apply regularly (usually unconsciously) in their daily lives. They usually call this "common sense." By learning more about each of these skills in academic settings or through a book such as this one, people can increase their ability to identify and carefully apply the rules that they formerly used unconsciously when attempting to make sense of their world. Persons without a college education but with well-developed common sense may often make excellent analyses of situations, although they may have difficulty explaining the process by which they made their analyses.

Some people label intuition as a fourth source of information. Their definition of intuition may go something like the following: "the direct apprehension of knowledge that is not the result of conscious reasoning or of immediate sense perception."[1] One could argue that intuition is nothing more than our experience of God's Word or God's world, filtering through our reasoning processes until an idea or proposition becomes definite enough that we can articulate it in words. If this is true, intuition is not a fourth source of information, but an early stage of truth discovery through these three other channels. Propositions derived through intuition should be considered as hypotheses that need to be proven by further research, just as any other hypotheses.

ONE'S RELATIONSHIP TO GOD: ANOTHER SOURCE OF INFORMATION?

Most evangelical Christians agree with the proposition that the most important differences between Christianity and other religions is that Christianity is primarily a relationship between God and human beings, and only secondarily a set of rules governing one's beliefs and behavior. Yet there is a way in which this relationship is different from most relationships.

The majority of Christians believe that God speaks to them indirectly through His Word, but that He rarely speaks to them directly, perhaps once or twice in a year's time. Often believers can cite only two or three instances in a period of several years where they believe God spoke directly to them.

Most believers speak to God regularly through prayer, but their prayers are almost exclusively monologues rather than dialogues between themselves and their heavenly Father. Most believers hunger for more dialogue between themselves and the Lord, but since it seems that monologue is the normal experience of other believers, they accept this as the norm for themselves.

In this chapter I will propose that prayer can become more of a conversation with our heavenly Father if we are willing to make some changes in the way we pray and if we wish for it to become so. Mark and Patti Virkler developed most of these ideas in their book *Communion with God*, which can be consulted for further details and discussion.[2]

Setting the Scene for Prayer to Become a Conversation

To have a good conversation with a special friend we often make certain arrangements. We schedule a time when we will not be distracted by other people or situations demanding our attention. We try to find a time when we will be alert and relaxed. We may think ahead of things we'd like to share with this friend. We probably would look forward to the time with eager anticipation.

We can do the same in preparing to meet with the Lord. It is helpful to find a time when we will be alert, relaxed, and free from other distractions or responsibilities. Early in the morning is often the best time, before the pressures of the day have begun, but this may not be feasible for everyone. It is best that we find a place that is private, so that we can shut out external distractions.

If we want to have a quality conversation with an earthly friend, it is important not to be thinking of something else during our time together. Similarly if we want to have a quality communion time with the Lord, it is important to shut out internal distractions. Some ways to quiet the internal distractions include:

- Before initiating a time of communion, spend some time in Bible study.
- Write down distracting thoughts, and put them aside so that they can be attended to later.
- Relax the parts of the body that are tense (slow breathing as part of this physical relaxation).
- If there is a picture of Jesus in the room that conveys His love and grace, focus on that for a moment, and then close the eyes and retain that image mentally.

- Imagine meeting the Lord in some biblical setting, such as a Judean hillside.
- Express love and thankfulness to Jesus through internal prayer or in spoken words or song.

The Communion Time Itself

- Have some writing materials available to write out our statements and the Lord's responses. (This is similar to the Psalms. The psalmist wrote out his requests or feelings, and then the Holy Spirit prompted him to write a response of encouragement or direction.)
- Date the page we will be using for journaling.
- Speak to the Lord about whatever is uppermost in our mind. This could be a desire to become more like Him, or for direction in a certain area of our life, help in dealing with anxious or depressing feelings, or even a theological question.
- Write the question down, then close the eyes, focus on a mental picture of Jesus, and wait for His response. (Perhaps one reason our usual prayer times resemble monologues is that we spend all the time talking, so there is no time for the Lord to respond.)
- Purposely do not try to solve the problem. Focus on the Lord. Pray that the Lord will not allow any thoughts to come from our own subconscious or conscious mind or from Satan, but that we would hear only His voice.
- If we hear no response, ask the Lord whether something is in the way of having fellowship with Him. If He brings to mind some sin, confess it and promise to discontinue it in His strength.
- When we receive a response, write it down. Do not try to analyze where it came from, for that will block the flow. Write it down, leaving one line between the question and the response we receive. There will be time later to evaluate its source.

• If we have one or more follow-up questions, write them down and wait for a response again. Leave one line between each statement and response in the conversation.

• If we have a question about whether something is from the Lord, we can ask Him whether it is from Him and how we can know it is from Him and not another source.

• After the conversation time, finish with any kind of response we want to make, whether thanksgiving, praise, a commitment to obedience in a certain area, or something else. Put the journal in a confidential place.

Some Reservations

If you are like most people who hear this proposal, you probably will have one or more questions. I will try to address some common ones.

How Can We Know Whether a Thought Is from Our Own Mind or from Satan Rather Than from the Lord?

Mark and Patti suggest that there are several ways in which thoughts from the Lord are different from one's own thoughts. I have found these distinctions to be true as I have used this method in my communion times with the Lord. Here are some of those ways:

- The Lord's responses are like your thoughts and musings except that you are not causing the thoughts to come together. They are spontaneous, not cognitive or analytical.
- They come easily, and as God speaking in the first person.
- They are often light and gentle, and easily cut off by any exertion of self (own thoughts, will, etc.).
- They have an unusual content to them, in that they will be *wiser, more loving* and *more motive oriented* than your thoughts (emphasis mine).

- They will cause a special reaction within your being, such as a sense of excitement, conviction, faith, life, awe, peace.
- When embraced, they carry with them a fullness of strength to do them, and a joy in doing so.
- Your spiritual senses become more sensitive as time goes on, and you more easily and frequently experience God speaking in this way.[3]

What Is the Relationship Between Journaling and Automatic Writing?

Since journaling bears some superficial resemblances to automatic writing, some Christians have concerns about whether they may be related. Here is Mark and Patti's answer:

> Those who have experienced automatic writing before becoming a Christian tell me that in automatic writing a spirit comes and controls the person's *hand*, whereas in journaling there is a spontaneous flow of ideas birthed by God in their *hearts* and then recorded in their journals by a hand freely under the person's own control. Therefore in journaling, the entire being is involved, the heart, the mind and the mind's guiding of the hand in writing, whereas in automatic writing only a limp hand is involved. The rest of the individual is bypassed by the evil spirit that controls the hand.[4]

Is This Not New Age Spirituality?

Mark and Patti make the following distinctions between what they teach and what the New Age movement teaches:

The Christian Believes:	*The New Ager Believes:*
The God of the Bible is the God of this universe.	The God of the Bible is not the God of this universe.

Salvation is by the blood of Jesus.	There is no need for salvation.
The Bible is the inerrant Word of God.	The Bible is not the inerrant Word of God.
One should be a student of the Bible.	There is no need to be a student of the Bible.
All Spirit encounter must be tested against the Bible.	Spirit encounter need not be tested against the Bible.
One should be linked to the body of Christ.	There is no need whatsoever to be linked to the body of Christ.
Each one must walk under the spiritual covering of a Christian pastor.	There is no need to walk under the spiritual covering of a Christian pastor.

What About Safeguards with This Method?

Mark and Patti suggest that every Christian who would try this approach to communion with God surround themselves with the following safeguards: that they be born-again Christians, that they use Scripture to judge any message they receive, that they use the criteria above to assess the source of any message they receive, that they share any message that they have questions about with one or more Christians whose spiritual judgment they trust, including their pastor, and not move forward on a message in question unless these other people and themselves all believe the message is from God.

A Personal Response to This Method of Communing with God

I have used the method of communing with God for the past two years. Here are some of my experiences and reflections upon those experiences:

"Communion time has helped make biblical truths experientially real in my life. Before learning to pray in this way I believed Jesus loved me, believed that He accepted me, and believed that He accepted me even when I made mistakes. I believed that He wanted to walk and talk with me daily. But these were primarily cognitive beliefs I had about God, not realities that I was experiencing in my Christian life. By having a regular communion time those theological truths have become daily realities."

"During my first few months of having a regular communion time with the Lord, I was very tentative about whether it was the Lord telling me these things or someone else. I would frequently say to my wife, 'I think the Lord said to me this morning...' As time has gone on, I have become more confident that it is the Lord speaking to me at those times. The insights I have learned about myself have been very accurate, and I've become aware of in my life spiritual areas that I didn't know I needed to grow in. It has definitely deepened my awareness of myself more so than any other kind of experience."

"It has always been hard for me to hear constructive criticism, even when I knew it was warranted and that it was given in love. Somehow the Lord can confront during our communion times in such a loving manner that it doesn't even seem to be a confrontation. And with the confrontation He seems to give a supernatural ability or grace to start changing in that particular area."

"The Lord has helped me see lifelong patterns that have become part of the way I lived my Christian faith. One of these was working things out using my ingenuity and interpersonal skills, rather than trusting Him to work. I've had much to learn about resting in the Lord. He's taught me that 'resting in Him' doesn't mean not working, but means learning to take His peace into a situation as I work."

"I've experienced difficulties in life, as everyone has. Through those difficulties I've learned some spiritual lessons. But journaling has helped me understand *much more* about the spiritual issues that Jesus wants me to be growing in as I go through a particular difficulty. If not for these times of communing with the Lord I would have experienced the stressful situation, but I don't think it would have been a catalyst to nearly as much spiritual growth as it has been since I've begun to talk with Him and listen to His responses in the midst of situations."

"Since learning about communion with God I have been tempted sometimes to ask the Lord to reveal the future to me, since I know He knows the future and could save me much unnecessary work. In a very gentle way He has told me that is not what He wants me to use this communion time for, but for developing our relationship. He has promised He would be with me as I worked and would guide me in the process. I'm glad He said that, because developing my relationship with Him is really much more important than knowing the future, and I could have developed some of the wrong motivations for our communion time if He had answered my request."

"One concern I had when I began journaling was whether Satan or my subconscious mind would enter the communion time and cause me to have difficulty discerning where a thought was coming from. I've found that the vast majority of thoughts I receive during my communion times do come from the Lord, using the criteria Mark and Patti have identified. The difference between the Lord's messages and my problem-solving thoughts is very easy to distinguish. There have been only two times in two years when I believe Satan tried to enter the process. Each time the voice had a harshness about it that made me quickly aware that there was something different (cf John 10:4–5). Another difference is that every time the Lord has said He will do something, He has brought it to pass. In contrast, these two instances of a harsher voice have been the only times that something that was predicted did not occur. I am increasingly confident that as I remain close to the Lord, He will give me discernment about the messages from Him and those that are not."

"I was reluctant to get started in journaling at first because several years ago I made a promise to the Lord to spend 30 minutes a day studying His Word. I didn't feel it would be right to take from the Bible study time for my communion time, but I didn't think I could afford to spend more than 30 minutes per day in Bible study and prayer. Here are some excerpts from my early journaling when I talked with the Lord about this issue."

"Jesus, what do you want me to be learning in my Christian life now?"

"I want you to be focusing on our relationship now. In the past you have gotten too busy doing things and reading things to have time for our relationship."

"Lord, how do you want me to do that?"

"Continue to read my Word, but then spend time with Me afterward. And you shall seek Me, and you will find Me, when you shall search for Me with all your heart."

"It's so easy for me to get distracted from this relationship time, or to think it's not important."

"Nothing could be more important than this, and no time will be easier to develop some new life habits than now."

"After that particular conversation with the Lord, I committed to having regular communion times with the Lord, usually ten or fifteen minutes, following my Bible study times. This time has definitely helped me experience the Lord's presence in my life regularly, and I have no regrets about this extra investment of time. As the Lord said, 'Nothing is more important than this.' "

"There are occasionally times when I don't hear the Lord speaking on a particular day. Usually this is due to something on my end—I've let external or internal distractions come into my communion time, and that blocks the flow of what the Lord wants to say to me. Occasionally I've allowed a sinful thought or motivation or behavior to enter my life, and that blocks our fellowship. When I can't hear the Lord speak, I've learned to ask Him what is in the way, and usually that day or the next He helps me see what it is. So I don't give up when I have a communion time that doesn't go anywhere, but I come back the next day and usually find that whatever was hindering it is gone."

"When I first started having a communion time I found myself a little afraid. I think I was afraid of the intimacy of conversing with the Lord, knowing that He knows everything about me. Yet as I've experienced His acceptance over the months, and experienced how loving His confrontations are, I've found I have nothing to fear. I'm experiencing Jesus as a Friend, as well as my Savior and Lord, as a daily reality in my life now."

SOME CONCLUDING THOUGHTS

The chapter that you have just read may seem out of place in a book on learning to think critically, although I don't think it is. We can become excellent critical thinkers, both in examining God's Word and God's world. But if we have no experiential reality of a loving, personal relationship with God, I believe we have an unbalanced Christian faith. We have all seen Christians who have an excellent understanding of doctrine but who show no evidence of a life-enriching personal relationship with a loving heavenly Father. For us to know the fullness of the Christian life our cognitive understanding of God's truths should be balanced by the experience of God's love and grace in a daily relationship.

Perhaps the method that I have discussed here is not the one that God will use to help you develop an experiential awareness of His presence in your life, but it may be. The method we've talked about is in actuality an expansion of Christian prayer. The primary difference is that instead of using all the time talking yourself, you spend a portion of the time talking with God and another portion listening to Him. That approach may be only a small change from how you have been praying for years.

If you are seriously wondering whether this might have a positive effect in your spiritual life, I would encourage you to try this as an experiment for three months and see what happens in your relationship with the Lord.

If you would like further information about the full-length book *Communion with God,* you will find it included in the notes for this chapter.[5]

CHAPTER 9

Using What You Have Learned

TRUTH, PERSONAL BELIEF, AND HUMILITY

At this point it may be helpful to review the distinction that Barry and Soccio made between truth and personal belief. A *true proposition* is a statement that describes an actual state of affairs. Our *perceptions* may at times be faulty. However, with the help of consensual validation and instruments that objectively measure variables, we can make statements that accurately reflect a state of affairs.

Belief refers to one's attitude toward a specific proposition. While we may agree that objectively true propositions exist, we recognize that our personal beliefs do not correspond exactly to them. For that reason it is wise to hold our beliefs (opinions) tentatively. There are many truths in Scripture and in the natural world that are so clear that we can have confidence in affirming them. However, there are also many things in Scripture and in the world that are not nearly so clear-cut. A measure of humility "wears well" on us all.

COMMON RESPONSES AFTER LEARNING CRITICAL THINKING SKILLS

There are two different sets of responses that occur with moderate frequency when Christians learn critical thinking skills. One of these relates to people who have been "heroes" to us in the past and present; the other relates to feelings generated within ourselves as we have to rethink issues that have been basic to our understanding of life. Let us discuss each of these briefly.

Disillusionment with Heroes

Christian graduate students who take a course in hermeneutics sometimes report that they become frustrated with their pastor, Sunday school teacher, or television minister. They find that these "heroes" use verses out of context, allegorize parables, or base their messages on an incidental detail in a passage rather than its teaching focus. The leader may commit logical fallacies such as *non sequiturs, ad hominem* arguments, or "proving" conclusions with examples. In response to their anger, some students withdraw from their heroes. What should we do in such a situation?

We can write letters (signed or unsigned), critiquing the message in the hope that the critiques will help the person improve his or her hermeneutics. However, writing critiques can take several hours per week, especially if one makes an effort to say things gently. Even then they may seriously strain a friendship or pastoral relationship. The person may become defensive and not read them.

Some people withdraw from a particular church, but often find that the hermeneutics of ministers and Sunday school teachers in other churches are no better than those of the church they just left. Withdrawal from all churches is not a biblical alternative (Heb. 10:25). Holding in a great deal of anger is not a very healthy or biblical alternative either (Eph. 4:26).

One approach that has helped many students is to purposely shift their focus from what is wrong with a sermon or Bible study to what is right with it. It is often true that even if speakers abuse a passage and draw points from it that the author never intended, those points can be found somewhere else in Scripture. Thus the points are biblical, but just should not be derived from that passage. By focusing on the biblical truths and not on the hermeneutical process, one can sometimes derive a spiritual blessing from a sermon or teaching that would not earn a passing grade in a hermeneutics class.

Another approach that some students have used has been to recognize that others may never have had the opportunity to take a course in hermeneutics, and to be thankful for the training one has, rather than angry with those who have not had it. Pastors and teachers who use poor hermeneutics rarely do so because they want to misinterpret Scripture, but because they are unaware of exegetical principles. Some students have taught an adult elective in hermeneutics at their church, using their frustration constructively to make a positive contribution. It obviously helps if the pastor sits in on or team-teaches such a class.

Dealing with Our Discomfort When Long-Established Beliefs Are Threatened

Think for a moment about how you feel when someone starts teaching a position different from what you believe. What are your usual feelings? Are there any feelings beneath the feelings that you first experience?

It is not unusual for us, when faced with ideas that contradict what we already believe, to experience some frustration. Beneath that also may be some anxiety, although we are usually much less aware of this second emotion. The amount of frustration and anxiety we experience varies with the degree to which the presented material challenges our core beliefs. Let us examine where these feelings come from. Before that, let us look briefly at one model of how emotions develop, then apply that model to an understanding of the feelings we might have in the specific context we're discussing.

The ABC Theory of Emotion. One widely-accepted model of how feelings are created comes from Rational-Emotive Therapy, a theory developed initially by Albert Ellis. Figure 9-1 describes this process.

A   +   B — — — — — —>   C

Activating Event   Belief   Emotional Consequence

FIGURE 9-1. The rational-emotive process.

A, the activating event, represents what happens. B, the belief, stands for the conscious or subconscious belief we have about the meaning of event A. C, the emotional consequence, represents the feelings we have as a result.

For example, one evening several years ago I visited some friends in another city for an overnight stay. I arrived after sunset, so I did not see the outside of their home before retiring for the night. I awakened in the middle of the night to the sound of a diesel train horn blowing just outside my window and the house shaking from the weight of the locomotive and the cars it was pulling (this was my A—the activating event). My B (belief), constructed in a few hundredths of a second, was that I was about to be run over by a several hundred-ton train, and I lay paralyzed with terror (C—my emotional consequence) at what I expected to be my imminent doom.

Notice that the emotional consequence was not caused by

the activating event directly, but by my interpretation or belief of the meaning of the activating event. The members of the family who resided there experienced no emotional upset (C) from the very same activating event (A), because they knew (B) that a slow freight passed right at the property line of their backyard every night around 2 A.M., and that it represented no danger. Thus the ABC theory of emotion asserts that the emotions we experience come, not from the events in our lives, but from the interpretations we make of those events. According to Ellis, over 200 research articles confirm this theory.

If it is true, this theory would suggest that the emotions we experience when someone begins teaching something that is contrary to our core beliefs are not a direct result of that teaching, but result from the conscious or subconscious beliefs we bring to that situation. Let us try to identify some possible beliefs that would produce frustration or anxiety in such a situation. The conscious or unconscious beliefs probably vary for each person. The following beliefs are illustrative only, and do not necessarily apply to everyone.

One possible subconscious belief is this: "They're teaching error, and I don't want others to be affected by that error." By subconscious belief I am referring to a belief that is normally below the level of conscious awareness. However, when someone points it out to us, and if we are in a setting where we feel comfortable being honest with ourself and others, we can recognize that it has been present in our thinking, perhaps for many years. We can call the statement above B_1. B_1 probably would produce the feeling of frustration (C) at someone for attempting to mislead others.

Another possible subconscious belief might be the thought that "I was comfortable with my previous worldview. I don't like it when someone challenges my basic assumptions or conclusions." We could call this B_2. This situation also could cause us to feel frustration.

A third possible subconscious thought would be, "Changing this one belief may cause all my beliefs to come tumbling down, since they are all related." This belief, B_3, of having all of one's beliefs undermined could cause anxiety.

A fourth possible subconscious belief could be, "I don't like to consider the possibility that I have been misunderstanding God's work in my life all these years, nor the possibility that my interpretation of these events has been wrong." This belief, B_4, also could cause anxiety. It is likely that we might cover our anxiety at this prospect by becoming frustrated with the person whom we perceive to be causing it.

Another possible subconscious thought would be, "I'm afraid that others will respect me less if they find that I have changed my mind on something. It would be difficult to admit that I have been wrong on something I taught or talked about so confidently." This belief, B_5, probably would produce some fear about others losing respect for us.

Disputing with Our Beliefs. Let us return to my situation of several years ago, thinking I am about to be run over by a 100-ton locomotive. I was quite anxious then, believing the runaway train would come crashing through the wall of my bedroom any second. Nothing happened for the next ten seconds, and when I heard the train whistle again it was moving away from me, rather than toward me as before. I heard the sounds of railroad cars passing by close to my bedroom but not through it. I gradually realized that my hosts must have a train track that passes very close to their house, but that I was not in mortal danger. I now had a new belief that I could use to dispute (D) with my former one (B), and feelings of relief (E) replaced my panic (C). See Figure 9-2.

My disputing self-talk did not cause me to be relaxed enough to go back to sleep immediately, since adrenaline was already pumping through my system, but it did release me from the paralyzing panic I had a moment earlier. By recognizing that I was in a safe place (D), I was eventually able to relax again (E).

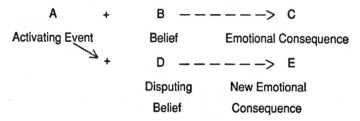

FIGURE 9-2. The rational-emotive process using a disputing belief.

According to practitioners of rational-emotive therapy, we also can learn to bring our emotional responses under control by learning to identify what we are saying to ourselves (frequently subconsciously) at B, and replace that self-talk with new, more functional, and more accurate self-talk at D. Here is how the approach might work with the five Bs we identified earlier.

In all of these, the activating event is information that raises questions about some belief that we have formerly believed was true. The first B was "They're teaching error, and I don't want others to be affected by that error." A disputing statement (D_1) that we might use against it could be: "What they're teaching disagrees with what I believe presently, but they may have some good data to back up their point of view. Let me listen to it with an open mind to see the quality of their arguments and data." Saying this kind of thing to ourselves, we can replace the frustration at C with a feeling of openness.

Before reading further, on a separate sheet of paper write down B_2 and the emotion likely to occur with it (C). Then write down a possible way to dispute with it (D_2) and the feeling you imagine would result (E). Do the same with B_3, B_4, and B_5. Then compare your answers with the following ones.

There is not one right D for each situation. The best D for you is one that would enable you to respond functionally in that situation.

B_2: I was comfortable with my previous worldview. I don't like it when someone challenges my basic assumptions and conclusions.

D_2: It's true that I was comfortable with my previous worldview. I don't particularly like it when someone comes along and forces me to reexamine my basic assumptions. However, if I don't reexamine my basic assumptions every once in awhile, I'll never know whether they are really true, or if I'm simply shielding myself from any information contrary to them. Without an occasional challenge, I could become intellectually lethargic and dogmatic, and I don't want that to happen.

B_3: Changing this one belief may cause all my beliefs to come tumbling down, since they're all related.

D_3: While it is true that many of my ideas are interrelated, it's not true that changing one will make the whole house come down. Usually changing one belief involves changing only that one, and occasionally one or two related ideas. The rest of my worldview remains intact and is not threatened.

B_4: I don't like to consider the possibility that I have been misunderstanding God's work in my life all these years, nor the possibility that my interpretations of these events have been wrong.

D_4: While it's not pleasant to think that I've been misunderstanding God's work in my life all these years, it's definitely better to change it now (if it needs to be changed) than to go through more of life expecting or believing something that is wrong.

B_5: I'm afraid that others will respect me less if they find that I've changed my mind on something. It would be difficult to admit that I have been wrong on something I taught or talked about so confidently.

D$_5$: I respect people who are open to new information more than those who cling to their former beliefs despite information that should cause them to reexamine and possibly change their beliefs (invincible ignorance). Therefore if I'm concerned about people's respect, I need to be open to new information and make changes when necessary.

You may find that you feel some frustration or anxiety when someone presents information that counters one or more of your core beliefs, yet none of the Bs described here seems to capture accurately the self-talk that is causing those feelings. If that is true, try to identify your personal Bs, and then develop Ds to dispute them using the examples given.

Tolerating Lack of Closure

Gestalt psychologists have shown that human beings dislike lack of closure. A simple closure experience that most of us are familiar with is when an artist draws the outline of something using dashed lines. We automatically fill in the lines mentally and see the object as a completed figure, sometimes not even recognizing that we have brought the closure ourselves until someone draws our attention to it.

In a similar way most of us want closure on intellectual questions. We want to know whether A or B is correct. A lack of closure is innately less comfortable than a state of closure. The amount of discomfort depends on the degree to which the issue is relevant to core issues in one's life. An issue that one's denomination is debating and that directly affects our future is more important to us psychologically than determining who is right in an intertribal conflict between two African tribes.

It may not be that there are conscious or subconscious Bs that cause us to be uncomfortable with lack of closure—this discomfort may simply come because God created us with an innate desire to make sense of (achieve closure in) our environment. In either event, it is possible to develop self-talk that helps us become more comfortable tolerating lack of closure. Some possible self-talk might include:

"While it's uncomfortable not to have closure on something important, it's possible to live with that discomfort for awhile."

"It's better to tolerate discomfort over lack of closure than to move to premature closure and make a poor decision or have to change one's mind a second time."

"There is nothing that should cause people to disrespect me if I occasionally say that I'm still researching an issue and haven't made a decision yet. If they do, that is more of an indictment of them than it is of me."

"With the tremendous amount of new information people are discovering each year on various issues, no one can stay abreast of it all. Trying to act as if I have a well-researched conclusion on all issues is not only humanly impossible, but also an illusion. I'm not willing to play the role of resident expert on every issue."

Millard Erickson gives us a model of someone taking a stance that allows for lack of closure.[1] On the issue of biblical inerrancy Erickson states that he believes the doctrines of God's holiness and God's inspiration of Scripture require a belief that Scripture, correctly interpreted, is without error. However, there are occasional examples within Scripture of statements that seem to be in error. One approach to this problem has been attempts to find resolutions using the linguistic and archeological data we now possess. Many difficulties have been resolved using this approach. However, a few of these attempts have produced explanations that are not very persuasive. Erickson thinks that a better approach is to affirm one's belief in inerrancy, affirm one's faith that as time passes more of the alleged contradictions will be satisfactorily solved, but recognize that, at the present, theologians have not developed satisfactory explanations (satisfactory closure) for every apparent contradiction. Perhaps a biblical scholar of the stature of Erickson saying that he has lack of closure on certain biblical texts can help us all have the courage and honesty to do likewise in our respective fields.

A LOOK AT DOGMATISM

Let us define what we mean by dogmatism. People are dogmatic when they selectively accept data that supports their position, reject data to the contrary despite the data's quality, and support their position with a confidence that is not proportional to the evidence supporting it. Nondogmatic people would be those who carefully review all data presented on an issue, only accepting that which is valid despite the position it supports, and who discuss a position with a confidence that is proportional to the evidence supporting it.

On a dogmatism scale from one to ten, probably few of us are ones or tens. However, there are probably more Christians who are in the upper half of this spectrum than we would wish. What causes Christians to be dogmatic? Are there things we could do within ourselves and within our social system so that we do not unwittingly encourage dogmatism?

Sometimes dogmatism may be a cover for fear. In a Sunday school class in an evangelical church recently a lay teacher was teaching on eschatology (the study of end times). During his lesson he said, without basing his conclusion on supporting evidence, that anyone who did not believe in the pretribulation rapture was demon-possessed. (What logical fallacy was this?)

This was abnormal behavior for this teacher. (This particular behavior was a ten on the dogmatic scale, while in general this person usually operated in the six to seven range.) The only plausible explanation that those who knew this person could make was that the thought that believers might experience some or all the Tribulation was so frightening to this person that it triggered an atypical outburst of dogmatism.

Sometimes dogmatism may be a learned habit. We may have had models (parental, pastoral, or theological) who spoke their opinions with high levels of certainty. We may unconsciously have interpreted that to mean that when we grow up and become leaders, we should do likewise.

Sometimes dogmatism may be a response to role expectations (this overlaps with the previous factor). In many conservative churches there seems almost an expectation that those who fill leadership roles should have clearly-defined opinions supportive of the denomination and be able to defend those opinions aggressively. Thus, as people mature and are asked to fill leadership positions, they may unconsciously feel the expectation to become more dogmatic. I believe this role expectation is more frequently present in conservative denominations than in liberal ones.

Sometimes dogmatism may be unwittingly reinforced because it "preaches well" in certain congregations. It is not uncommon for conservative ministers, from time to time, to have a stream of eloquent fervor within their sermon. This may be reinforced (rewarded) by increased numbers of "Amens!" and other affirming responses from the congregation. If several of these streams of eloquent fervor occur in one sermon, congregation members may describe the pastor as especially "anointed" during the sermon.

There are times when a pastor or Sunday school teacher does speak fervently and eloquently about a particular topic, and affirmation may be very appropriate. However, as I have experienced in various conservative congregations, I believe that those people most likely to say "Amen" often unwittingly reinforce dogmatic rather than thoughtful deliveries of sermons and lessons. Our pastors and teachers are human. If we reinforce dogmatic deliveries and sit quietly through thoughtful deliveries, we should not think it strange if the incidence of dogmatic deliveries increases.

I believe there is a mistaken belief in many conservative Christians' minds that a good sermon is one that the pastor delivers forcefully. We confuse volume and eloquence for depth and accuracy. Yet anyone who has ever heard an excellent Bible expositor such as John Stott knows that if a speaker, through careful preparation, helps an audience truly understand the meaning of a biblical passage and then thoughtfully apply it to twentieth-century living, that homiletical pyrotechnics are unnecessary and even distractive. Perhaps we need to encourage our pastors and Sunday school teachers more for thoughtful, careful preparation and delivery and less for dogmatic, forceful ones.

DEALING WITH NEW PREMISES OR CONCLUSIONS

What should we do when we are presented with new data, premises, or conclusions? What should be our epistemological process? If we want to apply what we have learned in this book, how should we go about it? Figure 9-3 presents one such way.[2]

We obviously do not need to use the entire model for each new proposition we encounter. Some ideas will be so obviously inaccurate that we reject them after finding that they are not compatible with reality (second step). However, we may be aware that in a specific area our subjective reality significantly differs from that of most other persons (for example, we may have a blind spot or undue sensitivity or rigidity). In that event we may want to continue to consider ideas within that specific area rather than rejecting them without further consideration.

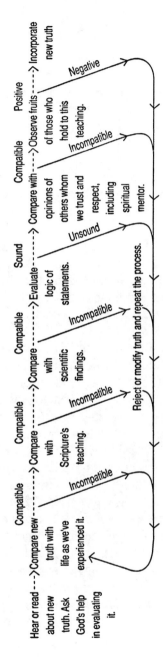

FIGURE 9-3. A model for dealing with new premises or conclusions.

We also may not go through all the steps if the idea seems sound, but is not significant enough to merit that amount of time and effort. Here we may go only through the second and third steps, accept it tentatively as true if it passes both these tests, and tentatively reject it as untrue if it fails to pass one or both.

The sixth step (comparing the proposition with the opinions of others whom we trust and respect, including our spiritual mentor) needs a word of elaboration. Mentors, both spiritual and otherwise, can often make us aware of new data that we had not considered before, especially if they are specialists in the area in which the new truth resides. To use input from others effectively, we should always ask them for the reasons (data or premises) on which they base their conclusions, and not just for their conclusions. In this way we have an opportunity to evaluate whether the data justifies their conclusions.

If one is married, one's spouse can often be a good consultant, and should always be consulted if incorporating the new truth is going to affect his or her life significantly. Particularly if one has had a history of impulsive decisions that have not turned out well, taking time to listen to mentors and consultants is very important. "In the multitude of counsellors there is safety" (Prov. 11:14 KJV).

What if a new proposition has passed all the previous tests and we are certain of those results, but one or more of our mentors or consultants disagree (step 6)? In that event I believe we should ask God's wisdom about moving forward on this new truth even if our mentors do not agree. Martin Luther would never have written his *Ninety-five Theses* had he not had the courage to confront his spiritual mentors when he believed they had departed from the true teachings of Scripture. Note though, that he did this only after he was thoroughly convinced that his spiritual leaders' teachings were at variance with Scripture. This was not simply a difference based on personal opinion or personal preferences.

The seventh step (observe the fruits of those who hold to this teaching) could be misinterpreted and misused. From earlier chapters you are aware of the fallacy of *ad hominem* arguments. The validity of an idea is not related to the character of the person or persons who champion it. Throughout Scripture and church history are many examples of believers who made significant contributions to the Christian faith in one area and made errors in other areas of their thinking or Christian life. We should only use the criterion of "fruit inspection" in considering the validity of an idea when it can be shown that there is a direct relationship between the idea and the fruit. If not, fruit inspection of the originator's life is not a valid criterion for judging the validity or invalidity of an idea. Even scoundrels come up with good ideas now and then, and all brilliant and morally upstanding men and women have their blind spots and vulnerabilities.

There may be occasional situations where, after going through all the steps in the above model, the wisest course may be to suspend making a decision, not to bring closure at this time because no proposal adequately accounts for all the data. In situations like this a goodness-of-fit criterion may be useful. This approach asks, "Which of the available hypotheses best accounts for the data we have?" That hypothesis may be used as a tentative explanation, with a recognition that it does not explain all the data, until someone develops a better hypothesis.

MY HOPES

In writing this book I have had the twin hopes that it could contribute to the process of Christians, especially evangelical Christians, becoming more known for their willingness to consider new information, and at the same time help them be better able objectively to critique the validity of that new information. We have looked at the critical thinking skills necessary to become a discerning thinker, a wise consumer of the ideas that constantly bombard us. To learn the names of these skills takes only a few weeks. To learn to use those skills effectively in checking one's own thinking and that of others takes much longer. To learn them and, in addition, learn the relationship skills necessary to help someone else see an error in his or her thinking without feeling personally attacked by us may take the better part of a lifetime. I hope this is a book that you will consult regularly in the coming years. Summaries of topics we have covered are included in the appendices for easy reference.

We have also looked at some reasons we as human beings sometimes have difficulty being open to new information, especially new information that conflicts with our present assumptions. I hope you now have some tools to help you deal with the subconscious self-talk that causes discomfort when you encounter new information that conflicts with your past assumptions.

Surely we have a theological basis for becoming known as open-minded scientists and professionals and laypersons. The God of the Word and the Creator-God of this world are one. The truths that He gives us through these two avenues will surely fit together if we continue to study them open-mindedly. But we must not let our personal worth become too attached to one theory, for then we become invested in protecting our reputation rather than in pursuing truth.

AN IMPORTANT DECISION

With critical thinking skills we have the potential to become professional critics or significant contributors. There are advantages and disadvantages to becoming either one. A few people choose, probably unconsciously, to become professional critics. By mastering the skills in this book it is possible to find something wrong with almost any idea, proposal, or human activity (including every sermon and church activity). The critic never has to put himself or herself on the line to be critiqued by others because he or she lets others take those risks. Thus they are relatively safe.

Professional critics can come out of their safety zones when they choose and wound or undermine those who are attempting to make a contribution. Many of their critiques will be valid—there will be an element of truth in them. The critic sometimes has the satisfaction of showing people their errors, and some of these people will have made errors, occasionally significant ones. Critics may have times of popularity, especially when they train their critical thinking skills on unpopular ideas or people, although much of the time few people will want to become close friends with them.

Another way to use these critical thinking skills is by trying to make a positive contribution to our world. We should be able, by using these skills, to be better pastors, Sunday school teachers, group leaders, group members, parents, supervisors, employers, or employees. We can make better proposals because we understand, better than most, the threats to validity that come from various sources. That does not mean that our proposals will be immune to criticism. Criticism, feedback, modification of proposals are part of being actively involved in life. Especially if our life is blessed with someone who has chosen to fill the role of professional critic, we, our ideas, and our methods will not escape criticism.

I hope you will choose to use your skills proactively to be a contributor. There are so many tasks that can benefit from concerned, committed, thoughtful Christians using their skills to help bring about God's kingdom here on earth. If you do make that commitment and follow through with it in God's strength, you will experience the fulfillment of knowing you've made a positive difference in your world.

Notes

CHAPTER 1

1. I am intentionally not including the names of those who commit the hermeneutical, statistical, or logical errors mentioned here in the text. My purpose is not to criticize specific people, but to teach readers to identify errors and fallacies.

2. "Family Life," *American Institute of Family Relations*, Jan. 1970, 7–8.

3. Shere Hite, *Women and Love: A Cultural Revolution in Progress* (New York: Alfred Knopf, 1987).

4. Andrew Greeley, "Faithful Attraction," *Good Housekeeping*, June 1990, 132–137.

5. The arguments given in the following paragraphs are not intended to be comprehensive or rigorous enough to convince a committed philosophical skeptic to change his mind on this issue. The arguments are intended to help the typical Christian affirm that the senses that God has created and placed within our bodies usually give us accurate and reliable information about ourselves and our surroundings.

The perceptual skeptic often takes the position that we cannot know that our sensory perceptions convey an accurate sense of reality. Our perceptions may be only illusions. It can be an interesting exercise to ask the perceptual skeptic about the discrepancy between what he says he believes and his behavior. Every perceptual skeptic I know of eats when he feels the sensation of hunger, drinks when he feels the sensation of thirst, and walks and converses with others *as if* his perceptions conveyed an accurate sense of reality. This is hardly consistent with his assertion that one cannot be certain that one's perceptions are anything more than illusions.

CHAPTER 2

1. Portions of chapters 2 and 3 are taken from or adapted from my full-length book on the subject, *Hermeneutics: Principles and Processes of Biblical Interpretation* (Grand Rapids: Baker, 1981). Used with permission of Baker Book House.

2. W. C. Kaiser, Jr., *Toward an Exegetical Theology* (Grand Rapids: Baker, 1981), 69–70.

3. Alexander Carson, *Examination of the Principles of Biblical Interpretation.* Cited in Ramm, *Protestant Biblical Interpretation,* x–xi.

4. Bernard Ramm, *Protestant Biblical Interpretation,* 3rd. rev. ed. (Grand Rapids: Baker, 1970), 136.

CHAPTER 3

1. Portions of this chapter are summarized from a more extensive treatment of the same topic in my book *Hermeneutics: Principles and Processes of Biblical Interpretation* (Grand Rapids: Baker, 1981). Used with permission of Baker Book House.

2. Lewis Sperry Chafer, *Dispensationalism* (Dallas: Dallas Seminary Press, 1951).

3. C. I. Scofield, *Rightly Dividing the Word of Truth* (Findlay, Ohio: Dunham, 1956).

4. John W. Bowman, "The Bible and Modern Religions, II: Dispensationalism," *Interpretation* 10 Apr. 1956: 172.

5. *Scofield Reference Bible* (New York: Oxford University Press, 1917), 5.

6. Charles C. Ryrie, *Dispensationalism Today* (Chicago: Moody Press, 1965), 57–64.

7. *Scofield Reference Bible* (Note accompanying John 1:17).

8. Ryrie, *op. cit.*, 123.

9. See H. P. Hook, "Dispensation," in *Zondervan Pictorial Encyclopedia of the Bible,* edited by Merrill Tenney (Grand Rapids: Zondervan, 1975),

vol. 2, 144 for an example of someone who believes that commands from one dispensation may apply to those in later dispensations. See Charles C. Cook, *God's Book Speaking for Itself* (New York: Doran, 1924), 31 for an example of someone who believes that commands from one dispensation have no application to those in later dispensations.

10. Louis Berkhof, *Systematic Theology*, 4th. rev. ed. (Grand Rapids: Eerdmans, 1941), 211–218, 265–271.

11. Walter C. Kaiser, Jr., *Toward an Old Testament Theology* (Grand Rapids: Zondervan, 1978), 14.

12. E. D. Hirsch, *Validity in Interpretation* (New Haven: Yale University Press, 1967), 70.

13. *Toward an Exegetical Theology* (Grand Rapids: Baker, 1981).

14. D. A. Carson, *Expositor's Bible Commentary* (Grand Rapids: Zondervan, 1984), vol. 8, 302–303.

15. Ibid., 303.

16. This is probably the same point intended by D. A. Carson when he said, "Most generalized conclusions about parables require painful exceptions; and on the whole it is best to deal inductively with parables...." (*Expositor's Bible Commentary*, vol. 8, 303).

17. The main ideas and some of the phraseology of these last two paragraphs were taken from R. C. Sproul, "Controversy at Culture Gap," *Eternity*, May 1976, 40. Sproul's discussion refers to a related, but slightly different issue.

CHAPTER 4

1. The definitions and examples in these four paragraphs are from Vincent Barry and Douglas Soccio, *Practical Logic: Third Edition* (New York: Holt, Rinehart and Winston, 1988), 121–126.

2. The first seven of these threats to internal validity are discussed in Schuyler Huck, William Cormier, and William Bounds in *Reading Statistics and Research* (New York: Harper & Row, 1974), 226–241. Some of the wording of these first seven threats was adapted from their book.

3. R. Rosenthal and K. L. Fode, "Psychology of the Scientist: Three Experiments in Experimenter Bias," *Psychological Reprints*, 1963, vol. 12, 491–511.

4. R. Rosenthal, "On the Social Psychology of the Psychological Experiment: The Experimenter's Hypothesis as Unintended Determinant of Experimental Results," *American Scientist*, 1963, vol. 51, 268–283.

5. R. Rosenthal and K. L. Fode, "The Effect of Experimenter Bias on the Performance of the Albino Rat," *Behavioral Science*, 1963, vol. 8, 183–189.

6. R. Rosenthal, G. W. Persinger, Vikan-Kline, L. Linda and R. C. Mulry, "The Role of the Research Assistant in the Mediation of Experimenter Bias," *Journal of Personality*, 1963, vol. 31, 313–335.

7. D. Rosenhan, "On the Social Psychology of Hypnosis Research," in J. E. Gordon, ed., *Handbook of Clinical and Experimental Hypnosis*, (New York: Macmillan, 1967), 495–496.

8. M. T. Orne, "The Nature of Hypnosis Artifact and Essence," In R. E. Shor and M. T. Orne, eds., *The Nature of Hypnosis: Selected Basic Readings* (New York: Holt, Rinehart & Winston, 1965).

9. D. Rosenhan, "On the Social Psychology of Hypnosis Research," in J. E. Gordon, ed., *Handbook of Clinical and Experimental Hypnosis* (New York: Macmillan, 1967).

10. M. T. Orne, *op. cit.*, 99–100.

11. Cited in Orne.

12. Orne, 1965.

13. For a fascinating illustration of this see D. Rosenhan, "On the Social Psychology of Hypnosis Research," in J. E. Gordon, ed., *Handbook of Clinical and Experimental Hypnosis*. (New York: Macmillan, 1967).

14. Reported by Linda Van Tuyl, RN, MSN, Neurobehavior Research Coordinator at Emory University School of Medicine, Atlanta, Georgia, 1991.

15. Stanley Milgram, "Behavioral Study of Obedience," *Journal of Abnormal and Social Psychology*, 1963, vol. 67, 371–378. This description of the experiment is adapted from Henry Lindgren, *An Introduction to Social Psychology* (New York: John Wiley and Sons, 1969), 341–342.

16. M. T. Orne and F. J. Evans, "Social Control in the Psychological Experiment," *Journal of Personality and Social Psychology*, 1965, vol. 1, 189–200.

17. M. T. Orne, "On the Social Psychology of the Psychological Experiment: With Particular Reference to Demand Characteristics and Their Implications," *American Psychologist*, 1962, vol. 17, 776–783.

18. D. Goleman, "A Conversation with Ulric Neisser," *Psychology Today*, vol. 17, no. 5, 1983, 62.

19. K. Farnsworth, *Whole-Hearted Integration: Harmonizing Psychology and Christianity Through Word and Deed* (Grand Rapids: Baker,

1985). A. Georgi, *Psychology as a Human Science: A Phenomenologically-Based Approach* (New York: Harper & Row, 1970). M. Merleau-Ponty, "What Is Phenomenology?" trans. Colin Smith, in *Phenomenology of Religion: Eight Modern Descriptions of the Essence of Religion*, J. D. Bettis (New York: Harper & Row, 1969), 13–30. D. Kruger, ed., *An Introduction to Phenomenological Psychology* (Pittsburgh: Duquesne University, 1981).

20. Many of the ideas in this section of the chapter are based on the discussion of Huck, Cormier, and Bounds, *op. cit.* 223–330, and D. Ary, L. C. Jacobs, and A. Razavieh, *Introduction to Research in Education*, 4th ed. (Chicago: Holt, Rinehart, and Winston, 1990), 322–324.

21. D. T. Campbell and J. C. Stanley, "Experimental and quasi-experimental designs for research on teaching," in N. L. Gage, ed., *Handbook of Research on Teaching* (Chicago: Rand McNally, 1963), 171–246, and Ary, Jacobs, and Razavieh, *op. cit.*, 324–330.

22. Huck, Cormier, and Bounds, 253, *op. cit.*, and Ary, Jacobs, and Razavieh, *op. cit.*, 336–341.

23. Huck, Cormier, and Bounds, *op. cit.*, 319.

CHAPTER 5

1. Madsen Pirie, *The Book of the Fallacy: A Training Manual for Intellectual Subversives* (London: Routledge and Kegan Paul, 1985), 72.

2. Runyon, *op. cit.*, 27.

3. Mark Twain, *Life on the Mississippi* (New York: Harper & Row, 1896).

4. Runyon, *op. cit.*, vii.

5. The following definitions and examples of various correlations are from Schuyler Huck, William Cormier, and William Bounds, *Reading Statistics and Research* (New York: Harper & Row, 1974), 30–36.

6. Darrell Huff, *How to Lie with Statistics* (New York: Norton, 1982), 98–99.

7. Ibid., 74.

8. These six methods are from Runyon, *op. cit.*, 37–47.

9. Huff, *op. cit.*, 19, 26.

10. Ibid, 19.

11. Huck, Cormier, and Bounds, *op. cit.*, 196–197.

12. The following threats to external validity are from Donald T. Campbell and Julian C. Stanley, *Experimental and Quasi-Experimental Designs for Research* (Chicago: Rand McNally College Publishing, 1963), 5–6, and Huck, Cormier, and Bounds, *op. cit.*, 259–267.

13. For further information, see Robert Rosenthal, *Experimental Effect in Behavioral Research* (New York: Appleton-Century-Crofts, 1966) or T. X. Barber, "Pitfalls in Research: Nine Investigator and Experimenter Effects," in R. M. W. Travers, ed., *Second Handbook of Research on Teaching* (Chicago: Rand McNally, 1973).

CHAPTER 6

1. Morris R. Engel and Ernest Nagel, *Logic and Scientific Method*, cited in Stuart Chase, *Guides to Straight Thinking: With 13 Common Fallacies* (New York: Harper & Row, 1956), 1.

2. Irving M. Copi, *Introduction to Logic* (New York: Macmillan, 1986), vii.

3. Ibid., 3–4.

4. Ibid., 28.

5. Vincent E. Barry and Douglas J. Soccio, *Practical Logic: Third Edition* (New York: Holt, Rinehart, and Winston, 1988), 323–328.

6. Chase, *op. cit.*, 13.

7. Copi, *op. cit.*, 90.

8. Chase, *op. cit.*, 39–150.

9. Barry and Soccio, *op. cit.*, 74–279.

10. W. Ward Fearnside and William B. Holther, *Fallacy: The Counterfeit of Argument* (Englewood, N.J.: Prentice-Hall, 1959).

11. Madsen Pirie, *The Book of the Fallacy: A Training Manual for Intellectual Subversives* (London: Routledge and Kegan Paul, 1985).

12. David Hackett Fischer, *Historian's Fallacies* (New York: Harper & Row, 1970).

13. Cited in Copi, 89.

14. Engel, 84. Copi, 116.

15. Copi, 92.

16. Cited in Chase, 60.

17. Pirie, 92.

18. Cited in Chase, 59.

19. From Engel, 81–83.

20. Pirie, 176–177.

21. Chase, 96. It is true that a writer may attempt to make a questionable thesis look more credible by overuse of footnotes. However, another use of extensive footnotes is to give credit to those whose thoughts the author has used or has built upon. The first is an abuse of footnotes, the latter an appropriate use.

22. Pirie, 40.

23. Pirie, 16–17.

24. Richard Whately, *Elements of Logic* (London, 1826), cited in Copi, 101.

25. Engel, 114–115.

26. Barry and Soccio, 84.

27. Copi, 120.

28. Engel, 90–91.

29. Copi, 113–114.

30. Cited in Chase, 126. Taken from *Reader's Digest* (October, 1934).

31. Chase, 87.

CHAPTER 7

1. Cited in Barry and Soccio, 101.

2. Ibid.

3. Copi, 103–104.

4. Runyon, 35.

5. Barry and Soccio, 246.

6. Pirie, 133–134. Barry and Soccio, 95.

7. Copi, 94.

8. Darrell Huff, *How to Lie with Statistics* (New York: Norton, 1982). Cited in Chase, 99.

9. Chase, 71.

10. Pirie, 43.

11. Chase, 78.

12. Adapted from Chase, 65.

13. Cited in Engel, 140.

14. Cited and adapted from Engel, 149.

15. Cited in Copi, 105.

16. Submitted by Mrs. F. M., Myrtle Beach, S.C. to the *Charlotte Observer*. Cited in Copi, 125.

17. Cited in Engel, 199.

CHAPTER 8

1. Barry and Soccio, 77.

2. Mark and Patti Virkler, *Communion with God: Student's Study Manual* (Shippensburg, Pa.: Destiny Image Publishers, 1990). There are

occasions where I do differ with Mark and Patti regarding interpretation of a Scripture, a specific psychological finding, or a line of reasoning. However, I believe that the method they are encouraging Christians to use in their prayer life is not significantly affected by differences of biblical interpretation, psychology or logic we might have.

3. Adapted from Mark and Patti Virkler, 42.

4. Ibid, 116.

5. The book *Communion with God: Student's Study Manual* by Mark and Patti Virkler can be special ordered through any Christian bookstore, or directly from the publishers (Destiny Image Publishers, P.O. Box 351, Shippensburg, Pa. 17257) or from Communion with God Ministries, 1431 Bullis Road, Elma, New York 14059. For the latter two addresses, include a check for $13.95 and $2.50 to cover shipping and handling costs.

CHAPTER 9

1. Millard J. Erickson, *Christian Theology* (Grand Rapids: Baker, 1985), 231–233.

2. Part of this model came from discussions with Mark Virkler, personal communication, December 23, 1990.

Answers to Exercises

I have given suggested answers to the exercises below. You may, on occasion, disagree with them. It is more important that you use these exercises to help you develop your skills than that you agree with each suggested answer.

EXERCISES: CHAPTER TWO

EX 1: Tunky 1 read a phrase from your letter that said "Please give your wife my regards" and stated, "I think this means that he misses his teddy bear." You object to his interpretation. Why?

The reason you object is that most of us hold an unconscious belief that the meaning of a statement is what the author intended it to mean. The listener cannot just apply his creative imagination to the speaker's words, insert any meaning he wants, and claim validity for his interpretation.

This belief recognizes that some people are more effective communicators than others, that is, we can understand their intended meaning more easily. When listening to poor communicators we have to work harder to understand their intended meaning. The more gaps there are between us and a speaker (historical, cultural, linguistic, and philosophical), the more effort we must make to enter the speaker's frame of reference and understand what he or she is trying to say.

Some contemporary writers have argued that the meaning of a text is what it means to the interpreter. If we accept their argument, Scripture could have as many possible meanings as it does readers. Some people assert that the meaning of a text is what it means to the reader. If we accept their assertion, we have no basis for differentiating orthodox interpretations of God's Word from heretical ones (every interpretation would be equally valid). The principle of interpretation that underlies orthodox Christian theology is that the meaning of the biblical text is what God, the author, intended it to mean.

There is a method frequently used in Sunday school classes and group Bible studies that contradicts the hermeneutical principle just mentioned. This is the practice of reading a passage of Scripture and asking "What does this mean to you?" The floor is then open for whatever creative inspirations come to participants' minds.

A better method, using good hermeneutics, would be to ask that question as two questions. The first question would be: "What do you think God intended to say as He spoke these words to these people?" After discussing the first question, the second question would be: "How does that meaning apply to us today?" Thus, our questions underscore the hermeneutical principle that there is one valid meaning (God's intended meaning). However, His meaning can have multiple applications in the lives of different group members and cultures.

Some might object that the author sometimes has a double intended meaning, as in allegories like *Gulliver's Travels* or *Pilgrim's Progress*. Certain jokes, like the following one, convey their humor by using a word that suggests an intended meaning, and then, as the conversation progresses, suggests another meaning.

> Peggy: "I caught my boyfriend flirting."
> Sharon: "Yes, that's the way I caught mine, too."

These examples point up the fact that they are exceptions to normal communication. Allegories and puns are interesting (or funny) because they are unusual. The principle of trying to discern the author's intended meaning holds true when interpreting allegories and puns. If the author intended to communicate on two levels, it is valid to interpret his or her meaning on both levels. If the author intended to communicate on a single level (as is true in most communication), we should interpret his or her meaning accordingly.

EX 2: Discussions of God's will often focus on two ideas. *God's general will* refers to His general moral commands that apply to all believers, (for example, marry only a believer). *God's specific will* refers to what God wants an individual believer to do in a specific situation (e.g., Julie should marry Jim). Does Colossians 3:15 support the idea that *intra*personal peace (peace inside ourselves) is one way of discerning God's specific will?

Historical-Cultural and Contextual Analysis: It appears that Paul wrote the letter to the church at Colossae to combat a heresy that had several diverse parts. Paul does not specify the exact nature of this heresy, but it can be deduced from the points he makes in his letter.

The first two chapters of the letter deal with refuting the theological errors found in this heresy. The third and fourth chapters (where the verse under consideration occurs) deal with practical guidelines for living the Christian life.

1. Read verses 12–15.

2. The context is talking about *inter*personal peace (peace between people), not about *intra*personal peace (peace inside ourselves).

3. Furthermore, Paul is not talking about how to find God's specific will for your life. He is talking about *inter*personal peace as part of God's general will for all Christians (we should all try to live peacefully with each other).

4. Therefore it would be invalid to say that this verse teaches that one way to find God's specific will for your life is whether you feel peace about your decision. Paul is not talking about finding God's specific will for your life in this passage, nor is he talking about intrapersonal peace.

5. This does not mean that intrapersonal peace may not be one way that God guides us, but only that we should not base that belief on this verse.

Hermeneutical principle violated: The person in question did not study how the passage under consideration fits into the flow of the author's argument. If you would like to study this issue further, you may find *Decision-Making and the Will of God* by Garry Friesen worthwhile. His hermeneutics are exceptional, although you may not agree completely with his conclusions.

EX 3: *Historical-cultural and contextual analysis:* This is a section from Jesus' Sermon on the Mount. Jesus was setting up a series of antitheses between the external, ritualistic "righteousness" that the Pharisees were practicing to impress men, and true righteous living that proceeds from a proper interpretation of the Old Testament. He stated that "unless your righteousness surpasses that of the Pharisees and the teachers of the law, you will certainly not enter the kingdom of heaven" (Matt. 5:20).

One area in which this was occurring was in the area of oath-keeping. The Scribes and Pharisees had become experts in casuistry. *Casuistry* involved making clever, petty legal distinctions that determined whether one's oath was binding or not. For example, if one swore by the temple, his oath was not considered binding. If he swore by the *gold* in the temple, he must keep the oath. If he swore by the altar he did not need to keep his oath, but if he swore by the *offering* that was on the altar, he must keep it (see Matt. 23:16–26).

Swearing by heaven or by earth was not binding, nor was swearing *by* Jerusalem, though swearing *toward* Jerusalem was. An entire tract was written on the subject and other rabbinic references suggest that this practice was widespread (see *Expositor's Bible Commentary,* vol. 8, pp. 153–154).

Jesus is condemning this casuistical approach to oath-keeping, and commanding His followers to practice a thorough and consistent honesty in all their dealings. In context He was saying: "Don't make false oaths. Let your word be a simple yes or no, and stick by it." He was not, even by the greatest stretch of our exegetical imaginations, stating that we should express our thoughts and feelings assertively. His teaching focused on dishonesty, not assertiveness.

This does not mean we should not discuss our feelings assertively in certain situations (e.g., Matt. 18:15–16). It does mean that we should not use the words of Jesus in Matthew 5 as the basis for doing so, since He wasn't talking about that subject in Matthew 5.

Hermeneutical principle violated: Understand the cultural circumstances that add meaning to given actions or commands.

EX 4: Does Romans 8:28 mean that if you lose your job, it is because God has a higher-paying one waiting for you?

There are two common misinterpretations of this verse. One is based on the King James Version translation, which says, "All things work together for good to those who love God." This seems almost to be teaching some kind of optimistic pantheism—that there is some force or principle that is working all things out for good. The NIV translation is to be preferred (on both textual and theological grounds): "And we know that in all things God works for the good of those who love him." This does not teach that by themselves all things work together for good, for we all know of situations that have caused people to become bitter, etc. What this does teach is that a caring God becomes involved in all the situations of our lives, helping us to reap good even from the tragedies and unfair situations that come our way.

The second common misinterpretation of this verse centers on the meaning of "good." This Christian, as many others before him, interpreted "good" from his human perspective to mean pleasure, absence of pain, higher salary, etc. "Bad," in his perspective, would mean pain, lower salary, lack of pleasure, etc. However, Paul goes on to describe what he means by good in the following verse. God works in every situation so that every circumstance helps us grow into more Christlikeness (v. 29). Thus sometimes "good" situations (from a human perspective) may be bad for us because they lessen our sense of dependence upon God and our desire to become more like Christ. On the other hand "bad" situations (from a human perspective) may be "good" from God's perspective. These are the times in which our spiritual growth is usually greatest, a fact that is almost universally affirmed by believers.

Hermeneutical principle violated: The believer mentioned in the exercise defined "good" from his perspective rather than understanding the authors' (God's and Paul's) intended meaning. He did not do a contextual analysis to find out their definition.

EX 5: If believers who deliberately sin have no possibility of repentance and forgiveness, heaven will be missing many biblical characters about whom we have read. Abraham deliberately lied, not just once, but twice about Sarah being his sister. Moses struck the rock and criticized the faithless Israelites in deliberate disobedience to God's command. David deliberately sinned by adultery with Bathsheba and by having Uriah murdered. Peter deliberately denied Christ, not just once, but three times.

If there is no possibility of repentance and forgiveness for believers who deliberately sin, most of us also have no hope of heaven. Which of us, when we are truly honest, have not deliberately sinned one or more times since our conversion?

However, a study of the context shows that the author of Hebrews is not talking about all types of sin when he states that "If we sin deliberately after receiving a knowledge of the truth, there remains no sacrifice for sins." Hebrews is an exhortation to Jewish believers who were undergoing severe persecution not to fall back into Judaism and try to be saved by keeping the Law. The immediate context (read vv. 19–39) strongly suggests that the specific sin to which the author is referring is the sin of professing salvation through the shed blood of Christ, and then repudiating that profession. This is a fatal spiritual error because, as Paul says in Galatians 3:11, "No one is justified before God by [keeping] the law."

Thus the author is not saying that if we deliberately sin after receiving salvation we cannot receive forgiveness. What he is saying is that if we profess to receive Christ and salvation through grace, but then deliberately renounce Christ and return to salvation by works, there remains no sacrifice for that sin. For other sins, we have the teaching of 1 John 1:8–9 that though we all sin, God promises forgiveness as we confess our faults.

Hermeneutical principle violated: The person did not look at the context of the whole book of Hebrews as well as the immediate context to understand what sin will not be forgiven.

EX 6: Why should we not encourage an oracular use of Scripture (consulting Scripture as one would an oracle, without studying passages in their context)? Many Christians claim that through this method God has often brought them comfort and guidance.

There are at least three points that can be made in response to this argument:

    1. God sometimes helps believers understand a passage in its

context even if they are not consciously trying to do so. For example, our knowledge of how Middle Eastern shepherds cared for their sheep allows many Christians to understand Psalm 23 and John 10 contextually without conscious effort.

2. People feel a sense of relief when they obtain closure on a problem, that is, when they find some way of making sense of the problem or question they are facing. This sense of relief comes because they have an answer, despite the objective accuracy or inaccuracy of that answer.

An extreme example of this is "psychotic insight." In this condition people who are clearly psychotic (out of touch with reality) feel a sense of relief because they believe that they finally understand why they have been feeling upset (e.g., the CIA was after them and that is who has been making noise outside their house at night and peering in their windows). People feel relief because they now have a way of making sense of their experience, even though the "closure" that they have obtained is clearly incorrect.

Christians who are experiencing trials sometimes open the Bible and interpret the first words they read as God's answer to them. They may feel a sense of relief at finally having a sense of direction about how to proceed, and may interpret this sense of relief as "God's peace." The reality is that what they have interpreted as God's peace following their oracular use of Scripture may not be God's peace at all. It may be the psychological relief of having closure on their problem of not knowing how to proceed.

3. Paul commands Timothy, and through him all of us, to "Do your best to present yourself to God as one approved, a workman who does not need to be ashamed and who correctly handles the word of truth" (2 Tim. 2:15). Therefore we should not handle the word of truth haphazardly, as the oracular method does, but carefully and thoughtfully.

EX 7: Most people assume that the girl spoken of in Matthew 9:18–26 was dead, but there is some reason to believe that she was comatose rather than dead.

(a) What facts would you look at in attempting to answer this question?

(1) Parallel passages
(2) The words "sleeping" and "dead"
(3) The words "her spirit returned to her"
(4) The words "she shall be healed"

(b) This is a good exercise for developing hermeneutical skills. It is not necessary to be dogmatic on either side. Whether Jesus raised the little girl from a coma or from death, the event is still a miracle of healing and compassion. I take the minority viewpoint that she was comatose rather than dead for the following reasons:

Arguments for Being Dead	*Arguments for Being Comatose*
The messengers said she was dead.	Death versus deep coma was difficult to distinguish before modern times. Jesus said she wasn't dead but only asleep.
Jews of Jesus' time sometimes used "sleep" as a metaphor for death.	When the biblical writers used "sleep" as a metaphor for death, they usually used *koimao* rather than *katheudo*.
Jesus used sleep as a metaphor for death regarding Lazarus (John 11).	When the disciples misunderstood Jesus' use of the word "sleep" in John 11, He corrected them and said Lazarus was not sleeping, but was dead. Here He said, she's not dead, but only sleeping.
The messengers laughed at Jesus, *knowing* that she was dead (Luke 8:53).	Knowing *(oida)* means "perceiving." This is a phenomenological (how it appeared to man) rather than a noumenological (how it appeared to God) description.
Her spirit returned, showing that she must have been dead.	*Pneuma*, translated spirit, can also mean breath. This could mean that her breath returned, i.e., she began breathing visibly again.

When Jesus said "She isn't dead," He could have meant "She isn't permanently dead."	Jesus didn't say: "She's temporarily dead, but I will raise her." He said: "She isn't dead."
	Sodzo meant to heal physically or spiritually. When used of physical healing it always meant either: (1) to restore something that is diseased, or (2) to save someone from dying. It never meant to bring someone back from death. *Sodzo* is the Greek word that describes what Jesus did to the little girl.

EX 8: *Historical-cultural analysis:* Paul probably wrote the book of Ephesians to a group of churches located near Ephesus during his two-year imprisonment in Rome. The first half of the book is doctrinal in nature, affirming and describing God's great redemptive plan. The second half includes practical exhortations regarding how believers, called out from the world, are to conduct their lives. Ephesians 4 is in this second section.

Contextual Analysis: Paul is drawing a sharp contrast between how the Gentiles live in sensual indulgence and spiritual darkness and how the Ephesian believers should live (vv. 17–21). He tells them that they are to put off the old self and put on the new (vv. 22–24). Paul is then going to describe several specific ways in which they can do this:

Old Nature	*New Nature*
Put away falsehood.	Let everyone speak truth (v. 25).
In your anger do not sin.	Do not let the sun go down while you are still angry, and do not give the devil a foothold (vv. 26–27).
Let the thief no longer steal.	He should be involved in honest, useful work (v. 28).
Don't let unwholesome words come out of your mouths.	But only what is good for building others up spiritually (v. 29).

Don't grieve the Holy Spirit.	With whom you were sealed until the day of redemption (v. 30).
Get rid of all bitterness, rage and anger, brawling and slander, with every form of malice.	Be kind and compassionate to one another, forgiving each other, just as in Christ God forgave you.

Thus the context suggests very strongly that Paul was not condoning human anger in verse 26. He was saying that anger, along with other manifestations of the old nature such as lying, stealing, evil-speaking, grieving the Holy Spirit, should no longer be part of the believer's life-style. He reinforces this in verses 30–32, where he covers the entire spectrum of angry emotions, and then says that these emotions should be put away (see below).

Lexical-syntactical analysis: Paul commands the Ephesian believers to put away all the following (v. 31):

> *thumos*—the outburst of anger
> *orge*—the settled emotion of anger
> *krauge*—clamor, self-asserting anger that makes sure everyone hears the grievance (aimed at the grievance)
> *pikria*—bitter feelings
> *blasphemia*—slanderous, abusive speech (aimed at the person with whom one is angry)
> *pasa kakis*—all other forms of evil, malice, or bad feelings not included above.

Because of the contextual analysis of the verses immediately surrounding verse 26 and verses 31–32, most expositors now agree that 4:26 should be translated as a permissive imperative (When you are angry do not sin) rather than a regular imperative (Be angry).

Thus, based on both a contextual and a lexical-syntactical analysis it is difficult to escape the conclusion that here Paul is saying that human anger is to be put away as part of the old nature. He did not intend this verse to be used as a justification for human anger, as some Bible commentators and some Christian psychologists have done. This doesn't mean that human anger is never righteous, but that we should not base such a belief or argument on Ephesians 4.

One further note: Ephesians 4:26 is often cross-referenced to

Psalm 4:4. This probably should be considered a verbal parallel rather than a real parallel. Although the words used are similar, the context shows that the authors are discussing different topics. In Ephesians 4, as we have seen, Paul is talking about putting off human anger as part of putting off our old nature. In Psalm 4 the psalmist is urging believers not to become exasperated or angry because some are turning away from God to worship idols (v. 2). They should continue to place their trust in the true God (vv. 3–5).

EX 9: What does 2 Corinthians 7:10 teach us about the meaning of godly guilt versus worldly guilt?

The characteristics of godly grief or godly guilt (*lupe*) are:

1. It is real grief, not some humanistic watered-down version of disappointment with oneself. *Lupe* means severe emotional or physical pain, as in the pain of childbirth (before anesthetics), or in the pain that Christ suffered before His death (Matt. 26:37, 38).

2. Godly grief, in contrast to worldly grief, produces repentance toward God and leads to reconciliation with Him through repentant actions (2 Cor. 7:9, 11).

3. Worldly grief uses the same word for grief (*lupe*) as does godly grief, so the intensity of the painful feelings is not the key difference. What is lacking in worldly guilt is that the person does not use those painful feelings to motivate him or her to a change in behavior.

4. A thorough understanding of the activity of conscience and guilt would, of course, have to include a discussion of several other passages. General conclusions should not be based on this passage alone.

EX 10: Does the word *yom* as used in the first chapter of Genesis mandate that we teach that the world was created in six twenty-four-hour days?

The Hebrew word *yom* has five possible denotations. It can denote (1) the period of light (as contrasted with the period of darkness), (2) the period of twenty-four hours, (3) a general vague "time," (4) a point of time, and (5) a year (*Theological Wordbook of the Old Testament*, pp.370–371).

In the first two chapters of Genesis, Moses uses it with the first three of these denotations:

In Genesis 1:5 (a) and 1:14 (a) it means "daylight as opposed to nighttime." In Genesis 1:14b it means "a twenty-four-hour period." In Genesis 2:4 it means "an extended period," as when we speak of "the day of the horse and buggy."

Genesis 2:1–4 reads:

> Thus the heavens and the earth were completed, and all their hosts. And by the seventh day God completed His work which He had done; and He rested on the seventh day from all His work which He had done. Then God blessed the seventh day and sanctified it, because in it He rested from all His work which God had created and made. This is the account of the heavens and the earth when they were created, in the day that the LORD God made earth and heaven (NASB).

[Notice in the last sentence that Moses uses the word *yom* for the extended period that covered the entire creation sequence.]

From the variety of ways Moses used *yom* in these first two chapters of Genesis we are not warranted in insisting that God created the world in six twenty-four-hour periods. It could have been that Moses intended the word to be understood so. He also could have intended to teach that God created the world in six creative epochs of unspecified duration (see *NIV Study Bible* concerning this text or *Theological Wordbook of the Old Testament*, p. 371).

Since the word *yom* can legitimately be interpreted to mean either "six twenty-four-hour days" or "six periods of time of unspecified duration" (the day-age theory), how do we decide which is likely to be the more accurate interpretation? One way to answer this is to apply the "goodness-of-fit" approach, i.e., which possibility best fits with other data that we have available to us?

One argument that suggests that these were longer than twenty-four-hour days is the biblical record of the events that occurred on the sixth day. On this day God created all the species of land animals except the birds (Gen. 1:24–25). He then created man and gave him dominion over all the animals (vv. 26–30). God planted a garden for Adam and caused all kinds of trees to grow in it (2:8–14). He then gave Adam instructions about what he could and could not do in the garden (vv. 15–17).

On this "day" God also brought all the animals and all the birds to

Adam and had him name them. Since the Hebrew practice of naming involved studying something's character and giving it a name based on that character, it is likely that Adam spent considerable time studying and naming all the species of birds and animals that God had created.

After these events had all transpired, it became evident that none of the created animals was a suitable helper for Adam (v. 20). (We don't know how long it took for Adam to become aware of this fact: God obviously knew it before Creation.) When Adam developed this awareness, either through experience or through God telling him, God put Adam under divine anaesthesia, did some major surgery, and created Eve. After Adam woke up God performed the first marriage ceremony.

These events could have happened in the space of fourteen hours (one twenty-four-hour day minus time for sleeping and major surgery), but it seems likely that they required more time. If we allow that the sixth *yom* was probably not a twenty-four-hour period, we no longer need to insist that the other five *yoms* were also twenty-four-hour periods.

Hermeneutical principle violated: A dogmatic stance on this issue fails to recognize the variety of ways the Genesis author used the word *yom.*

EXERCISES: CHAPTER 3

EX 11: *Historical-cultural analysis:* In the Old Testament loans were charitable, not commercial. They were given to tide a peasant farmer through a time of financial difficulty. Taking out a loan was not forbidden. What was forbidden was an Old Testament Israelite extracting interest from his poverty-stricken brother (interest rates of 25 percent to 33 percent annually were not uncommon in the times and surrounding cultures of the Old Testament). Since the extracting of interest was forbidden, the allowable loans were charitable, not commercial. The taking out of a loan was not forbidden.

This idea of charitable loans continued into New Testament times. In Matthew 5:42 Jesus commands his followers, "Give to the one who asks you, and do not turn away from the one who wants to borrow from you." If the taking out of any kind of loan was a sin, Jesus' command here would have been encouraging His followers to allow others to sin by allowing them to borrow from them.

In New Testament times the growing commercial economy introduced the idea of loans as an investment to earn income (e.g., Matt. 25:27 and Luke 19:23). When people made loans for commercial purposes, Jesus did not prohibit taking interest. This is implicit in His parable of the three servants. If the taking of interest was sinful, Jesus probably would not have upbraided the lazy servant by saying that at the very least he should have deposited his talent with the bankers, so that when the Master returned he would have received the principal back with interest.

Contextual Analysis: Paul is talking about the application of the Golden Rule in civil and personal relationships. We are to pay taxes because those who govern give their full time to governing. Therefore we are to give them the respect and taxes they deserve as God's servants in maintaining a peaceful and law-abiding society (vv. 1–7).

Likewise if we take out loans from someone else, we are not to let any debt remain outstanding (we are not to defraud others by failing to repay our debts), since this shows a failure to love others as ourself.

Lexical-syntactical analysis: Opheilo could mean either "Don't owe anyone anything" or "Let no debt remain outstanding (unpaid)." The NIV translators have opted for this second denotation because the taking out of commercial or charitable loans was not forbidden in the Old or New Testaments, and because there is nothing about the taking out of a loan that would contradict the Golden Rule, unless the debtor fails to repay the loan as promised.

Theological analysis: Proverbs 22:7 states: "The rich rule over the poor, and the borrower is servant to the lender." This proverb does not say that there is anything immoral about taking out a loan, but only that when people do so, they subject themselves to a servitude of sorts until they repay the loan. In a nonindustrialized society there was little profit from commercial ventures. If interest rates were between 25 percent and 33 percent annually, it was unwise to take out loans, and the borrower frequently did become the slave to the lender.

It is probably unwise to acquire loans for things we want, but do not need. It is wise to curtail our spending so that we can save ahead for necessities such as cars, business ventures, etc. However, it is probably impossible for most individuals and couples to save ahead enough to buy a house and other major purchases with cash.

I believe it is more biblical to encourage believers to differentiate more clearly their needs from their wants, not to go in debt unnecessarily, and not to develop a debt load that makes it impossible to repay their loans as promised. It is the non-repayment of loans, rather than the acquiring of a loan, that Paul prohibited in Romans 13:8.

EX 12: *Contextual Analysis:* Paul, in the verses all around this one, is strongly arguing that Christians are not to lead immoral lives (read vv. 9–20). This husband's interpretation of verse 12 is in direct contradiction to the flow of Paul's argument as found in all the verses surrounding it.

How do we explain Paul's use of the phrase "All things are lawful for me" when some things are definitely unlawful (e.g., violation of any of the Ten Commandments)?

Most religions taught that one earned salvation by doing good works. Christianity was unique in teaching that salvation came through God's grace rather than by doing good deeds. Since Paul had preached and taught that salvation was by grace and not by works, some in the Corinthian church may have begun teaching that believers could do anything and still be saved. They may have even developed a slogan such as "All things are lawful for me" which Paul is quoting.

Paul quotes the slogan, but then puts three very important qualifiers on it. Yes, Christians probably could commit nearly any sin and still go to heaven, but before embarking on any activity, they should first ask these questions:

1. Is it beneficial? (Everything is permissible for me—but not everything is beneficial, v. 12)

2. Will I become enslaved by it? (Everything is permissible for me—but I will not be mastered by anything, v.13).

3. Will it cause our bodies, which are temples of the Holy Spirit, to become impure? (vv. 13–20)

Although we could conceivably engage in any behavior and still go to heaven, we should not engage in it unless it passes the above three tests. Most sinful behavior fails to pass this test on all three counts.

Theological Analysis: The interpretation of this verse made by the husband is contradicted by several other clear passages of Scripture (e.g., Romans 6:1–23; 1 Cor. 5:9–13; Gal. 5:16–21).

EX 13: Psalm 37 focuses on a contrast. The worldly person who is constantly pursuing earthly possessions will soon find that he or she has nothing. The believer who delights himself in the Lord will soon find himself rich in Him.

It is important to remember the first half-verse when interpreting the second half: Delight yourself in the Lord, and He will give you the desires of your heart. As we delight ourselves in the Lord, this will change the desires of our hearts. We will not be obsessed with acquiring earthly possessions, but with pleasing Him. As we delight ourselves in Him, He will grant us the desire of our hearts, i.e., He will help us develop in ways that will truly please Him.

Another verse in this psalm clearly says that this is not a guarantee that we will become rich in this world's goods: verse 16 states "Better the little that the righteous have than the wealth of many wicked."

Mark 11:24 also needs to be read in context. The full passage reads:

> The next day as they were leaving Bethany, Jesus was hungry. Seeing in the distance a fig tree in leaf, he went to find out if it had any fruit. When he reached it, he found nothing but leaves, because it was not the season for figs. Then he said to the tree, "May no one ever eat fruit from you again" (vv. 12–14).
>
> [The next morning], as they went along, they saw the fig tree withered from the roots. Peter remembered and said to Jesus, "Rabbi, look! The fig tree you cursed has withered!"
>
> "Have faith in God," Jesus answered. "I tell you the truth, if anyone says to this mountain, 'Go, throw yourself into the sea,' and does not doubt in his heart but believes that what he says will happen, it will be done for him. Therefore I tell you, whatever you ask for in prayer, believe that you have received it, and it will be yours. And when you stand praying, if you hold anything against anyone, forgive him, so that your Father in heaven may forgive you your sins" (vv. 20–25).

This is a difficult passage to explain: the story contains the only miracle of destruction recorded in Jesus' earthly ministry. It was common for fig trees to leaf out in March or April, but not to have ripe figs until June. Why then did Jesus curse the tree for doing the normally-expected thing?

A historical-cultural analysis provides a clue to answer this question, particularly as we bring in data from the parallel passage in Matthew 21:18–22. The *Expositor's Bible Commentary*, vol. 8, pp. 444–445 makes the following explanation:

> Somewhere on the road between Bethany and Jerusalem, Jesus approached a fig tree in the hope of staunching His hunger (v.18). Mark tells us that though it was not the season for figs, the tree was in leaf. Fig leaves appear about the same time as the fruit or shortly thereafter. The green figs are edible, though sufficiently disagreeable as not usually to be eaten till June. Thus the leaves normally point to every prospect of fruit, even if not fully ripe. Sometimes, however, the green figs fall off and leave nothing but leaves. All this Matthew's succinct remark—"He... found nothing on it except leaves" (v. 19)—implies; his Jewish readers would infer the rest....
>
> Why should Jesus curse a tree for not bearing fruit when it was not the season for fruit?... That it was not the season for figs explains why Jesus went to this particular tree, which stood out because it was in leaf. Its leaves advertised that it was bearing, but the advertisement was false. Jesus, unable to satisfy His hunger, saw the opportunity of teaching a memorable object lesson and cursed the tree, not because it was not bearing fruit, whether in season or out, but because it made a show of life that promised fruit yet was bearing none.

A second clue that helps to explain the meaning of Jesus' miracle of destruction is the story that the incident with the fig tree encircles (read Mark 15–19). This fig tree incident may be an acted-out parable. The fig tree looked to be full of fruit, but had nothing. So also the hypocritical Israelites looked as if they were religiously fruitful, but in reality they were barren. God's curse would eventually fall on the spiritually-barren Israel even as Jesus' curse fell on the barren fig tree.

Let us return to a discussion of what implications this passage has for a theology of prayer. In interpreting the meaning of this passage's teaching on prayer, four hermeneutical principles need to be kept in mind:

Theological analysis: Trench's excellent words: "We are not to expect, in every place, the whole circle of Christian truth to be fully stated.... No conclusion may be drawn from the absence of a doctrine from one passage which is clearly stated in another" (*Notes on the Parables*, pp. 17–18). Thus we should not take these verses to mean that God will give us everything we ask, for He repudiates this belief in other places in Scripture.

Contextual analysis: Jesus is not trying to give a complete treatise on prayer. He is making one point about prayer, namely, the importance of believing in God's power to answer our prayers. (See verse 21: Peter's astonishment points to his lack of faith that anything would happen after Jesus had cursed the fig tree. Verses 22 and 23 teach us explicitly the importance of trusting in God's power to do anything.)

Lexical-syntactical analysis: Jesus is using a figure of speech here. He is using *hyperbole* (exaggeration) to make a teaching point more memorable. Jesus was standing on the Mount of Olives, from which the Dead Sea could be seen. But He was not intending that we try to pray literal mountains into the sea. He was instead teaching that even the greatest possible difficulties can be removed if we pray in faith.

Contextual and theological analysis: Scripture reveals several conditions for answered prayer, including the following:

1. Asked in faith, believing, vv. 22–24.
2. Asked after having forgiven our brothers, vv. 25–26.
3. Not asking for the wrong motives, (read James 4:3–4).

"Prayer is not simply asking God for the pleasant things we desire, but an earnest yearning for, and entering into, the will of God for ourselves and others, be it bitter or sweet" (*Tyndale New Testament Commentaries, in loco*, pp. 180–181).

In summary then, these verses are not intended to teach that we can "claim" whatever we want in faith, and it will be ours.

EX 14: Read the passages noted in EX 14. Luther had great difficulty with this apparent discrepancy, and called the book of James "an epistle of straw." Is there any better way to resolve this problem?

Lexical-syntactical analysis and contextual analysis: Paul and James are writing to different audiences. They have different intentions and so use three crucial words (works, justify, and faith) in slightly different ways.

Works: Paul, when referring to works, is speaking of legalistic works as a way of gaining salvation, and thus soundly denounces such. James is speaking of works as evidence of a true faith in God, and thus strongly encourages such.

Justification: Paul is the only writer in the New Testament to use the word justification in a technical sense. When Paul refers to justification, he is referring to a judicial act of God by which God remits our sins and declares us righteous in His sight. James uses justify in the more general sense of proving oneself genuine before God and men in the face of possible doubt that one was all one professed to be. A true believer shows the genuineness of his faith by righteous actions. This sense of justification is a manifestation of the justification that concerns Paul (*New Bible Dictionary*, p. 686).

Faith: Paul makes faith the ground of our salvation. James agrees. What he is criticizing is the type of faith that even demons have—intellectual assent only—without a corresponding change in life-style (James 2:26).

Vern Lewis ("A Psychological Analysis of Faith" in *The Journal of Psychology and Theology*, Spring 1974) suggests that faith can be likened to an attitude. An attitude can be held at one of several levels:

1. Cognitive level only: persons affirm that they believe a certain truth.

2. Cognitive reorganizational level: persons not only affirm that they believe a certain truth, but also reorganize other beliefs so that other beliefs are consistent with the identified belief.

3. Cognitive reorganizational and behavioral level: persons affirm their beliefs, reorganize other beliefs to be consistent with them, and alter their behavior to be consistent with their beliefs. Lewis suggests that saving faith (as identified by James) is an attitude that one holds at a minimum of some level between 2 and 3.

EX 15: *Contextual Analysis:* To understand the meaning of Deuteronomy 19:21, it is crucial to read its context. The surrounding verses 16–21 teach:

> If a malicious witness takes the stand to accuse a man of a crime, the two men involved in the dispute must stand in the presence of the Lord before the priests and the judges who are in office at the time. The judges must make a thorough investigation and if the witness proves to

> be a liar, giving false testimony against his brother, then do to him as he
> intended to do to his brother. You must purge the evil from among you.
> The rest of the people will hear of this and be afraid, and never again will
> such an evil thing be done among you. Show no pity: life for life, eye for
> eye, tooth for tooth, hand for hand, foot for foot.

Thus, this verse is teaching that if somebody falsely witnesses against
someone else and the court discovers this, whatever penalty the innocent victim would have received shall instead be applied to the false
witness(es).

Theological Analysis: Exodus 21: 22–25 states:

> If men who are fighting hit a pregnant woman and she gives birth prema-
> turely but there is no serious injury, the offender must be fined whatever
> the woman's husband demands and the court allows. But if there is
> serious injury, you are to take life for life, eye for eye, tooth for tooth,
> hand for hand, foot for foot, burn for burn, wound for wound, bruise for
> bruise.

[Note: the Hebrew means serious injury to mother *or* baby. See Keil
and Delitzsch, *Commentary on the Old Testament in loco* or *NIV Study
Bible* text note.]

Leviticus 24:17–22 states:

> If anyone takes the life of a human being, he must be put to death.
> Anyone who takes the life of someone's animal must make restitution—
> life for life. If anyone injures his neighbor, whatever he has done must be
> done to him: fracture for fracture, eye for eye, tooth for tooth. As he has
> injured the other, so he is to be injured. Whoever kills an animal must
> make restitution, but whoever kills a man must be put to death. You are
> to have the same law for the alien and the native-born. I am the Lord
> your God.

The point of the Exodus and Leviticus passages was that the penalty should fit the crime, not be lesser or greater. Preferential treatment
should not be given to those who were rich and powerful, or to citizens
of Israel versus foreigners living among them. There is historical evidence to suggest that courts did not apply these commands literally
(e.g., the courts did not literally gouge out eyes). People understood
that these commands were teaching that the punishment should fit the
crime.

In Matthew 5:38–42 Jesus states:

You have heard that it was said, 'Eye for eye, and tooth for tooth.' But I tell you, Do not resist an evil person. If someone strikes you on the right cheek, turn to him the other also. And if someone wants to sue you and take your tunic, let him have your cloak as well. If someone forces you to go one mile, go with him two miles. Give to the one who asks you, and do not turn away from the one who wants to borrow from you.

The Pharisees had apparently taken commands regarding how judges were to deal with those who are maliciously bringing false witness against a person and how judges were to mete out punishments for crimes, and turned them into justification for taking personal revenge. God gave these commands to judges to ensure impartial judging: the Pharisees were using them as license for personal vengeance.

Jesus had said that unless a person's righteousness surpasses that of the Pharisees and teachers of the law, he will not enter the kingdom of heaven (Matt. 5:20). Jesus' followers were to overcome the law of personal retaliation with the law of love.

EX 16: *Historical and Contextual Analysis:* Paul had given Timothy the role of an overseer (bishop) over several churches. Thus it seems likely that these were general instructions for all churches rather than for specific ones only.

In verse 8 Paul gives instructions to men. In verses 9–11 he gives instructions to women. In verse 12 he says: "I do not permit a woman to teach or to have authority over a man: she must be silent."

The two prohibited activities were *didaskein* and *authentein*. *Didaskein* referred to authoritative teaching in the corporate meetings of the congregation. *Authentein* referred to having authority over someone else.

In 1 Corinthians 11:5 Paul indicates that women prayed and prophesied in the public gathering of believers. Since prophecy was a Holy Spirit-initiated activity, this did not contradict Paul's prohibition of women engaging in *didaskein*. Prophecy originated from God: the person (male or female) who spoke it was only a vessel. *Didaskein* was something initiated and prepared by a person—authoritative instruction for the congregation. Women could participate in prophecy (and therefore probably also in speaking in tongues and interpretation of tongues, which are also Holy Spirit-inspired activities). Women also could pray in public worship, as this did not contradict *didaskein*. The early church often designated its leaders as either teaching elders or ruling elders. There were apparently multiple elders in each church, so that a group of people shared the responsibility of leading the congregation. It seems likely that what this passage is prohibiting is women functioning in the role of either teaching or ruling elder.

What application should this prohibition have for us today? Some believe that this command is time-bound and culture-bound. Their reasons are as follows: (1) Paul labels these as personal commands, e.g., I do not allow women to preach or teach, and (2) the women of that day did not receive formal education. Only men received an education, and therefore having women in these positions would be detrimental to the growth of the church. Since women now have possibilities for education equal to that of men, this prohibition should be regarded as culture-bound.

Others believe that these commands should be regarded as transcultural. Some of their reasons are that Paul gives two grounds for women not being involved in *didaskein* or *authentein*. Paul bases both reasons in the early chapters of Genesis. First, creation order: God created Adam first, then Eve. Second, Eve was the one deceived. The last verse in this passage (women will be saved through childbearing), suggests (to these people) that childbearing rather than church leadership is the role best designed for use of her gifts.

If Paul had based his prohibitions on the fact that the women of his time did not receive a formal education, there would be stronger reason to suggest that these prohibitions are culture-bound rather than transcultural. Because he roots his arguments in creation order and in the Fall, this gives somewhat greater support to the idea that they are transcultural.

Another approach to understanding these commands as temporary was described by Bruce Barron recently. (Bruce Barron, "Putting Women in Their Place: 1 Timothy 2 and Evangelical Views of Women in Church Leadership." *Journal of the Evangelical Theological Society*, Dec. 1990, pp. 451–459.) Basing his work on earlier work by classicist Catharine Kroeger, he argues that Paul was giving instructions to Timothy on how to guide the Church through some of the difficult situations posed by Gnosticism, or the early developments of Gnosticism. Gnosticism had a number of doctrines that conflicted with Christianity. It also had a tendency to elevate women as favored instruments of revelation. The Gnostics reinterpreted the story of Adam and Eve in a fairly radical way that made Eve the heroine. In one gnostic version Adam, after taking the fruit from Eve, is enlightened and thanks her for giving him life.

According to this view, the reasons that Paul returns to the Creation narrative and reminds his readers that Adam was created first and Eve fell into sin first may not have been to place his commands about women not being church leaders in a transcultural setting. The reason may have been to refute the Gnostic heresies regarding the prominence of women as recipients of revelation and as heroes in the Fall. If this is true, then Paul may have been commanding women not to teach or lead the Church for a particular time in church history (until some of the threats of Gnosticism were passed) and his commands should be considered time-limited. It will remain for other evangelical theologians to respond to Mr. Barron's thesis before we can decide whether this is a plausible explanation for his commands in 1 Timothy 2.

What are the implications for female Sunday school teachers? God encourages women to instruct younger women and children, so they definitely would not be prohibited from teaching these groups. Sunday schools did not arise until the 1800s, so Paul definitely did not have them in mind when he wrote. Sunday school does not carry with it the same level of authority as leading the congregation in corporate worship. Therefore some would argue that 2 Timothy 2 does not prohibit women teaching men in Sunday school.

The same argument could be made for women serving as hospital chaplains or seminary teachers (i.e., that this text does not prohibit either of these activities). Concerning women serving as missionaries, it would be easier to comply with this teaching if there were at least one male missionary with good preaching gifts in any group of missionaries. Female missionaries could be involved in personal witnessing and home Bible studies. As the fruit of their labor increases in numbers, a male missionary can lead in corporate worship until nationals have matured enough spiritually to take over this function.

The issue of whether women should serve as ordained ministers today remains a hotly-contested one. There probably will be greater clarifications of the 1 Timothy 2 text in the coming years as theologians continue to discuss and debate this issue.

EX 17: Read Acts 4:31–35. Luke is describing what happened, not prescribing this as a requirement for all believers (this is descriptive truth, not prescriptive truth).

Compare verse 32 with verse 34. It seems that this passage is not saying that everyone sold everything they had and developed a socialistic system. Instead, believers adopted the attitude that personal possessions were to be shared with brothers and sisters who were in need. The phrase "from time to time those who owned lands or houses sold them" suggests that believers retained personal ownership of some things, and only sold them as there was need within the body of Christ.

Conclusion: This is not stating that socialism is an ideal Christian economic system. It is stating that voluntary sharing of the good things God has given to us personally is one example of God's grace among us (cf. James 2:14–24).

EX 18: I believe this teaching is not a valid understanding of the text as Paul originally gave it, based on lexical-syntactical analysis. The word for "child" is *teknon.* Its common meaning is young offspring. *Teknion,* the diminutive form of the word, means "little child," or "infant." Paul and John both use this to refer to spiritual children.

The implied denotation of *teknon* means someone young, not having reached adulthood themselves. We will always be our father's son or daughter, but we are not forever his child: eventually we become adult sons and daughters.

Paul did not use *huios* (son), which might have included the concept of obeying our parents as long as they're alive. Instead he uses *teknon,* teaching that while we are children, we are to obey them. We are always to honor our parents, but we are not bound by Scripture to obey them once we reach adulthood.

EX 19: *Logical and Theological Analysis:* 1 Timothy 3:2 and 12, and Titus 1:6 state the principle that pastors and deacons are to be "the husband of one wife." For this reason many believers have concluded that those who for any reason are now divorced and remarried, or those who have never been married, are to be excluded from ministries with the church because they are not "the husband of one wife."

Altough the English translation of these verses is ambiguous, many Greek scholars agree that the Greek wording does not mean never having been married before, but rather not presently bigamous (e.g., A. T. Robertson, *Word Pictures in the New Testament*, 1931, vol. 5, p. 572; Guy Duty, *The Right to Remarry*, 1967, p. 140). Persons who have remarried following the death of a spouse should not be excluded from service based on these verses (see 1 Cor. 7:39; Rom. 7:2–3; 1 Tim. 5:14), even though they have been, throughout their lifetime, the husband of more than one wife.

Also, it would not be biblical to exclude someone from the ministry because he has the gift of celibacy (1 Cor. 7:1–40). If this were true both Christ and possibly Paul could not have participated in church ministry. Thus it seems that to translate the phrase *mias gunaikos andra* (literally, a "one-wife man") as meaning that those who serve the church must have at least one wife, but never have been married previously, must be inaccurate because such an interpretation contradicts the clear teachings of the above passages, and the examples of Christ and Paul.

Contextual Analysis: Let us look at the context to try to ascertain a more accurate understanding of the phrase. We find that all the other qualifications in this list refer to present character, not past history (Stanley Ellisen, *Divorce and Remarriage in the Church*, 1977, pp. 83ff.). The church leader must be above reproach, temperate, self-controlled, respectable, able to teach, gentle, etc., all of which are present characteristics.

Putting contextual evidence with that cited in the previous paragraphs, it seems likely that this verse requires that a church leader is one who, in the present, is "faithful to his own wife" (*Expositor's Bible Commentary, in loco.*). The potential church leader must not be a person of wandering affections, but must be known for his fidelity to his wife or to his celibate life-style.

For these reasons it seems to me that we should not automatically exclude from consideration for church service those who have been married previously. Often such persons may have been the innocent party in a biblical divorce (Matt. 5:31–32; 19:1–9). They may have been the unwilling recipient of a divorce. In either of these cases I think they should be allowed to participate in those ministries for which they are qualified.

Even in those cases where persons have been the initiators or contributors of an unbiblical divorce some time past, this is not an unpardonable sin, although many of our church practices implicitly label it as such. Of the dozen criteria for elders, some elders must not have been successful at keeping all of them throughout their entire lifetime. What Paul says is that, with God's renewing grace, candidates for elder should possess these traits now.

Therefore I believe that, even as with other sins, if people show evidence of genuine repentance, the church should minister grace and forgiveness as representatives of Christ. If sufficient time has elapsed, and the person shows consistent evidence of the other qualities of a church leader as found in 1 Timothy 3 and Titus, I believe such persons should be considered for positions of service and ministry.

EX 20: This method suggests that the minister has an inaccurate understanding of the principles of hermeneutics in several regards:

Historical-cultural analysis. Since a large gap separates us from biblical times and culture, we need help from those who have researched these areas to understand historical and cultural allusions correctly.

Lexical-syntactical analysis. In translating from one language to another, translators attempt to find words that have similar denotations. It is frequently impossible to find a word in the second language that carries the exact meaning as the first word had in the original language. This is why studying the works of linguistic scholars is important in fully understanding God's intended meaning.

Theological analysis. It is almost impossible to do a comprehensive theological analysis without referring to the works of other biblical scholars. Also, the Holy Spirit has been illuminating the minds of serious Bible students for many centuries. There is a certain kind of spiritual pride involved when a person claims that he or she can bypass the accumulated truth the Holy Spirit has revealed to others over many centuries, and find truth solely on his or her own.

Genre analysis. The Bible contains many genre that we rarely find in English (e.g., parables, many Hebrew figures of speech, etc.). If the preacher interprets these in a literal way without recognizing them as specialized genre or figures of speech, he will often distort God's intended meaning.

For all the above reasons it is important to recognize that the best exegesis will depend on a careful study of the text aided by the work of biblical scholars who have gone before us.

EXERCISES: CHAPTER 4

EX 21: Sigmund Freud's observations as he worked with patients (sometimes called "clinical research") failed to control for the following threats to internal validity:

1. History: Psychoanalysis usually takes several years. There is no control group to control for the effects of the historical events that could affect the client's mental health during this time.

2. Maturation: Same criticism as above. Because of the length of typical psychoanalytic treatment, the threat that biological or psychological maturation might cause changes in the client's mental health significantly increases.

3. Instrumentation: Freud drew his own conclusions about whether a patient's mental health improved because of therapy. The criteria he used were not validated by others, nor was his ability to measure these criteria validly and reliably ever proven; therefore, his instrumentation was extremely weak.

4. Statistical regression to the mean: Since those who chose to see Freud for therapy (when this was not a culturally-accepted thing to do), probably would have received extreme scores if an objective test of mental health had been available then, we would expect those persons to move toward the mean naturally because of statistical regression. However, since Freud never used objective measures before or after treatment, this is a moot point.

5. Mortality: Freud gives us no data about the number of patients who did not stay in therapy until their treatment was complete. Therefore we do not know whether those treatments he considered clinical

successes represent 80 percent of those he started with, or 60 percent, 40 percent, or 20 percent.

6. Selection: Since there was no control group, there was no nonrandom selection.

7. Experimenter expectancy transmitted by the experiment itself: The experiment in this situation was the experience of therapy. Throughout human history doctors have assumed that if a patient comes for appointments as scheduled and follows their advice, they will get better. Therefore we have no reason not to assume that this factor was operative in Freud's clinical work. We do not know whether it, rather than the method of therapy, may have produced the improvements Freud noted.

8. Experimenter expectancy transmitted through the experimenter's actions, responses, and interrogations: Freud believed that his method of therapy would improve the mental health of his patients. He was unaware of many factors that can affect an experiment's validity that we are aware of today. Therefore probably he took few pains to hide from his patients his expectations that they would get better.

9. Effect of subject's preconceptions and expectations: This is the patient's counterpart to factor (7) above. Even as the doctor expected the patient to get well, patients also expect to get well when they were treated by a doctor. Without a true experimental design, we do not know how much of any alleged improvement in mental health is due to the patient's expectation that he or she will get well (remember the power of the placebo effect), versus improvement due to the specific treatment Freud offered.

10. Effect of role context: We have seen the effect that the role differential between researcher and subject can have on the subject's willingness to do things he or she would not do under any other circumstances (remember Milgram's electrical shock experiments). The power differential between doctor and patient in Freud's time was, if anything, even greater than the power differential between scientific researcher and subject in our own time. This role context, then, could have exerted tremendous influence on patients, and may have been the cause of patients' improvement, rather than the treatment itself (thus the need for double-blind studies).

There are other historical facts that raise questions about the validity of Freud's claims (I do not expect you to have known the following information). At a recent conference of the American Association for the Advancement of Science, Frank Sulloway, professor of science history at the Massachusetts Institute of Technology, presented a paper that claimed the following facts to be true:

One of Freud's major works is an accounting of how he treated six patients. Psychoanalysts consider this book to be a pillar in the field of psychoanalysis. But historical research has shown that of these six patients, "one involved a patient who fled therapy in disgust, Freud did not treat two of them himself, and a fourth involved no real therapy."

Freud claimed to have cured two of the patients, yet when researchers interviewed one of those patients at length later, they found the reported cure to be "a complete misrepresentation of the facts," said Solloway. He added that Freud's case histories "are rampant with censorship, distortions, highly dubious reconstructions and exaggerated clinical claims." Studies by several experts have shown that "Freud's logical inferences and conclusions about his research and empirical evidence are simply not justified." (Excerpts from "Scientists Questioning Psychoanalysis Theories," *Associated Press*, February 19, 1991.)

General conclusion: Freud's personal discussions of clients' improvements ("clinical research") fall far short of a true experimental design. His research design fails to control for almost every threat to internal validity. There is additional evidence that Freud, either consciously or unconsciously, misrepresented some of his clinical data. Therefore the basic formulation of psychoanalytic theory and treatment cannot be considered proven by Freud's research.

EX 22 and EX 23: The answers to these exercises will differ based on individual experiences, and so no general answer can be given.

EX 24: There are several possible reasons for the discrepancy. People were not randomly assigned to the Hite and Greeley surveys, so there may have been some differences in the two samples. To assess whether differences in the samples may have caused the differences in results, it would be necessary to obtain full information about how the two researchers selected their groups and the mortality rate for each. In an area as sensitive as whether one has been faithful, it is very possible that those who have been unfaithful will be anxious about completing such a survey. Thus those who do not complete the survey might have significantly higher levels of infidelity than those who do. Also, women who have been unfaithful may be more comfortable being truthful about this in the anonymity and impersonalness of a written survey than in a telephone conversation with someone they do not know.

Second, the two research questions were not identical. Shere Hite said that 75 percent of the women in her survey married five years or longer had had or were having an affair. Greeley reported that 90 percent of the women he had contacted said they had been faithful during their present marriage. This factor may explain some of the difference between a 10 percent and 75 percent infidelity rate, but is not likely to cause this large a difference.

Third, and this is probably the major contributing factor to the difference, is instrumentation. Hite mailed her survey to respondents, who could complete it at a time they considered safe. It was totally anonymous. Greeley's assistants telephoned women at their homes. If any of these women had been or was being unfaithful, she may have feared that the telephone call from an unknown "surveyor" was a clever attempt by her spouse to gather incriminating evidence against her. Another factor that may have affected Greeley's results is the likelihood that someone else was home at the time of the telephone survey. Women may not have answered questions honestly for fear that someone would hear. Lastly, even if Greeley's research team did pick women's telephone numbers randomly, there probably would be few unfaithful women who would believe an unknown caller's affirmation that this was so. Thus it is probable that differences in instrumentation (methods for gathering the information) accounted for the large differences in responses between the two surveys.

EX 25: This "research" did not include a control group. If it had, people would have recognized a fact noted by humorist Henry G. Felsen: "Proper treatment will cure a cold in seven days, but left to itself a cold will hang on for a week." [Quoted in Darrell Huff, *How to Lie with Statistics* (New York: Norton, 1982), p. 8.]

EXERCISES: CHAPTER 5

EX 26: While this table accurately reports the results, it gives us no information about the three programs in terms of their differential effectiveness. The ENRICH inventory gives information about fourteen different areas of marital functioning. It would be useful to know which programs produce the greatest change in the various areas of marital functioning. In this way couples with difficulties in a certain area of their marriage might be assigned to the program that appears to produce the greatest improvement in that area.

More important, though, is the possibility that this table and its caption may mislead the reader about the extent of improvement caused by the various programs. For example, the table includes only the percentages from 50 to 70, rather than 0 to 100. This exaggerates visually the amount of change that did occur. Since the scale only covers 20 percentage points rather than the 100 points that exist, it magnifies the changes by a factor of five.

The caption also may mislead the casual reader, for it suggests that the marital enrichment programs caused significant positive changes on six of the fourteen ENRICH scales. However, when you look at the magnitude of the positive changes, most changes represent only 2 or 3 percentage points out of 100. When a researcher has a sample of 198 subjects (99 couples), it is possible to achieve a statistically significant change even though the numbers do not represent a meaningful change. This is the case here.

Also, one wonders why the author did not mention that there were not statistically significant changes on eight of fourteen scales. The article could easily mislead the casual reader into believing that these three marriage enrichment programs caused more improvement in couple's marriages than they did, although I do not believe the authors' intention was either to deceive or mislead.

EX 27: I will note each possible threat to internal and external validity, and briefly remark about its relevance to this experimental design.

History: Since members of all three treatment groups and the control group experience the same history, this design controls for this factor. (All clients are exposed to the same general historical events outside therapy as they are treated.)

Maturation: We will assume that all three therapists use brief therapy methods and their treatment of phobias is essentially complete in fifteen sessions or less. Since subjects in all four groups experience roughly similar amounts of maturational time, the effect of maturation is equalized.

Effect of testing: All subjects receive the same testing at the same intervals, so the effect of this factor is equalized.

Reliability of instrumentation: The counselors tested all clients with a validated assessment instrument. One secretary, who has been trained to give the instructions in a standardized way, will introduce clients to the tests. Clients will complete the testing in a private room free of distractions.

Statistical regression to the mean: Because of random assignment, there should be equivalent regression to the mean in all groups.

Mortality: Because of random assignment, there should be equivalent mortality. However, there is no way to predict this, so it is a factor that the researchers should watch. If there is significantly more mortality with one therapist than with the others, it would be helpful to interview those who dropped out of therapy to see what their reasons were.

Non-random selection: Clients are randomly assigned.

Experimenter bias or experimenter expectancy transmitted by the experiment itself, by the experimenter's actions, responses, and interrogations, or by the phrasing of questions on surveys: Since all three therapists believe in their approaches, this factor would, one hopes, be equalized. Also, they made a commitment not to compete with each other in terms of the efficiency of their respective treatments, but to focus on how healing occurred in their clients. This also should reduce the amount of experimenter expectancy that would impact the client.

Subjects' preconceptions and expectations: Equalized by research design.

Effect of role context: Equalized by research design.

Effect of natural science techniques: Avoided through choice of methods of therapy and assessment.

Experimentally-accessible population and target population are different: Target population is those with a phobia who seek Christian therapy. Experimentally-accessible population is the same.

Interaction between treatment and specific subjects: Controlled through random assignment.

Inadequate description of the treatment variable: It would be up to the three clinicians to decide whether they are willing to invest the time to describe their respective approaches thoroughly for others.

Inaccurate method of measuring the dependent variable: The counselors measured all clients using the same validated instrument and standardized administration procedures.

Multiple-treatment interference: Some guideline could be developed such as saying that any client in the research program could not have been in therapy during the six months before becoming part of the research project, and could not have received prior treatment for the phobia. (If they did not meet these two criteria they could still receive counseling, but would not be part of the research project.)

Interaction of time of measurement and treatment effects: Counselors would control this factor by having standardized times of measurement.

The Hawthorne Effect: Equalized by having all groups, including the control group, know that they are part of a research project.

Novelty and disruption effects: Equalized since therapists in all groups would have an equal number of treatment experiences. This could be a threat to external validity if the therapists had significantly different amounts of prior experience using their particular approach to treatment of phobias.

(I did not discuss some threats to external validity if I had already addressed that factor as a threat to internal validity.)

EX 28: No, random assignment does not reduce this threat to external validity. Random assignment of an accessible population does not reduce the differences that may exist between the accessible population and the target population. The only way to reduce this threat to external validity is for the researcher to make sure that the random sample is drawn from the target population.

EX 29: The mean class attendance is 30.38 persons. The mode is 31 and the median is 31. The distribution of scores is neither positively-skewed nor negatively-skewed: it is very close to a normal distribution of scores.

EX 30: There is inadequate evidence to conclude that these two factors would change the church's negative-growth situation. A person would have the evidence to come to cause-and-effect conclusions like the ones this man is making only if he had conducted an experiment using a true experimental design. If he had evidence from some correlational research he could identify certain co-relationships, but he still could not state cause and effect relationships.

This person has not even done correlational research. His statements might be called, if we are generous, "observational research." He has not developed any objective way of validating his observational methods—they may be as much a product of his projections as they are of the objective realities of your church situation or that of the three Baptist churches. It is totally improper, from a scientific point of view, to take one's personal, unvalidated observations and attribute cause and effect relationships to them. Scientifically, it is also improper to begin suggesting action plans before one has carefully diagnosed the problems in one's specific situation. The same solutions that have worked well for three Southern Baptist churches in their specific situations may not be the answer for your church.

Any scientific study should first start with a review of the research that others have done on the subject. Remember that the second step of the scientific method is to collect facts that relate to the question or problem. The committee could do this by reading the research done by church growth specialists such as Peter Wagner and others. The committee also could develop an anonymous survey that would ask present church members for their thoughts about the reasons for the decline in attendance, and for the factors that have made them consider a move in the last two years. (Not all of them will have thought of moving, but some of them probably have. Finding out their reasons can be important in reducing future membership losses.)

It would be particularly useful to either survey or interview those who used to attend the church who are still in the community but no longer attending it. Most surveys or interviews will gain more information if the interviewer promises confidentiality regarding the answers. It also may be helpful to interview denominational officials to see whether the local trend in your church reflects a national trend. If so, what suggestions have denominational officials at the national level made?

From all the above, you can generate several hypotheses about the possible causes of decline in your church's attendance. From your group discussion and data gathering, you can rule out some of these hypotheses, and retain others as possible, partial explanations. Probably you will conclude that people have left your church for a variety of reasons, and that no one solution (such as "get a more dynamic preacher"), is a comprehensive answer. Multiple regression analysis recognizes that few things in human life are affected by only a single factor. Your study should reflect whatever level of complexity is accurate in your situation.

One way of responding to the governing body's request would be to list several reasons for the lack of growth, starting with those that the committee feels most certain of, and then moving to those for which you have less confirmatory data. (Let the governing board know about this progression from more certain to less certain.) Your committee could follow this with a list of recommendations, again starting with those about which you feel most certain, and then moving to those about which you feel less certain. The certainty with which you identify the problems and recommend solutions should be directly related to the amount of confirmatory data you have on each problem or solution.

EXERCISES: CHAPTER 6

EX 31: The middle-aged man is using both appeal to antiquity and appeal to authority (in this case the denomination). The fallacy here is that simply because the church has done something a certain way for many years does not guarantee that it will continue to be spiritually meaningful to teenagers today. The fallacy of the appeal to the denomination's authority is that even if the entire denomination does it a certain way, this is no guarantee that it is spiritually meaningful to Christian teens. The entire denomination's teenagers may be feeling bored and unchallenged.

EX 32: The daughter is using both an appeal to popularity and an *ad hominem* argument. The proposition that all her friends are experimenting with drugs does not reduce the dangers involved. Trying to go over Niagara Falls in a barrel is dangerous no matter how many friends go with you.

From a logical standpoint, the daughter pointing to the mother's tranquilizer use is an *ad hominem* argument. Whatever medication her mother takes or does not take is irrelevant to the danger of her experimentation. While logically irrelevant, her mother's use of tranquilizers is psychologically relevant in this daughter's eyes. Physicians often over-prescribe minor tranquilizers, and many people unintentionally become addicted to them.

Since medical drugs are prepared in carefully-controlled laboratories rather than somebody's bathtub, they are much safer than drugs purchased off the street. However, if the mother wants to have her daughter become serious about saying "No" to drugs, she probably should get some help with her addiction, if it turns out that she has become addicted.

EX 33: This is probably an example of appeal of the poor, helped because Mandela became a symbol of those who maintain their dignity and principles in the face of the oppressive governments. The respect accorded his conclusions were based, less on the facts he had used to develop his arguments and his philosophies, than on his status as a symbol of the poor and oppressed.

EX 34: Answer to both questions: The conclusion of either argument may be either true or false. It is possible for a person to start with inaccurate premises and still arrive at a true conclusion. It is also possible for a person to reason badly and still state a true conclusion. In either case, though the conclusion was true, the premises or argument do not prove it to be so.

EX 35: This group committed the fallacy of false analogy. Though Christ was like a vine in one respect, it does not then follow that He was like a vine in all respects. The point of that analogy was to underscore the importance of believers (branches of the vine) abiding in Christ. They could not successfully live the Christian life through their own commitment and resources. The focus of Christ's analogy was the process of sanctification, not ontology.

EX 36: He is making an *ad hominem* argument, among other errors. The validity of the portions of the book this theologian wrote depend on how well he understood and summarized the content in his field of specialization. The activities of his personal life, whether noble or sinful, do not affect the validity of his writings.

EX 37: The hermeneutical error this man was committing is part of lexical-syntactical analysis. He was supplying his own definitions of these words, rather than the definitions Paul was using in these chapters. There is at least one place where Paul discusses natural talents that God can use as believers dedicate those talents to Him (Romans 12). Also, the Old Testament makes reference to skilled craftsmen whose skill was due to the Spirit of God. However, the content of 1 Corinthians 12 and 14 clearly shows that in this passage Paul is talking about supernaturally-given manifestations of the Holy Spirit.

The logical error this teacher was making is parallel to the hermeneutical one. It is the error of equivocation. However, he does not change the definition he is using partway through his argument. Instead he takes a word that someone else was using, changes the definition, then claims to be giving an exposition of that person's writing.

EX 38: The above abortion-rights argument assumes that women have a right to abortions, and therefore this right should be equally available to all women, whether rich or poor. However, in so doing, it bypasses the central issue of whether abortion involves terminating an innocent human life. Our constitution grants certain rights and freedoms to all citizens, as long as the exercise of their freedoms do not deprive another person of his or her freedom.

The argument mentioned above assumes that women have the right to an abortion. It therefore makes the prior assumption that exercising this right does not violate the rights of any other person. However, abortion does not deprive anyone of his or her rights only if the unborn child is not a human being. Therefore abortion-rights activists are including as a premise in their argument the conclusion they want to prove. This is an example of begging the question. The conclusion rests on a premise that the activist has not proven to be true.

Premise: Every woman has a right to an abortion, since the exercise of this option does not violate the rights of any other person.

Conclusion: All women, rich or poor, should have equal access to abortion.

EX 39: From a hermeneutical standpoint, there is much in this passage that misrepresents the God of the Bible and the way He views and feels toward us. From a logical standpoint, Edwards is using the fallacy of an appeal to fear rather than giving any number of more biblical and valid reasons for turning to God.

EX 40: Amphiboly.

EXERCISES: CHAPTER 7

EX 41: This argument could be critiqued as an example of the fallacy of irrelevant conclusion or as a *non sequitur*. The fact that hunting gives pleasure and employment to many people is irrelevant to whether it is cruel to animals.

EX 42: Those who believed that our involvement in the Persian Gulf War was right could say that the Soviets were using the fallacy of You Too. Those who were against the U.S. involvement in the Persian Gulf War or who criticized the way President Bush conducted it might accuse the U.S. of the fallacy of provincialism.

EX 43: There are several possible fallacies that could be named here. One would be *non sequitur*—illustrations can be used to clarify something, but they do not prove something. This is also an example of hasty generalization (also known as overgeneralization or unwarranted extrapolation), which occurs when one constructs a rule based on too few cases. One swallow doesn't make a summer: one anecdote does not prove a point.

EX 44: This argument is invalid. It commits either the fallacy of irrelevant thesis or a *non sequitur*. The presence of conflict in the church does not prove that use of our mental and critical capacities is to blame. More likely causes would be our sin natures, our tendencies to become rigid about the beliefs with which we have become accustomed, and our fears of new data that might threaten the established beliefs we hold. There are scriptural commands we cannot obey without the use of our mental and critical capacities (e.g., 1 Tim. 3:2; 4:11; 2 Tim. 2:14–15; Matt. 7:15–20).

EX 45: To answer this question it is necessary to do some historical investigation to see whether denominations that have taken the approach of "limited inerrancy" have eventually abandoned their trust in God's Word. Harold Lindsell's book *Battle for the Bible* contains some factual data about this question. His data suggests that once a denomination begins to teach and believe that the Bible contains errors, usually the categories where errors are assumed to occur increase in number, and gradually the denomination moves away from the Bible as its authority. If his analysis is correct, then this issue would *not* be an example of a fallacious use of slippery slope.

EX 46: This is an example of the fallacy of guilt by association. The primary concern of the Pharisees was that a spiritual man might become ceremonially defiled by associating with someone who did not obey the Pharasaic laws strictly. Jesus completely changes the metaphor, likening Himself to a doctor who regularly goes out among those who are sick. He changes the emphasis from the Pharisees' concern of staying away from the spiritually sick to the physician's concern of seeking them out and ministering to them.

EX 47: These two scientists just committed the logical fallacy called appeal to ignorance or shifting the burden of proof. We expect someone presenting a new idea to present proof for it. Our inability to disprove it does not establish its validity.

EX 48: This is an example of equivocation. There is a difference between the way Chesterton is using the word "incompatibility" in the first sentence versus the second and third. In the first he is using it in the sense of two people whose differences have hardened into a chronic state of dislike. In the second and third sentences he is referring to the general truth that men and women usually see some things from different perspectives. By suggesting that there are marriages composed of people who are "not compatible" yet nonetheless happy, he clearly shows that he has changed his definition of "not compatible" from the way he used this word in the first sentence.

EX 49: The best way to discover whether this situation is an example of legitimate fear of the slippery slope or an invalid fear would be to look at the history of what the federal government has done in this regard with other Christian colleges that have faced this problem. Officers of the Christian College Coalition or the Christian College Consortium might be aware of other historical precedents. It also might be possible to come up with some sort of "workable compromise" in which the college does not sign a federal form, and thus does not create a precedent, but does express in an official way that it does comply with the Title IX guidelines, but out of its biblical commitments rather than because of a federal mandate.

The other possible logical fallacy that may be present in this situation is false analogy. Without having personal contact with the Department of Health, Education, and Welfare, it is impossible to know whether the comparison of their behavior to that of camels is valid or not.

EX 50: Freud was a personality theorist. While he considered himself a scientific researcher, the scientific validity of much of his research has been thoroughly criticized, as we have seen in previous sections of this book. So at most we can say that Freud was a personality theorist who believed he was a researcher, and who developed theories, many of which have been rejected by the majority of mental health professionals today. For Strachey to say that Freud has "stated with simple clarity the impossibility of religious belief for the educated man of today" is an exorbitant example of the fallacy of appeal to "false" authority. Freud lacks credentials to make statements about the validity or invalidity of religious belief. His *Illusions* book is full of conjectures and hypotheses without supporting facts. (For an interesting refutation of much of what Freud says in his book, read R. C. Sproul's book *The Psychology of Atheism*.)

EX 51: Amphiboly.

EX 52: Poisoning the well.

EX 53: The fallacious use of humor and ridicule. Admittedly, good guys sometimes stoop to invalid methods. Don't be one of them.

APPENDICES

APPENDIX A:

Summary of Hermeneutics

Historical-Cultural and Contextual Analysis

1. Discover the general historical and cultural milieu of the writer and his audience.
   a. What is the general historical situation facing the human author and his audience?
   b. What knowledge of customs will clarify the meaning of given actions or given commands?
   c. What was the level of spiritual commitment of the audience?
2. Identify the purpose(s) the author had in writing the book by:
   a. Noting explicit statements or repeated phrases.
   b. Observing exhortations he gives.
   c. Observing issues the author omits or focuses on.
3. Understand how the passage fits into its immediate context.
   a. Identify the major blocks of material in the book and show how they fit into a coherent whole.

    b. Show how the passage fits into the flow of the author's argument.

    c. Decide if the author's perspective is noumenological or phenomenological.

    d. Distinguish between descriptive and prescriptive truth.

    e. Distinguish between incidental details and the teaching focus of the passage.

    f. Identify who the biblical author is addressing in this passage.

Lexical-Syntactical Analysis

1. Identify the general literary form or genre.
2. Trace the development of the author's theme and show how the passage under consideration fits into the context.
3. Identify the natural divisions (sentences and paragraphs) of the text.
4. Identify the connecting words within the paragraphs and sentences and show how they aid in understanding the author's progression of thought.
5. Decide what the individual words mean.
    a. Identify the multiple meanings (denotations) a word possessed in its time and culture.
    b. Determine the single meaning intended by the author in a given context.
6. Analyze the syntax and show how it contributes to an understanding of the passage.
7. Put the results of your analysis into nontechnical, easily-understood words that clearly convey the author's intended meaning.

Theological Analysis

1. Select the view of salvation history that you believe best fits the biblical data.

2. Identify the implications of this view for the passage you are studying.
3. Assess the extent of theological knowledge available to the original recipients of the letter.
4. Decide what meaning the passage possessed for its original recipients in light of the knowledge available to them.
5. Identify the additional knowledge about this topic that is available to us now because of later revelation.

Genre Analysis

1. Identify the literary genre and apply an appropriate analysis.
   a. Look for explicit references that show the author's intent regarding the method he was using.
   b. If the text does not explicitly identify the literary form of the passage, study the characteristics of the passage to ascertain its form.
   c. Apply the principles of genre analysis carefully but not rigidly.
      (1) Similes, metaphors and proverbs: Look for the single point of comparison.
      (2) Parables: Identify the focal teaching and the details of significance surrounding it.
      (3) Allegories: Look for the multiple points of comparison intended by the author.
      (4) State your understanding of the meaning of the passage.
      (5) Check to see if your stated meaning "fits" into the immediate context and total context of the book. If it doesn't, recycle the process.
2. Compare your work with that of others.

Transculturation

1. Discern as accurately as possible the principle behind the given behavioral command.
2. Discern whether the principle is timeless or time-bound (transcultural or culture-bound).
3. If a principle is transcultural, study the nature of its behavioral expression within our culture.
4. If the behavioral expression of a principle should be changed, suggest a cultural equivalent that would adequately express the God-given principle behind the original command.
5. If after careful study the nature of the biblical principle and its attendant command remain in question, apply the biblical precept of humility.

Internal and External Threats to Validity

Internal Threats

1. History
2. Maturation
3. Effect of testing
4. Reliability of instrumentation
5. Statistical regression to the mean
6. Mortality
7. Nonrandom selection
8. Experimenter bias or expectancy transmitted by the experiment itself
9. Experimenter bias transmitted by the experimenter's actions, responses, and interrogations
10. Experimenter bias transmitted in the phrasing of questions on surveys
11. Subject's preconceptions and expectations
12. Effect of role context
13. Effect of natural science techniques

External Threats

1. Experimentally-accessible population and target population are different
2. Interaction between treatment and specific subjects
3. Inadequate description of the treatment variable
4. Inaccurate methods of measuring the dependent variable
5. Multiple-treatment interference
6. Interaction of history and treatment effect
7. Interaction of time of measurement and treatment effects
8. Pretest sensitization
9. The Hawthorne Effect
10. Novelty and disruption effects
11. Experimenter bias or expectancy

List of Logical Fallacies

Accent
Accident
Ad hominem
Amphiboly
Appeal to Antiquity
Appeal to Authority
Appeal to the Crowd
Appeal to Moderation
Appeal to Newness
Appeal to Pity
Appeal to Popularity
Appeal of the Poor
Appeal to the Stone
Appeal to Wealth
Apriorism
Begging the Question
Bifurcation
Blinding with Science
Catastrophizing

Classical Syllogism Fallacies
  • Contradictory Premises
  • Exclusive Premises
  • Positive Conclusion from
      Negative Premises
  • Fallacy of Four Terms
  • Illicit Process
  • Undistributed Middle
Cliche Thinking
Complex Question
Composition
Concealed Evidence
Converse Accident
Damning the Alternatives
Dismissal
Division
Emotional Appeals
Equivocation
Every Schoolboy Knows

False Analogies
Fear or Force
Gambler's Fallacy
Genetic Fallacy
Guilt by Association
Humor and Ridicule
Intuition
Invincible Ignorance
Irrelevant Thesis or
    Irrelevant Conclusion
Loaded Words or Name-
    Calling
Magical Thinking
Meaningless Claim
Non Sequitur
One-Sided Assessment
Oversimplification
Poisoning the Well
Provincialism
Red Herring
Refuting the Example

Shifting the Burden of Proof
Slippery Slope
Special Pleading
Statistical Fallacies
  • Biased Question
  • Biased Sample
  • Concealed Quantification
  • False Precision
  • Figures Prove
  • Hasty Generalization
  • Post Hoc Fallacy
  • Sweeping Generalization
Straw Man
Traditional Wisdom
Trivial Objections
Two Wrongs Make a Right
Unaccepted Enthymemes
Unobtainable Perfection
Wishful Thinking
You Too!

APPENDIX D:

Suggestions for Further Reading

Hermeneutics

D. A. Carson, ed., *Biblical Interpretation and the Church: The Problem of Contextualization.* (Nashville: Thomas Nelson, 1985).

D. A. Carson and John Woodbridge, eds., *Hermeneutics, Authority and Canon* (Grand Rapids, Zondervan, 1986).

Tremper Longman III, *Literary Approaches to Biblical Interpretation* (Grand Rapids: Zondervan, 1987).

A. Berkeley Mickelsen, *Interpreting the Bible* (Grand Rapids: Eerdmans, 1963).

Vern Poythress, *Science and Hermeneutics* (Grand Rapids: Zondervan, 1988).

Bernard Ramm, *Protestant Biblical Interpretation* (Grand Rapids: Baker, 1970).

Samuel Schultz and Morris Inch, eds., *Interpreting the Word of God* (Chicago: Moody, 1976).

Statistics and Research Design

I am including some dated textbooks because they still continue to be recommended by statistics professors and students. Those books marked with an asterisk are written for the layperson.

Donald T. Campbell and Julian C. Stanley, *Experimental and Quasi-Experimental Designs for Research* (Chicago: Rand-McNally, 1963).

Thomas H. Cook and Donald T. Campbell, *Quasi-Experimentation* (Chicago: Rand-McNally, 1979).

Robert V. Craig and Allen T. Craig, *Introduction to Mathematical Statistics*, Fourth Edition (New York: Macmillan, 1978).

John Freund, *Modern Elementary Statistics*, Seventh Edition (Englewood Cliffs, N.J.: Prentice-Hall, 1988).

William L. Hayes, *Statistics for the Social Sciences* (New York: Holt, Rinehart, and Winston, 1973).

Paul G. Hoel, *Introduction to Mathematical Statistics*, Fifth Edition (New York: Wiley, 1984).

Schuyler Huck, William Cormier, and William Bounds, *Reading Statistics and Research* (New York: Harper and Row, 1974).

*Darrell Huff, *How to Lie with Statistics* (New York: Norton, 1982).

Richard Light, Judith Singer and John Willett, *By Design: Planning Research in Higher Education* (Cambridge: Harvard University Press, 1990).

Edward W. Minium, *Statistical Reasoning in Psychology and Education*, Third Edition (New York: Wiley, 1988).

Frederick Mosteller and John Tukey, *Data Analysis and Regression* (Reading, Mass.: Addison-Wesley, 1977).

*John L. Phillips, *How to Think about Statistics* (New York: Freeman and Company, 1988).

Robert Rosenthal, *Experimenter Effects in Behavioral Research* (New York: Appleton-Century-Crofts, 1966).

*Richard Runyon, *How Numbers Lie: A Consumer's Guide to the Fine Art of Numerical Deception* (Lexington, Mass.: Lewis, 1981).

Richard Runyon, *Fundamental Behavioral Statistics*, Sixth Edition (New York: McGraw-Hill, 1987).

James P. Stevens, *Applied Multivariate Statistics for the Social Sciences* (Hillsdale, N.J.: L. Erlbaum Associates, 1986).

Logic and Logical Fallacies

Vincent E. Barry and Douglas J. Soccio, *Practical Logic*, Third Edition (New York: Holt, Rinehart, and Winston, 1988).

Stuart Chase, *Guides to Straight Thinking: With 13 Common Fallacies* (New York: Harper and Row, 1956).

Irving M. Copi, *Introduction to Logic* (New York: Macmillan, 1986).

S. Morris Engel, *With Good Reason: An Introduction to Informal Fallacies*, Second Edition (New York: St. Martin's Press, 1982).

C. L. Hamblin, *Fallacies* (London: Methuen, 1986).

Madsen Pirie, *The Book of the Fallacy: A Training Manual for Intellectual Subversives* (London: Routledge and Kegan Paul, 1985).

Topic and Author Index

Scripture Index